Additional Praise for
Managing Foundations and Charitable Trusts

"This is an outstanding book. I have been practicing law for 50 years, and have been involved with foundations and other tax-exempt organizations throughout the entire time, and I have never seen a publication that is as well written and covers this area as completely and succinctly."

—Thomas L. Norris, Jr., Of Counsel, Poyner Spruill LLP

"After nearly four decades of counseling wealthy families with respect to their tax planning, I have finally found the perfect tool for my clients in the implementation and maintenance of their charitable giving. ... This well written book has all the key characteristics that I have been seeking for my clients; it is comprehensive, easy to read, and skillfully addresses all of the questions that philanthropically inclined individuals and families routinely ask of their advisors."

—Robert D. Borteck, Partner, Borteck, Sanders and Torzewski, LLP

"This is the best resource I have yet seen on [private foundations]. It is sufficiently detailed to be useful to attorneys, accountants, and others who seek to advise clients regarding private foundations, yet it is still quite readable and should be very helpful to the interested layperson."

—Eric N. Holk, Law Office of Eric Holk

"The book includes a clearly written overview, simple and succinct explanations about donations, differing methods of giving to charities, and forceful descriptions of the difficulties in giving money away. ... Technical issues and philosophical discussions are helpful."

—Eileen Sharkey, President, Sharkey, Howes & Javer

"I have been an estate planning attorney for over twenty five years. I wish that I had this book to refer to earlier on in my career. I find that it was well written for the experienced practitioner as well as those lacking experience in this field and wanting a resource to help them."

—Gregory C. Hamilton, Esq., Hamilton & Associates, PLLC

"This book has merit to those who are already operating a private foundation and those who are considering the establishment of a private foundation. ... I will keep this book for reference to be available when clients consult me on the issue of a private foundation."

—John W. Cooper, Of Counsel, Lindabury, McCormick, Estabrook & Cooper, P.C.

"This will be a great resource for anyone involved with charities including foundations, whether they serve on the board, work as an officer or staff or are a professional guiding a charity."

—Jean Carter, Partner, Hunton & Williams LLP

"This book is a must have resource for all professionals who practice in the area of charitable giving, including private foundations. It is thorough for the professional but it is also written in an understandable and readable style for the layperson. I plan to give a copy to every client for whom we create a private foundation or charitable trust."

—David J. Harowitz, David J. Harowitz, P.C.

"This is a terrific book. It is more than a textbook, it is a guidebook for those interested and involved in charitable planning. It has a wealth of information and educational stories. I will be happy to recommend it to all of my charitable planning professionals and high net worth clients."

—Jim Van Houten, CLU, ChFC, MSFS, CFP, Stonegate Financial Group, LLC

"*Managing Foundations and Charitable Trusts* by Silk and Lintott is an excellent source for the seasoned professional or those new to this field. The book concisely sets forth the various charitable tools available to the practitioner/advisor and administrator alike. This resource clearly explains the charitable mindset, the techniques to reach a particular client's goals and the possible pitfalls of one method over another."

—Brian Kirby, Partner, Bangs, McCullen, Butler, Foye and Simmons, LLP

"I [found] this text [to be] a very good balance between the technical and informative such that that it would be useful for the practitioner community, as well as individuals considering the concept of a foundation. For the donor it summarizes in a readable and understandable fashion the technical aspects of operating a foundation, as well as the social good that a family foundation can provide to the community at large. It was an enjoyable read."

—Kimon P. Karas, Principal, McCarthy, Lebit, Crystal & Liffman Co., L.P.A.

"The combination of stated principles and story-based support is effective, avoiding the sluggishness of too much detail. It enables an energetic reading pace and a sense of productivity on the part of the reader."

—Dennis Branconier, Senior Vice President, M Advisory Group

"Silk and Lintott have done it again!"

—Marc Lane, President, Marc J. Lane Wealth Group

"Great work on how foundations can influence family development and functionality."

—Peter Brown, Partner, Lathrop & Gage LLP

"Every person who wants to become an intentional philanthropist should read it. It is not only very readable, but it is comprehensive and full of generalized advice. ... I want to have copies available to give to seriously motivated clients."

—Chris Johnson, Of Counsel, Buchanan & Stouffer, P.C.

"Bravo to the authors of an intelligent yet fast-reading primer on charitable giving."

—Roy A. Krall, Partner, Weston Hurd LLP

MANAGING FOUNDATIONS AND CHARITABLE TRUSTS

Since 1996, Bloomberg Press has published books for financial professionals on investing, economics, and policy affecting investors. Titles are written by leading practitioners and authorities, and have been translated into more than 20 languages.

The Bloomberg Financial Series provides both core reference knowledge and actionable information for financial professionals. The books are written by experts familiar with the work flows, challenges, and demands of investment professionals who trade the markets, manage money, and analyze investments in their capacity of growing and protecting wealth, hedging risk, and generating revenue.

For a list of available titles, please visit our web site at www.wiley.com/go/bloombergpress.

MANAGING FOUNDATIONS AND CHARITABLE TRUSTS

Essential Knowledge, Tools, and Techniques for Donors and Advisors

Roger D. Silk
James W. Lintott

BLOOMBERG PRESS
An Imprint of
WILEY

Published by John Wiley & Sons, Inc., Hoboken, New Jersey.
Published simultaneously in Canada.

This book is a revised edition of *Creating a Private Foundation: The Essential Guide for Donors and Their Advisers* published by Bloomberg Press in 2003.

For general information on our other products and services or for technical support, please contact our Customer Care Department within the United States at (800) 762-2974, outside the United States at (317) 572-3993 or fax (317) 572-4002.

Wiley also publishes its books in a variety of electronic formats. Some content that appears in print may not be available in electronic books. For more information about Wiley products, visit our web site at www.wiley.com.

Library of Congress Cataloging-in-Publication Data:

Silk, Roger D.
  Managing foundations and charitable trusts: essential knowledge, tools, and techniques for donors and advisors / Roger D. Silk and James W. Lintott.
     p.   cm. — (Bloomberg financial series)
  Includes index.
  ISBN 978-1-118-03826-0 (hardback); ISBN 978-1-118-09349-8 (ebk);
  ISBN 978-1-118-09350-4 (ebk); ISBN 978-1-118-09351-1 (ebk)
     1. Nonprofit organizations—Management.   2. Charitable uses, trusts, and foundations—Management.   I. Lintott, James W.   II. Title.
  HD62.6.S5575 2011
  658.'048—dc22   2011006384

Printed in the United States of America

V10017931_031120

To Janie Block, z'l, Susan Pohl, and Susan Maher.

Contents

Preface

When we wrote *Creating a Private Foundation* in 2002, the world had just finished one of the most ebullient decades in history. The long decade from 1989 to 2000 was one of almost unbroken good news for many of the peoples of the world. Following the fall of the Berlin Wall in November of 1989, the 60-plus-year night of Communism was lifted from most of Eastern Europe. And farther east, China, thanks to the introduction of market reforms, was in the early stages of one of the most remarkable flowerings of wealth in history.

In the West, the peace dividend, along with the significant roll-back of government intervention during the Reagan/Thatcher years, was a significant factor in helping the economies of the West grow steadily with few significant hiccups from the early 1980s all the way through the year 2000.

Then, we hit a rough patch. As we all know, the dot-com bubble burst in 2000, causing grievous losses to tech investors around the world. Many have still not recovered. Many may never recover. In 2001, Islamic terrorists murdered thousands of people in New York and Washington, plunging the United States and much of the world into a series of wars that still continue.

It is perhaps not surprising then that charitable giving (in the United States, for which data is available) declined in real terms in each of the years 2001, 2002 and 2003, before recovering in 2004, and reaching an all time high in 2005.[1] Our view is that 2005's giving, which was significantly higher than 2004's, was driven at the margin by the immense charitable response of Americans to Hurricane Katrina.

In the eight years since we wrote *Creating a Private Foundation*, much has changed in the world of philanthropy. Many of those changes have been driven by a decade of the worst financial performance since the Great Depression.

---

[1]Charitable giving statistics in this chapter are from the Giving USA Foundation 2010 Giving USA report.

You are already familiar with the dismal statistics. As we write, the major market averages are well below the levels they reached in 2000, over 10 years ago. Many of the risks in the financial system have proven to be much greater and much more widespread than was previously understood by most people.

And the years 2008 and 2009 saw the U.S. stock market lose about two-thirds of its value from peak to trough with similar losses around most of the world, real estate markets around the world seize up, the banking business come to the brink, the failure of the two of the three big U.S. automakers, and the near-failure of many of the largest companies in the United States and around the world.

So things must be pretty bad for charitable giving, right?

Well, no.

In fact, as of the end of 2009 (the most recent year for which data are available at this writing), total charitable giving in the United States, adjusted for inflation, was nearly 10 percent higher than it had been in the peak year of 2000. In other words, while the Dow Jones Averages *declined* by more than 20 percent in real, inflation-adjusted terms, charitable giving in the United States *increased* 10 percent in real, inflation-adjusted terms.

The bottom line? Despite a very difficult decade for many people, including people with wealth invested in the stock market, charitable giving is alive and well and even thriving.

What's New

The changes in philanthropy over the past decade have mostly been difficult. As Warren Buffett has observed in connection with the stock market, "You only find out who's been swimming naked when the tide goes out." During the past 10 years, the tide went out.

And it revealed plenty of ugly. Some of the ugliness was very widely reported, such as the Madoff scandal (see new Chapter 12). But other equally serious economic and philanthropic, if not moral, problems got less showy press.

We are speaking particularly of the emerging understanding of the law of unintended consequences to the field of philanthropy. Perhaps by chance, and perhaps by the operation of what we might call the "Pride goeth before a fall" principle, both of the first two charities we mentioned in our introduction to the first edition—the Bill and Melinda Gates Foundation and the Susan G. Komen Foundation—have stumbled badly over the equal-opportunity scourge of unintended consequences. (See new Chapter 8.)

These revelations, along with more mundane changes in the economic and regulatory environment, have added new challenges and new opportunities for philanthropists.

Among the more important changes are the increased prominence of donor-advised funds (see new Chapter 14), the blossoming of a market for Charitable Remainder Trust income interests (see new Chapter 18) and the seemingly inevitable growth and elaboration of tax rules relating to charitable organizations.

As noted, another major feature of the past decade has, alas, been the loss of billions of dollars of charitable funds to fraud. As foundation managers face the future, they add fraud-avoidance to the list of must-do items. Similarly, with the yawning U.S. fiscal deficits and stated Federal Reserve policy of inflation, foundation managers must make themselves aware of the potential for devastating price inflation, and take appropriate steps. (See new Chapter 12.)

Perhaps not surprisingly given the economic turbulence of the last decade, the formation of new foundations has slowed. New foundations have, of course, been forming, and continue to be formed. But relatively more attention has been given and needs to be given to the effective management of those foundations and charitable trusts after they have been formed.

To best serve the needs of readers, both those contemplating creating a new foundation and those who already have a foundation, a charitable remainder trust, a donor-advised fund account, or other charitable entity, we have elected to keep most of the material that comprised *Creating a Private Foundation* and incorporate it in the present volume. Thus, although it has a new title, technically this book is a highly revised and expanded edition of *Creating a Private Foundation*.

Acknowledgments

We thank Laura Walsh, our Wiley editor, as well has the many members of her very capable team, including Judy Howarth, Adrianna Johnson, and Vincent Nordhaus.

We also thank a great number of clients and advisors with whom we have worked over the years, and from whom we have learned a great deal. For privacy reasons, we cannot name many of them, but you know who you are and we thank you.

We owe a large "thank you" to all of the professionals who helped, in one way or another, develop the ideas and information in this book. Among these, in alphabetical order, are Jeff Albrecht, Bob Alexander, Grace Allison, Garry Armstrong, Brian Barker, Richard Berner, Andy Bewley, Bill Billimoria, Rob Borteck, Dennis Branconier, Peter Brown, Brodie Burwell, John Cady, Tim Carroll, Jean Carter, Geoff Close, Harry Colmery, John Cooper, Guy Cumbie, Trigg Davis, Frances Gaver, Cynthia Dupont, Ruth Easterling, Dick Greene, Greg Hamilton, David Harowitz, Leigh Harter, Steve Hartnett, Todd Healy, Vaughn Henry, Rich Hoholik, Eric Holk, Paul Hood, Rick Huff, Mark Jaeger, Jared Jameson, Mark Jarasek, Chris Johnson, Kimon Karas, Ira Karlstein, Douglas Kerr, Brian Kirby, Mark Kornblau, Roy Krall, Sal LaMendola, Michael Lampert, Marc Lane, Dick Lang, Richard Lehrman, Bill Linkous, Jonathan Lurie, Ronald Lyster, Dennis Mainerd, Norman Manley, Earl Mar, Bruce McClanahan, Jerry McCoy, Dipakkumar Mehta, Michael Millman, Derek Misquitta, Helen Modly, Read Moore, Jim Nepple, Terry Norris, Tom Norris, Tom Olofsson, Georgianna Parisi, Bob Petix, Ron Philgreen, Dean Phillips, Jeff Pickard, Tim Savage, Jack Sawyer, Jim Schmidt, John Scully, Eileen Sharkey, Tom Sigmund, Karen Sinchak, Fredric Sjoholm, Carolyn Smith, Vern Sumnicht, Robert Sweeney, Don Twietmeyer, Chris Valentine, Jim Van Houten, Raymond Vay, Henry Veit, Bob Wacker,

Don Weigandt, John Weil, Jeffry Weiler, Mark Weinberg, and Jason White. If we have omitted anyone, please accept our apology.

Any opinions expressed may or may not be the opinions of any one or more of the people who gave us input. No opinion, in one way or another, should be attributed to any of them, unless directly cited or quoted in the text. Any errors are ours.

CHAPTER 1

The Basics of Charitable Giving

You need no special knowledge to write a check to charity. But if you are a serious philanthropist, someone who wants to have an impact, to take advantage of tax breaks, and to exercise control, you need to know how the system works. Specifically, you need to know about the ways in which you can give to charity.

Charitable vehicles are legal structures that make effective charity possible. For people who are new to the world of philanthropy—and some who aren't so new—the range of charitable instruments can seem overwhelming. The first step in understanding them is to review all of the options with their advantages and disadvantages. In this chapter, we will look at four approaches to philanthropy: direct gifts, supporting organizations, donor-advised funds, and private foundations. We examine two other popular vehicles, charitable lead trusts and charitable remainder trusts, in greater detail in Chapter 4. Our aim is to provide a working overview of the available options so that donors and their advisers will be able to make choices appropriate for their specific situations.

Of course, we'll be focusing on the private foundation, the vehicle of choice for 75 percent of the country's wealthiest 400 families and truly the gold standard of charitable vehicles. However, to understand why private foundations work so well, it's important to know something about the other three approaches for a basis of comparison.

Direct Gifts

A direct gift of money is the simplest, easiest, and perhaps most familiar way to support a cause. Essentially, you write a check to the charity of your choice, and you're done. Large direct gifts are usually endowment gifts—money that will be held and invested by the charity or invested into bricks and mortar. Over time, the charity will spend the income generated by those assets. For example, anyone who's attended a class at any one of dozens of U.S. universities has probably seen the name "Kresge" on a hall or auditorium. "Kresge" is the "K" in "Kmart," and the Kresge family has given large amounts to numerous schools, where the family name is now carved in stone. Kresge obviously favors using direct gifts as a means of supporting select charities and organizations. And for having buildings named after you, there's probably no better way to go.

But direct gifts often are not the best strategy for an effective long-term program. Here's why. Once a donor makes an endowment grant, he or she may have an opportunity to advise the board of the charitable organization, but will no longer have control over how the funds are used. Charities with large endowments—classic examples being Harvard University, with an endowment approaching $30 billion at last count, and Yale, with over $15 billion—are often less than responsive to the donors who created those endowments. Yale famously returned a $20 million gift from Texas billionaire Lee Bass, saying that Bass wanted too much control over how his money was used.

Unresponsiveness is no problem for donors who don't want a lot of involvement and are willing or even happy to give control over the money they have donated to the organization they've chosen. Many donors, though, especially those whose gifts are large, want to use their donations to create and implement a specific vision or to encourage a specific project. It is important for these donors to have control.

In the best cases, donors make large endowment gifts because they conclude that doing so will put the money to the best possible use. In many cases, however, donors may be interested in the publicity, the kudos, and the goodwill that attend the announcement of such gifts. The reader may recall Ted Turner's $1 billion pledge to the United Nations in 1997. It's hard to know what really went on in Turner's mind, but it's not unreasonable to believe that favorable publicity may have factored into his decision.

It can be very frustrating to make a large endowment gift only to watch the charity change its mission or act contrary to the donors' wishes. Even having your name on the door does not guarantee that a charity will always do what you want. In 2000 in New York City, this was illustrated in an ugly and public battle between Marylou Whitney and the Whitney Museum over a work of art by Hans Haacke entitled *Sanitation*. Marylou Whitney, a daughter-in-law of Whitney Museum founder Gertrude Vanderbilt Whitney, was a director and member of the museum's national fund-raising committee. But when she and other family members raised objections to the planned exhibit because of the exhibit's appallingly insensitive use of Nazi iconography, the museum dismissed her concerns and proceeded to mount the show. Whitney resigned from the museum's fund-raising committee and removed the museum from her will. The Whitney was "free to associate itself with trash," she told the BBC, but she did not want people to think she approved of it. Marylou Whitney also cancelled a planned $1 million gift to the Whitney Gallery of Western Art.

Another problem with large endowments is that they can make it feasible for the people running the charity to focus more on their own positions or on raising still more funds than on the immediate needs of the charity's beneficiaries. In our view, the actions of many large, privately endowed universities in the United States are a case in point. Schools such as Harvard, Stanford, and Princeton continue to aggressively seek new funds for their endowments, and continue to raise the pay levels of senior faculty and administration, even as they continue to raise tuition at rates far exceeding the rate of inflation, without using the endowment to moderate these costs. Some universities pay their presidents what many would consider to be astronomical salaries. For example, Rensselaer Polytechnic Institute, in Troy, New York, paid its president, Shirley-Ann Jackson, $1,598,247 in fiscal 2008 according to the New York *Times*. But she has company. The *Times* reported that 23 presidents of private universities earned more than $1 million in 2008.

Jon Van Til, a professor at Rutgers University, told the *Chronicle of Philanthropy*, seen by many as the newspaper of record for the philanthropic community, that such salaries often allow the people running the organizations to lose touch with the people they're supposed to be serving. James Abruzzo, who heads nonprofit headhunting for the New Jersey–based firm DHR International, draws the link explicitly. Many of the largest nonprofits tie executive pay to fund-raising success, he says.

Some cases of a charity actually violating a donor's intent are particularly blatant and egregious. If you haven't heard such stories, it's because they rarely reach the courts or show up in the press. Donors are too embarrassed to go public with their complaints. And even if the donors seem to have a good legal argument, it's difficult and expensive to meet the legally required standards of evidence on something as subjective as intent.

One case that did go to court involved Manhattan's St. Luke's Roosevelt hospital and a donor named R. Brinkley Smithers. Smithers dramatically influenced the treatment of alcoholism in the second half of the twentieth century. During the 1970s and 1980s, he pledged $10 million to St. Luke's Roosevelt in order to establish the Smithers Alcoholism and Treatment Center. Smithers was a strong supporter of an approach that encourages alcoholics to give up drinking entirely and to rely on group support from other alcoholics, the same approach pioneered by Alcoholics Anonymous. Smithers spent millions of dollars funding research on this form of treatment. He naturally expected the Smithers Alcoholism and Treatment Center to support his views on abstinence.

Smithers' theories were generally supported during his lifetime. But a year after he died, in 1994, St. Luke's developed an intervention clinic that accepted and supported a "controlled drinking" treatment. In addition, the hospital, heavily in debt, decided to sell the town house on Manhattan's Upper East Side that had housed the program for years. Smithers' widow Adele sued St. Luke's, but she lost, and before she could get an appeals court ruling, St. Luke's sold the building for $15.9 million. Smithers and her son were so displeased with St. Luke's that they now publicly disavow the program that bears the family name. The trial court ruled that Mrs. Smithers lacked standing to sue. She appealed, and won. St. Luke's finally agreed to settle the case in 2003, by agreeing to give almost $6 million to another nonprofit, which is expected to carry out Brinkley Smithers' original intentions.

As foundation managers, we've seen a number of similar cases up close, involving donors who felt mistreated and saw their money used in ways they'd never wanted. To protect our clients, we have removed identifying detail from these stories. But they are worth hearing.

In one case, during the 1970s, a well-known university raised $20 million from a prominent donor to finance research in a then-arcane area of finance called "derivative contracts" by a distinguished professor. When the university accepted the funds, it seemed to be in complete agreement with the donor's wishes that the money be spent on this particular area; the funds were put in a separate endowment account. Time passed, and the endowment grew. For a number of years, the research went on as intended.

But when the university changed hands in the 1990s, so did its priorities. The administration eliminated the entire research program and even the department for which the funds had been raised. A primary motive was to get their hands on the endowment funds. The donor had already died, but the finance professor, now retired, decided to fight. Over a period of several years, he expressed concerns quietly, and then made formal protests. He tried his best to gather allies against the administration, but he still hadn't made any headway when he died from a stroke in 1997. The assets were commingled with the endowment of the university.

In a second case, which also involves a university, a donor agreed to endow a chair for an economics professor. Endowed chairs, which establish a named professorship in a given field, are a staple of university fund-raising. They are created by universities as a fund-raising tactic, or by a donor who wants his or her name associated with a chair in exchange for funding. Perhaps the most famous is the Lucasian chair in mathematics at Cambridge University, now held by Stephen Hawking and once held by Sir Isaac Newton. That chair was created in 1663 by a gift of land from a Member of Parliament named Henry Lucas. The land yielded £100 a year, which was a lot of money in those days. These days, it costs a lot more than £100 a year to endow a chair. The price varies from school to school and even department to department, but it generally runs into six or seven figures. (The price may be negotiable, although this is a fact that schools would prefer remained secret.)

In our case of the economics chair, which occurred in the late 1990s, a wealthy donor who was already a supporter of a well-known eastern school decided to give an additional $1 million to endow a chair in economics. It was up to the university to make the appointment, and it chose one of the university's well-known professors. The professor was chosen partly because of work he had done to establish an important academic organization within the university—an organization that was endowed by the same generous donor who now wanted to endow the chair.

Receipt of a chair (which is always tenured) is both an honor and a sinecure for any professor, who has a public platform and cannot be fired. In this instance, the professor started a very public attack on an academic organization supported and funded by the same donor who had endowed the professor's chair. As a result, the organization's ideology changed dramatically, and in opposition to the donor's beliefs.

The donor was furious and extremely disappointed that his intentions for the organization and for the endowed chair had gone awry. There was nothing he or the university could do. He had no choice but to live with his mistake. But it is certain that he doesn't plan to endow another chair anytime soon. In all his future giving, the donor has been careful to attach strings and fund programs only a year at a time.

Stories like these are not unusual. We urge donors to weigh decisions carefully before making endowment grants to charities, whether these charities are universities, arts organizations, hospitals, or any other large institution. If donors have no doubt that a charity will be responsive to their wishes, or accept the idea that a charity should be free to modify its use of the funds as it thinks best, an endowment grant may be appropriate.

If you like the idea of your name carved in stone or on a plaque, and you believe in the mission of the organization and have confidence in its leadership, go ahead and make an endowment. You will be in a lot of good company. But if you want more control over the use of your money, we believe that there are better alternatives.

To encourage one-time endowment gifts, charities often tell donors that they need such gifts to ensure funding for long-term programs. In certain cases, this logic may be justified. But there are ways that a donor can arrange to provide long-term funding and still retain control. As we shall see later in this chapter, a private foundation is an ideal way to get the immediate tax benefits that come from an endowment-level gift, but still exercise the control and judgment you want (and that you believe can benefit the charities over the long run).

As you've seen, we are particularly cautious about universities. Even under the best of circumstances, in our view, universities are no longer good places to make big donations. Despite the popularity of university endowment funds, we do not usually advise large endowments for universities if a donor wants to have significant control over how that money is spent.

Supporting Organizations

Another charitable vehicle that can be appropriate in certain situations is a supporting organization. A supporting organization has some characteristics of a private foundation and some of a public charity. Like a private foundation, a supporting organization is a separate, freestanding legal entity. But it is often associated with a charitable organization that supplies it with certain services, such as money management and administration. The founder can often be on the board of the associated charity. However, unlike with a private foundation, the founder cannot have control. Control must rest with one or more public charities.

Recently a number of fund-raising organizations such as community foundations, universities, and Jewish federations have been marketing supporting organizations as "family foundations." That creates some confusion, so it is worth examining these organizations in some depth.

For example, the Associated Jewish Charities in Baltimore, Maryland, in cooperation with Zanvyl Krieger, a very wealthy Baltimore businessman, created the Zanvyl Krieger Fund as a supporting organization in 1978. The Associated named Krieger and several of his family members, as well as a larger number of nonrelated people, to the board of the fund. For many years, until his death in the late 1990s, Krieger treated the fund much as he would have his private foundation. However, unlike with a foundation,

Krieger had to take into account the desires of the Associated—the supporting organization—which at times conflicted with his own.

The rules describing supporting organizations are, not surprisingly, fairly complex. They are laid out in the Internal Revenue Code (IRC)'s Section 509(a)3. In essence, the rules state that a supporting organization must have a relationship with one or more public charities as follows. The supporting organization must be:

- Operated, supervised, or controlled by,
- Supervised or controlled in connection with, or
- Operated in connection with the principal organization.

In practice, "operated, supervised, or controlled by" means that the directors or officers of the supporting organization are selected by the associated group. Thus, a donor can be on the board of a supporting organization, but the donor and related people (generally the same people who would be disqualified persons under the private foundation rules, as discussed in Chapter 11) cannot constitute a majority of the board. The selection of these board members would be entirely in the hands of the associated organization.

"Supervised or controlled in connection with" generally means that the same people who control the associated organization also control the supporting organization. This requirement can be met, for example, by having the board members of the supporting organization be the same people who are on the board of the associated organization.

"Operated in connection with" is probably the most complicated of the three types of relationships, in that to qualify for this type of relationship, a supporting organization must meet both a so-called responsiveness test and an "integral part" test. Since these, in turn, have more tests, we will not go into full detail here. It is sufficient to note that this relationship will qualify only in cases where the supporting organization works very closely with, for the purposes of, and under the control of the primary group.

As the above makes clear, a charitable entity organized as a supporting organization is not a family foundation in the sense that most people use that term. That is, it is not an independent, private foundation. People charged with raising funds for the associated organization may reason that, since they will allow the donor's name to be attached to the fund and since the donor may be allowed to sit on the board, the organization is like a private foundation and can be called one. Since there is no legal definition of the term, this practice is legal. However, it may mislead some donors. Anyone considering a vehicle that purports to offer the benefits of a private foundation (without the restrictions) should fully investigate what he is getting. If it's a supporting organization, the donor must, by definition, give up control.

In practice, a supporting organization can be much like an outright endowment gift in that the donor may have an advisory role but is not allowed to maintain control. Our experience is that most donors do not use supporting organizations if their circumstances allow a private foundation. When donors choose on their own to form supporting organizations, it is most often a situation in which a private foundation simply won't work because of one or more regulatory or tax considerations.

Perhaps the most salient issues for a donor considering a supporting organization are the choice of the primary organization and the manner in which that group will exercise control. Note that the rules permit the control to be vested in more than one public charity. From the donor's point of view, a supporting organization controlled by several public charities can give the donor more flexibility and influence than is possible with just one charity in control. With several public charities, it may be easier to prevent any single organization from dictating terms on its own.

There are several circumstances that may cause a donor to select a supporting organization as the charitable structure of choice—usually in cases where something precludes the use of a private foundation. These include situations where a donor wishes to contribute closely held company stock, where a donor wants to contribute appreciated property that is not publicly traded stock and get an income tax deduction at fair market value, or where a donor expects to carry out transactions with the organization that would be deemed self-dealing (see Chapter 11) if done with a private foundation.

In such circumstances, a supporting organization can be the best alternative, allowing the donor to achieve a central goal and still maintain sufficient influence over how the funds are used. With an informed donor driving the process, a supporting organization can be a useful and satisfactory tool for all parties over the long run.

Donor-Advised Funds

Donor-advised funds are public charities or subsidiaries of public charities that give donors the ability to make a large gift to the charity and then "advise"—without the legal right to actually direct—the fund on how and when to make specific charitable gifts. Several donor-advised funds, such as the Fidelity Gift Fund and the Vanguard Charitable Endowment Program, have been very successful in raising money on a commercial basis. In addition, a growing number of community foundations, including most of the larger ones, such as the California Community Foundation and the Central New York Community Foundation, offer donor-advised funds.

The donor-advised fund area, once a sleepy backwater of charitable giving, has in recent years gained tremendous acceptance, driven in part by Fidelity's marketing machine. There are several reasons. First, a donor-advised fund, whether a commercial or a community foundation, offers the donor the ability to make a gift immediately for tax purposes and decide later when and where to make grants to the charities that will eventually spend the money.

Second, gifts to donor-advised funds qualify as gifts to a public charity for tax deduction purposes. Depending on the specifics of the donor's situation, this advantage may be worth anything between zero and a large number.

Third, it is simple. A donor simply writes a check or sends money, not unlike opening a mutual fund account, and may sign an agreement covering the way in which she will advise on grants to be made. There is no further paperwork for the donor, because the fund takes care of it all.

Because a donor-advised fund is treated as a public charity for purposes of income-tax deduction limitations, it can offer some benefits for donors who want to give more than 30 percent of their income to charity each year or to donate appreciated property other than publicly traded stock. If this is the only reason for considering a donor-advised fund, however, a donor may wish to consult an adviser about other possibilities that can allow him to give a higher percentage of income and maintain better control.

Donor-advised funds can offer some savings in certain situations. For example, they do not pay excise taxes, as private foundations do. However, because the excise tax rate for foundations is only 2 percent of earnings (not assets), this advantage is typically very small—a few hundred dollars a year on $500,000 of assets. A donor-advised fund may also save money on annual fees for donors who will never have more than $200,000 or so in a charitable entity.

Donor-advised funds spare donors some paperwork, because the funds handle the compliance work. But with professional foundation management, donors to private foundations are also spared paperwork. For charitable commitments of about $500,000 or greater, such a donor can have all the benefits of a private foundation and none of the headaches, for about the same costs.

In spite of, or perhaps because of, these benefits, some donors are confused about what a donor-advised fund actually is. Some donor-advised funds encourage the confusion by calling a donor's account a "foundation." A donor-advised fund is itself a charity. When you give money to a donor-advised fund, you are giving away your money—irrevocably. The charity that receives it—that is, the donor-advised fund—then owns the money. "Once a contribution is accepted, it's an irrevocable charitable contribution to the Gift Fund, to be owned and held by our Trustees," says the nation's largest commercial donor-advised fund, Fidelity Gift Fund.

While usually there is no issue, occasionally the donor might end up out-of-luck. For example, the National Heritage Foundation for years offered donor-advised fund accounts that they called "Foundations." As with all donor-advised funds, contributions to National Heritage Foundation's donor-advised fund are considered legal contributions to the National Heritage Foundation. Donor-advised contributors learned the significance of this distinction the hard way in January 2009, when National Heritage filed for bankruptcy. The bankruptcy court in that case reaffirmed the fact that donor-advised fund donors have no legal claim to the assets, and have merely an "advisory" role. In other words, "sorry, fellas."

National Heritage Foundation is the exception. A donor-advised fund will generally take the donor's advice, but is not *required* to take such advice. In fact, the Internal Revenue Service (IRS) takes a negative view of any pledge by a donor-advised fund to follow donor advice. In the Tax Reform Act of 1969, which established the current laws dealing with private foundations, Congress made quite clear that it considered control over a foundation to be a privilege, and that in exchange for that privilege, foundations had to adhere to a complex set of requirements and limitations. The agency objects to attempts to offer the benefits and avoid the rules. In accordance with those rules, Fidelity makes it very plain that Fidelity, not the donor, controls the money. "As a donor, you may recommend grants," states Fidelity's marketing material. That recommendation is then reviewed by the fund trustees or staff. "If the recommendation is not approved, we will try to notify you and obtain a recommendation for a grant to an alternative charitable organization." In other words, they'll try to accommodate you, but your funds become their money, and they'll ultimately do as they see fit.

A private foundation, in contrast, gives the donor full, legal control. And if a foundation is managed by a full-service professional management firm, administration is nearly as simple for the donor as it would be with a donor-advised fund. The difference is that the donor need not worry about whether his wishes will be followed.

While most donor-advised funds follow donors' advice most of the time, this could change. The IRS, in its 2001 Exempt Organizations Instruction Program (EOIP), said that it "will look closely at" donor-advised funds that say they will "follow donor advice as to charitable distributions all the time." They finally got around to issuing further clarification in 2006. We review those changes in some depth in Chapter 14.

Another concern about donor-advised funds is that they are susceptible to public pressure to avoid controversy. A popular "Mom-and-apple-pie" charity can quickly become highly controversial, as the Boy Scouts has. Once that happens, public and political pressure may be placed on donor-advised funds to stop directing funds to such charities—regardless of the donor's wishes. Private foundations, in contrast, can support any cause as long as it is a recognized charity.

A new potential problem for donor-advised funds has been created by the antiterrorism measures enacted since September 11, 2001, targeting charities that support—or are believed to support—terrorism. A donor-advised fund is legally a single charity. But it might agree to make a grant to any charity that a donor to the fund designated. What happens if one of those recipient charities turns out to be a supporter of terrorism? Will the government freeze the assets of the donor-advised fund? While this is probably not likely, it still applies and does raise the possibility that those who give money to a donor-advised fund are linking their fate to the actions of hundreds or thousands of other people whom they do not even know.

A number of people who have put money into donor-advised funds found that the sponsors made it difficult to distribute money to unpopular causes, or causes they didn't deem important. One of the largest disputes between a donor and a community foundation has dragged on for several years between the Chicago Community Trust and the Searle family, led now by Daniel Searle. He is the son of pharmaceutical magnate John G. Searle (most famous for his company's Nutra-Sweet products) who provided the funding in question. The Office of the Illinois Attorney General states, "The issue centers on whether and to what degree [John G.] Searle intended the Chicago Community Trust to defer to the Searle 'family consultants' in the granting of monies from the fund."

While the relationship between the Searles and the Trust is not exactly a donor-advised fund relationship, it shares the critical element of donor advice without legal control. Under the will of the elder Searle, the Chicago Community Trust was to administer certain funds, currently about $20 million a year, in conjunction with advice and input from the Searle family. In 2001, about $40 million was frozen in an account at the Harris Bank in Chicago, and the dispute resulted in a lawsuit. Ironically, the Searles argued that the Chicago Community Trust should behave *more* like donor-advised funds and the Trust countered that it was attempting to act in the best interests of everyone. "Really what this all comes down to ... is a relationship that has deteriorated over time," Tina-Marie Adams, a spokeswoman for the Searle family, told the *Chicago Tribune*. That's as good as any comment for an implied warning to those considering entering into such long-term, nonbinding relationships.

Searle's lawsuit dragged on until 2004, when it was settled under terms that were kept quiet. The Searle Fund continued at the Chicago Community Trust, where it remains. However, whether by coincidence or not, shortly after the suit was settled, the President of the Chicago Community Trust, Donald Stewart, stepped down after only four years in the position.

While this case is notable for its magnitude, it is hard to know exactly how often donor-advised funds disregard a donor's wishes. Again, disputes are often embarrassing for both sides, so that neither has much desire to publicize them. And, usually, donors have no standing to complain. After all, they agreed to the terms specifying that they didn't have control, and to attempt to assert a legal claim would be tantamount to admitting that they obtained improper tax benefits.

There are other limitations to commercial donor-advised funds. One is that they offer few investment options. Financial services companies that run donor-advised funds generally require donors to put their money into their own mutual funds or other investment vehicles. A donor cannot hold stock in a donor-advised fund; if he donates stock, the fund will sell it and invest the proceeds in its own mutual funds. Furthermore, the choice of mutual funds is restricted not just to that company's funds, but to specified funds—which impose additional costs, beyond the administration fee charged by the donor-advised fund itself. Fidelity Gift Fund, the largest commercial donor-advised fund, offers only four investment choices, each consisting of a pool of its own mutual funds. Even among these four, Fidelity has the ultimate say as to where the money is invested. As we see in Chapters 9 and 10, limited investment flexibility can sometimes be quite costly.

Private Foundations

In essence, a private foundation is a tax-exempt charity that is funded and controlled by an individual or a family. A private foundation may be set up as a not-for-profit corporation or as a trust. Whichever arrangement you choose, a private foundation is treated the same for tax purposes. However, there are certain advantages that usually make the not-for-profit corporation more appealing than the trust.

The Not-for-Profit Corporation

Establishing a foundation as a not-for-profit corporation is a routine matter. As with a for-profit corporation, incorporation requires filing a certificate of incorporation with the state and adopting by-laws, which describe the internal workings of the organization. The primary difference is that a not-for-profit corporation usually has no shareholders. Instead, it may have members who elect a board of directors, which in turn appoints the officers. Alternatively, the board of directors can elect its own successors.

There are several advantages to the corporate form for a foundation: limited liability for officers and directors, greater flexibility (than a trust would have) to adapt the organization's structure as circumstances change, and the ability to have perpetual life (still not available for trusts in most states). Another feature of the corporate form is that it permits changes in the foundation's charitable goals. While some founders view this flexibility as a negative, we have found that you can have the best of both worlds by using a corporate form but maintaining control by having the donor make restricted grants to the foundation. Not-for-profit corporations, just like for-profits, are managed by their directors or officers. Certain management tasks, such as investment management and administration, may be delegated to professional advisers. Officers and directors, including family members, may be paid reasonable compensation for services actually performed.

Corporate form requires that the usual corporate formalities be observed, such as annual meetings and minutes. While these can be done simply, even perfunctorily, many families view them as a useful way to expose younger members to corporate workings.

The Trust

To establish a private foundation as a trust, the founder must sign a written document making a gift, in trust, to one or more trustees. The founder himself can be the trustee. A trust is generally located in the founder's home state. The registration rules vary from state to state.

Within limits, the terms of the trust can be broad or narrow, as desired. For example, a founder could write very narrow language into the trust document (see Chapter 7), or very broad language. For this reason, some founders believe that a trust gives them more control because it can be more difficult to change a trust, as compared to a corporation. However, structuring a trust very narrowly is not inherently better than making restricted gifts to the foundation, and may inadvertently (because of the difficulty of making changes) tie the hands of the trustee—even if the trustee is the founder—when unforeseen changes occur.

A trust has one or more trustees, just as a corporation has directors. Trustees generally select their successors. Trustees may receive reasonable compensation for services actually performed, although some states have more restrictive rules for trustee pay than for corporate director pay. Conversely,

California imposes strict rules that often make the corporate form a bad choice for foundations in that state. Because investment management is traditionally seen as part of the trustee's duty, payments to professional investment managers may reduce the amount that can be paid to trustees under state law. These kinds of rules vary from state to state.

There are other drawbacks to creating a foundation as a trust. Perhaps the most important is that trustees have a fiduciary duty to the beneficiaries. This is a higher standard than the "business judgment" rule that applies to corporate directors, and can make it more difficult to attract outsiders as trustees. In addition, beneficiaries of a trust may have standing to sue that they would not have if the foundation were a corporation.

Because some foundations are trusts, and are therefore governed by trustees, and some are corporations and therefore governed by directors, the terms "trustee" and "director" are commonly used interchangeably in the nonprofit world. We generally use the term "director" in this book.

Private Foundations: Why the Gold Standard?

For a donor with substantial assets, no other charitable vehicle can match the unique combination of flexibility, control, and tax advantages offered by private foundations. A private foundation offers its founder the ability to make a difference in the world, build a permanent legacy, gain personal satisfaction and recognition, and keep control in the family forever. (It also offers an array of tax and financial benefits, which we cover in greater detail in the next chapter.)

• **Make a Difference.** A truly effective foundation is much more than a sum of money set aside for philanthropic use. It is the carefully cultivated, ever-evolving product of the founder's vision, drive, and ethical will. The ways in which foundations make a difference are as varied and interesting as their founders.

For example, the Arthur Schultz Foundation, headquartered in western Wyoming, is dedicated to promoting environmental conservation and providing access to recreation for the disabled. The Russell Sage Foundation, founded in 1907 by Margaret Olivia Sage in New York, funds research into the social sciences with the goal of improving social policies. The James S. McDonnell Foundation, founded in 1950 by the aviation pioneer and cofounder of the McDonnell Douglas Corporation, aggressively encourages the "improvement of mankind" through its 21st Century Science Initiative.

When Congress was debating restrictions on foundations in the 1960s, a supporter of foundations, noted philanthropist Irwin Miller, the former

CEO of Cummins Engine who built the company into a major player in its market, commented that "while foundations are the most peculiarly American manifestation of the philanthropic impulse, they do not operate as simply as traditional charity; taking the long view, and working with professional skills, they have grown more sophisticated and specialized in their approach to problems."

• **Create a Legacy.** Charitable foundations have a long and honorable history. When Plato died in 347 B.C., he left income from his estate for the perpetual support of his academy. Control passed through heirs who each designated their successor, and the academy thrived until 529 A.D., when Roman emperor Justinian terminated it for spreading pagan doctrines. While 856 years is not exactly forever, Plato's foundation surely ranks among the most long-lived individual institutions in the history of humankind.

When Benjamin Franklin died, he left 1,000 pounds sterling to the cities of Boston and Philadelphia with detailed instructions for use of the money. Franklin directed that some of the earnings be used initially for loans to young married couples, allowing principal and interest to grow, with the first use of the accumulated funds to be made 100 years later. The endowment helped finance the Franklin Institute of Philadelphia and the Franklin Institute of Boston, and the remainder continues to grow today.

Andrew Carnegie and John D. Rockefeller are often viewed as the pioneers of the modern charitable foundation. In 1899, Rockefeller told a group gathered to commemorate the tenth anniversary of the University of Chicago, "Let us erect a foundation, a trust, and engage directors who will make it a life work to manage, with our personal cooperation, this business of benevolence properly and effectively." The foundations established by Rockefeller and Carnegie are still active today, doing good work and carrying on their founders' names.

But a private foundation offers more than a long-lasting legacy. Because it is private, it can be and do exactly what the founders and directors want—even if what they want is considered unconventional by others. The John D. and Catherine D. MacArthur Foundation pursues an unconventional path. Founded in the late 1970s upon the death of industrialist John D. MacArthur (his wife died in 1981), it has become known for its "genius" grants—unrestricted grants, with no required reports or expected outcomes, given to "exceptionally creative individuals, regardless of field of endeavor." The MacArthurs' son, Roderick, a trustee of the foundation, revels in the foundation's freedom to pursue its own vision. "This [the private foundation] is the only institution in our society that does not have constituencies that it has to keep looking to. All the others have to worry about pleasing a lot of people, so they're bound to tend toward conventional wisdom, respectability, and the lowest common denominator.... Foundations should be striving to do the kinds of things that the government cannot do. I repeat, cannot do: things that are not politically popular, things that are too risky, things that are just too far ahead of what the public will put up with.... A private foundation, where the board of directors is answerable only to itself, is in a completely different situation, and if it doesn't take advantage of that uniqueness, it's just blowing its opportunity, and perhaps even its moral obligation."

• **Achieve Personal Satisfaction and Recognition.** In the late 1990s, Karen Maru File, an associate professor of marketing at the University of Connecticut, conducted a survey of philanthropists who had established their own private foundations. She found that 86 percent said their giving had become much more gratifying, and 79 percent said they felt less barraged by solicitations from charities.

Another important benefit is the recognition that comes from having a private foundation. Researcher Teresa Odendhal, author of several books on philanthropy and foundations, quotes one donor who created a private foundation: "If you are an individual making small contributions, you are magically transformed when you become a foundation making small grants. I feel that I am taken very seriously."

A 1999 article in *Scientist Magazine* predicted that in the coming millennium, the private foundation would become the status symbol of choice. And in the first decade of this millennium, the number of foundations has continued to grow, despite two of the worst stock market dives in the past century, as seen in Figure 1.1. In 2011, the *New York Times* reported that status is a major factor for some donors. "Of course," says the January 28 Wealth Matters column, "There are reasons that go well beyond charitable giving ... Status is the obvious one ..."

Donors who intend to have their children eventually run their foundations will also benefit—not merely by having a status symbol, but by being able to give more. As one adviser who also has his own foundation told the authors, "It's a great way to give my kids my influence, and it makes good financial sense, too."

• **Maintain Family Control.** As we saw in the discussion of other charitable vehicles above, control over how money is spent is often an issue. With private foundations, the donor retains full control. Indeed, the Searle family learned its lesson, and the current generation, led by Dan Searle, has an active private foundation, the D&D Foundation, which was created in 1983. A spokesperson for D&D speculated that the elder Searle made the now-troublesome arrangement with the Chicago Community Trust only because

FIGURE 1.1   Growth in Domestic Private Foundations

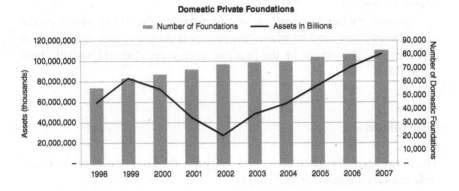

Domestic Private Foundations*

Asset Range	Number of Returns	% of Total
Zero or unreported	2,259	3%
$1 to under $100,000	20,630	24%
$100,000 to under $1,000,000	31,081	37%
$1,000,000 to under $10,000,000	24,083	28%
$10,000,000 to under $25,000,000	3,581	4%
$25,000,000 to under $50,000,000	1,421	2%
$50,000,000 to under $100,000,000	788	1%
$100,000,000 or more	769	1%
Total	**84,613**	

Source: http://www.irs.gov/taxstats/charitablestats/article/0,,id=96996,00.html
*Based on tax year 2007 data, the most recent year for which data is available as of 2011.

at the time, in the mid-1960s, his generation did not see control as such an important matter.

Control extends to all aspects of a foundation: the name; who is on the board; when, how, and to whom the money is donated; how the money is invested; and the choice of the bank or institution that will actually hold the funds.

Conclusion

The following table summarizes and compares the key features of the charitable vehicles discussed in this chapter.

Comparison of Charitable Vehicles

	Private Foundation	Direct Gift	Supporting Organization	Donor-Advised Fund
Immediate income tax deduction	Yes	Yes	Yes	Yes
Gift exempt from estate tax	Yes	Yes	Yes	Yes
Donor retains legal control	Yes	No	No	No
Legally controlled by donor's family in perpetuity	Yes	No	No	No
Builds charitable wealth free of income tax	Yes	No	Depends	Yes
IRS attitude	Supports	Supports	Supports	Supports
Investment options	Broad	Not applicable	Depends	Limited
When to use	When the amounts are large; When control is important	In special situations	In special situations	When amounts are small; When control doesn't matter

As this table shows, only the private foundation offers legal control along with its tax benefits. A private foundation also offers more flexibility—in how to invest and how to spend the money—than the alternatives. As for eventual disposition of assets, if a donor creates a private foundation but later changes her mind and wants to stop running it, she can still give some or all of the foundation assets to a donor-advised fund. The reverse is not true: A donor-advised fund may not contribute to a private foundation.

In addition, if its assets are large enough, a private foundation can be very cost-effective. While it is possible to spend upwards of $20,000 to set up a foundation, it does not necessarily cost that much. It may be $10,000 or less. Many full-service foundation companies—especially those providing financial management services, grants administration, and full foundation management—set fees based on a foundation's assets. For example, a foundation might pay an annual fee of 1 percent of total assets to a company that handles all the foundation's financial and administrative operations.

Most donor-advised funds do not impose a setup fee, but they tend to charge higher annual fees. Fees for donor-advised funds vary quite a bit, with the typical cost running about 1.5 percent of assets, which consists of an administrative fee of 1 percent of assets, plus investment management fees of approximately 0.5 percent.

Private foundations and donor-advised funds both play an important role in the charitable universe, and in general neither can be decisively preferred on the basis of cost alone. Donor-advised funds and private foundations each offer a unique combination of grant-making control, investment flexibility, and tax benefits. The next chapter looks at these tax benefits in greater depth and discusses several ways to take advantage of them.

CHAPTER 2

Tax Incentives
and Limitations

Philanthropy and tax breaks have gone hand-in-hand for thousands of years. In fact, the very word *philanthropy* tells this story. Just looking at the word, you might guess that it related to two Greek words: *philos* meaning "love" and *anthropos*, meaning "man." That is correct. But our word philanthropy traces its descent to the word *philanthropa* (same roots). The word *philanthropa* was in use in Egypt when Egypt was ruled by the Greek Ptolemies (305 B.C.E. to 30 B.C.E.). (You know the last Ptolemy to rule Egypt—her name was Cleopatra.) Under Ptolemaic rule, the word *philanthropa* referred to specific acts of royal "beneficence," including tax exemptions.[1]

Since 1913, when the Sixteenth Amendment introduced the income tax, Americans have found themselves with financial incentives for charity. When the estate tax was introduced three years later, more incentives for charitable donations were created. Although tax rates change—rising and falling with the political tide—the one perfectly legal, actively encouraged way to save on taxes has been to contribute to charity. (All references to tax rates—income tax or estate tax—unless otherwise noted, are as of 2011.)

Four Powerful Tax Incentives

Private foundations, as well as public charities, benefit from four tax incentives designed to encourage charitable giving:

---

[1] *Hellenistic History and Culture*, by Peter Green, University of California Press, 1996. See, e.g., p. 191. See also *For Good and Evil: The Impact of Taxes on Civilization*, by Charles Adams, Madison Books, 2001.

1. Current-year income tax deductions.
2. Income-tax-free growth.
3. Exemption from estate and gift taxes.
4. Ability to avoid capital gains tax on appreciated stock.

Income Tax Deductions

A donor to a private foundation can take an immediate deduction on both federal and state taxes. Like all charitable deductions, these are subject to some limits. At the federal level, contributions of cash (or other so-called basis property) are deductible up to 30 percent of the donor's adjusted gross income.

The immediate income tax deduction for contributions lowers the cost of giving to charity. For example, if a donor is in a 50 percent combined state and federal income tax bracket, it will cost him just 50 cents, after taxes, to put a dollar in his foundation. We further explore the implications of this benefit later in this chapter.

Income-Tax-Free Growth of Assets

Returns on assets in a private foundation are not subject to income tax. The source of the investment return does not matter: Interest, dividends, capital gains, and other forms are all free of income tax when earned within a foundation. This is a valuable benefit, making all returns (except 2 percent payable as excise tax, as described below) available for the foundation to use. And add to that the power of tax-free compounding. For example, one dollar invested at a return of 8 percent a year will take 15 years to double in value if it's subject to a tax rate of 40 percent. If the returns are exempt, the dollar will double in just nine years.

Gift and Estate Taxes

All assets in a private foundation are exempt from estate and gift taxes. Currently both the gift and estate tax are at 35 percent, through 2012 when the current law expires. During most of the past 70 years, the top federal estate tax rate has been well over 50 percent, and was 77 percent for about three decades. 2010 was the only year since the adoption of the modern tax system almost 100 years ago with no estate tax. With an estate and gift tax in effect, this exemption is obviously quite valuable.

Capital Gains Tax

Contributions of appreciated publicly traded stock that has been held by the donor for at least one year will qualify for an income tax deduction at the stock's fair market value. In addition, neither the donor nor the foundation will pay capital gains tax when the stock is sold. For stock that was acquired much below its current price, this greatly increases the value of the contribution. For example, consider a donor in a 50 percent combined income tax bracket and 30 percent capital gains tax bracket (combined state and federal) who gives $100,000 of zero basis stock to his foundation.

If the donor were to sell the stock first, he would pay $30,000 of capital gains tax, leaving just $70,000 for charity. But if the donor gives the stock to the foundation, and the foundation sells the stock, it keeps the entire $100,000. (It should be noted that while there are no income or capital gains taxes on private foundation asset returns, there is an excise tax on net investment income. This excise tax is usually levied at the rate of 2 percent of net investment income, but under certain conditions can be just 1 percent.)

The cumulative value of these tax benefits over time is staggering. In one generation, proper use of the tax incentives can double the amount available for charity without reducing the amount the donor keeps for his own use. Over two generations, of course, the value of the savings compounds even further. The following four examples illustrate the wealth-building power of these tax incentives for the philanthropically minded.

• **Example 1—Income tax benefit in a single year.** In any given situation, creating a foundation will usually result in both an immediate and a longer-term increase in net assets for the donor and his foundation. That's because of the deduction the donor gets.

For example, suppose a donor, whom we'll call Bill, is in the 45 percent income tax bracket (combined federal and state), has $1 million of income, and is considering a $300,000 contribution to his foundation. If he does not make the donation, Bill will be taxed on the full $1 million. He will pay $450,000 in taxes, leaving $550,000 of assets. He plans eventually to leave 25 percent of his estate to charity.

If he does make the $300,000 contribution, he pays tax on just $700,000 of income. The foundation gets the full $300,000. Bill keeps $700,000, on which he pays income tax of $315,000—a decrease of $135,000. After he pays income tax, Bill keeps $385,000 in personal assets. The total of Bill's assets and the foundation's assets is $685,000, which is $135,000 more than if Bill hadn't funded the foundation.

• **Example 2—Income tax benefit is greater when appreciated stock is gifted.** In Example 1, we assumed that Bill gave cash to his foundation. The income tax benefit will be even greater if he uses appreciated stock. Let's assume Bill gives $200,000 of stock (appreciated property is limited to 20 percent of AGI), for which he had paid $50,000. He also gives $100,000 of cash. His income tax deduction is still $300,000, saving him $135,000 of income taxes. But he also avoids a capital gains tax on the $150,000 of unrealized appreciation. At a 15 percent capital gains rate, he saves another $22,500 of income taxes.

• **Example 3—Income tax advantages over time.** The advantage grows over time because, as we said above, private foundations pay only a minimal excise tax, not income taxes.

Let us illustrate the effect of these savings by expanding on the previous example. Suppose Bill is 55 years old and has assets of $12.5 million, which return 8 percent a year, giving him $1 million in income. Also assume that each year he contributes 30 percent of his income to his foundation. His foundation also earns 8 percent, makes the required minimum annual distribution, and pays excise taxes of 2 percent of investment income and foundation management fees of 1 percent of assets. Using a standard life expectancy, let's assume that Bill dies at 82. After those 27 years, his net worth will be $27.7 million, and his foundation will be worth $20.8 million, for a total of $48.5 million.

Now consider the same scenario with Bill's identical twin Bob, who has no foundation, but each year gives to charity the same amount that Bill's foundation gives. After that same 27-year period, Bob will have $35.2 million, which is more than Bill, because Bob didn't fund a foundation. However, Bill, by funding his foundation each year during his life, can increase the total assets under his own control and in his foundation by over $13.3 million.

• **Example 4—The estate tax advantage.** Now let's look at the advantage created by the estate tax exemption. Again, let's assume that both Bill and Bob die at 82. Bill leaves no additional assets to charity because he is already leaving a sizable foundation. Bob decides to leave 25 percent of his estate, or $8.8 million, to a newly created foundation. This leaves his estate with $26.4 million (that is, $35.2 million, less the $8.8 million to his new foundation).

Because the current estate tax rate is temporary, and to make the numbers easier to follow, the following example uses a hypothetical estate tax rate of 50 percent. Estate taxes will take 50 percent of each man's personal assets. Neither foundation will be affected by estate taxes. Bill's estate of $27.7 million will go half to estate taxes and half to his son, Joe, who will receive

$13.85 million. Bob's estate, $26.4 million, also goes half to the government and half to his daughter, Carla, who gets $13.2 million.

When Joe and Carla compare notes, they go back over the histories of their father's financial lives. Both are surprised to discover that the only difference in the twins' conduct was Bill's annual funding of his foundation for 27 years. Not only has Bill left Joe half a million dollars more than Bob left Carla, but Joe will now run a foundation with $20.8 million; Carla will run a foundation with less than half that amount.

Details on Tax Deduction Limits

The deduction limits for estate and gift taxes are beautifully simple—there are no limits. Up to 100 percent of a donor's assets can be given to a foundation, completely free of gift or estate taxes. Alas, the rules for charitable income tax deductions are not so simple. There are a number of rules, and the interplay of these rules can become complex. It's probably best to get expert advice on any program for charity other than the most elementary (or see the Master Tax Guide cited in Resources). But here's a general preview.

All charitable contributions (whether to private foundations or public charities) are subject to limits on the amount that can be deducted. The overall maximum is 50 percent of adjusted gross income (which, for the sake of simplicity, we'll call "income"). This means that the most any donor can deduct in a single year is 50 percent of income. For example, if Tom's income this year is $1 million, the maximum total contributions he can deduct is $500,000.

But from here on, the rules become more complicated. There are two further sets of limits: one for gifts being made to public charities, and one for gifts to private foundations. For gifts to public charities, the deduction limit is the same as the overall maximum, 50 percent of income. If Tom's income is $1 million and he gives $500,000 in cash to a public charity, he can deduct it all. Alternatively, he could give $500,000 consisting of up to $300,000 in the form of appreciated long-term capital gain property (such as stock held for more than a year) and the balance in cash, and he could still deduct the entire $500,000. If Tom wanted to give only appreciated long-term capital gain property, he could deduct only 30 percent ($300,000 in this case) of his income.

Deductions for contributions to private foundations are limited to 30 percent of gross income. So, if Tom's income is $1 million, he can deduct up to $300,000 for gifts to a private foundation. Of this amount, up to

20 percent of income ($200,000 of the $300,000) may be in the form of appreciated publicly traded stock held for more than a year. (See Chapter 17 for a discussion of what kinds of property can qualify for fair market value deductions.)

There are also rules that allow excess deductions to be carried forward and used in future years. An example illustrates this. Suppose Tom's income this year is $1 million, and he gives $2 million to a public charity. He will be able to deduct $500,000 this year and carry forward the unused amount, $1.5 million. If Tom's income next year is $1.2 million, he will be able to deduct $600,000 (50 percent). This would leave him with a remaining carry-forward of $900,000. He has up to five years after the year he makes the contribution to use it all up.

If Tom gives both cash and appreciated property, he must deduct all his cash gifts before he is permitted to deduct any of the appreciated property. For example, if in years 1 through 3, Tom's income is steady at $1 million a year, and in year 1 he gives $800,000 in cash and $400,000 in appreciated property, he will be able to deduct the following amounts in each year:

Year	Deduction for Cash	Deduction for Appreciated Property
1	$500,000	$0
2	$300,000	$200,000
3	$0	$200,000

For gifts to private foundations, the carry-forward rules work similarly, except that the overall limit is 30 percent.

Because unused contribution deductions can be carried forward for up to five years, these limitations usually mean a deduction is deferred, not lost. For example, if a donor earns $1 million a year and wants to contribute $1 million to his foundation and deduct it all, the carry-forward rules allow this. In year 1, the donor contributes the $1 million. He would then deduct $300,000 (30 percent of income) in years 1, 2, and 3. In year 4, he would deduct the remaining $100,000. Alternatively, he could contribute the $1 million to a public charity. He would then be able to deduct $500,000 a year for two years. In either case, he gets the same tax deductions. The only difference is that he gets the deductions sooner with the gifts to public charity.

A donor may also deduct contributions to both a private foundation and a public charity in the same year. The overall limit is still 50 percent of income. For example, Tom could give 30 percent of income, in cash, to a private foundation, and another 20 percent in cash to a public charity, and deduct it all. Alternatively, he could give 20 percent of his income in the form of appreciated publicly traded stock to a foundation and another 10 percent of his income in the same form to a public charity and deduct it all.

If a donor wants to maintain maximum control and still take advantage of the 50 percent maximum deduction, he should consider contributing 30 percent of income to a private foundation and 20 percent to a public charity. This gives him control over the 30 percent and also allows him to deduct the maximum 50 percent immediately. If he does not plan to contribute over 30 percent of income every year, he can make a 50 percent contribution in year 1 to his foundation and carry forward the unused 20 percent to the following year, when he then deducts it. This approach is commonly used when a donor has a large block of appreciated stock that he wants to get into his foundation so that it can be sold without capital gains tax.

Finding the Best Giving Strategy

Here we will discuss the financial benefits of lifetime funding of a foundation. In Chapter 6, we look at some of the philanthropic benefits.

A study we conducted several years ago, analyzing various donation strategies, looked at ways to meet two different goals: maximizing the amount given to charity and maximizing the amount left to heirs. The best way to meet either goal, we found, is for a donor to establish a private foundation or other charitable entity while she is alive, and add money to it every year. After we crunched all the numbers, we came up with some rules of thumb.

Maximizing Money for Charity

If a donor's goal is to leave as much as possible to charity—while not leaving her heirs any worse off—the best strategy is to make annual contributions to her foundation. Each contribution should be a percentage of income equal to 1.25 times the percentage of the estate the donor wants to leave to charity. For example, if a donor wants to leave 20 percent of her estate to charity, the optimal funding strategy would be to contribute 25 percent (1.25 times 20 percent) of income to the foundation each year. In a typical situation, this strategy would more than double the amount of money a donor would give to charity if compared with simply leaving the money in her estate.

Maximizing Money for Family

Some donors want to keep as much as possible in the family—either for themselves or their heirs—while not leaving any less to charity than they would have by simply making a donation upon their death. Annual contributions to a foundation are again the best approach. Of course, these contributions will be considerably smaller than when the donor is seeking to maximize the money for charity. As a rule of thumb, here's the equation: Contributions should equal income times one-half the percentage of the estate that the donor wants to leave to charity. For example, if a donor had planned to leave 25 percent of his estate to charity, but wants to optimize his tax benefits and keep the charity's dollar amounts the same as before he optimized (with the additional savings going to heirs), he should contribute about 12.5 percent of his annual income to his foundation each year.

This second strategy would give the donor's family about 20 percent more money than if he did not create a foundation and instead donated 25 percent of the estate to charity at his death.

Extra Benefit — Buy Time

Having understood the tax benefits of annual giving, busy people will immediately recognize another benefit of a private foundation: It allows them to take the tax deduction now, and then continue, through the foundation, to invest the money and to give it out to charities at their leisure.

The $1.6 Trillion Loss

These examples illustrate the enormous amount one family can protect from taxation through the proper use of a private foundation. If you multiply the results for just 1 percent of the nation's wealthiest families, the potential is staggering. Our study reinforced the point that any high-net-worth donor wanting to leave part of her estate to charity should create a foundation and fund it annually. Most of the very wealthiest families have figured this out. But only about 1 in 10 of the 500,000 other families, with assets of $5 million, has followed suit. This means that most donors are forfeiting money to taxes and thereby will collectively cost charity about $1.6 trillion dollars over the next 30 years, according to our estimate. Extrapolating from available IRS data, we project that approximately 52,500 foundations (with assets of at least $100,000) will be created over those three decades. However, a U.S. Trust Survey of Affluent Americans shows that more than half of the wealthiest Americans plan to leave at least part of their estate at death to charity (whether a private foundation or public charity). If only the wealthiest 200,000 families (those worth approximately $10 million or more) are considered potential foundation creators, that means that 100,000 people (i.e., half of the total potential) might be creating and funding foundations during the next 30 years if they were fully informed.

Here's how we arrived at our $1.6 trillion estimate. We assumed, conservatively, that the typical member of this class of wealthy individuals has a beginning net worth of $12.5 million. In scenario 1, we assume that the individual starts a foundation out of an assumed income of $1 million per year and funds it annually with the maximum amount that he can take as a deduction, $300,000. In scenario 2, we assume the same individual waits until he dies in 30 years and funds his foundation via his will. To do these calculations, we assumed that the long-run average top tax rates remain at about what they are today, that the average investment return over the period is about 10 percent, and that the donor will contribute 25 percent of his estate to charity. Given these and some other minor assumptions, we conclude that over the 30 years, the individual will accumulate an additional $35 million for charity by funding his foundation annually. And he will still accumulate the same amount for his family.

This tremendous benefit derives from a modest annual contribution to his foundation of about 2.5 percent of net worth each year. This $35 million of potential additional charitable resources, multiplied by the 47,500 foundations we estimate should be formed, yields the $1.6 trillion estimate.

The point is not whether the $1.6 trillion estimate is correct. It may be high or low. The point is that good planning can capture a tremendous amount of resources for charity.

Estate Taxes

The decades-long debate in Washington over the estate tax continues. While there is concern from some in the philanthropic community that eliminating the estate tax would harm charitable giving, our analysis suggests that if the estate tax were lowered or eliminated, charitable giving would increase. The following analysis sheds some light on the importance of the estate tax for charitable giving.

Dozens of real-life discussions with clients and prospective clients who are actively considering a foundation indicate that there are four basic ways people think about how much of their estates they will allocate to charity. These are (1) a specific dollar amount to charity, with the remainder to their heirs; (2) a fixed dollar amount to heirs, with the remainder to charity; (3) a fixed percentage of their wealth to charity, with the remainder to the heirs;

and (4) a fixed percentage of their wealth to heirs, with the remainder to charity. In our experience, not many people who create private foundations do it in order to avoid estate taxes.

The following table shows how lower estate taxes would affect charitable contributions.

How Charitable Bequests Strategies Would Be Affected by Elimination of the Estate Tax

Strategy	Effect on Contributions to Charity
Specific $ to charity; remainder to heirs	No effect
Fixed $ to heirs; remainder to charity	Increase
Fixed % to charity; remainder to heirs	No effect
Fixed % to heirs; remainder to charity	Increase

If these results are surprising, think of the founder's estate as a pie to be split between heirs, charity, and the government. Whenever the government's share is less, more is left to be split among the remaining two groups. Paul Schervish, director of the Social Welfare Research Institute, a multidisciplinary research center specializing in the study of spirituality, wealth, and philanthropy at Boston College, used to oppose lowering the estate tax because he believed it would hurt charity. Then, in 2000, he conducted a study of people with net worths of $5 million or more. He concluded that if the estate tax were eliminated, the portion of these people's estates that would go to charity would increase from 16 percent to 26 percent, an increase of about 60 percent.

In 2006, Schervish published additional findings. Using data from the late 1990s and first half of the 2000s, Schervish found two significant trends affecting charitable bequests. He found that the larger the estate, the larger the percentage given to charity. For estates with assets of between $1 million and $2.5 million, about 17 percent was left as a bequest on average. For the largest estates, this percentage was more than double, averaging around 40 percent of the estate. Second, he found that estates are tending to grow over time.

Putting these facts together, Schervish expects the amount going to charity from estates to continue to grow.

Conclusion

"The avoidance of taxes is the only intellectual pursuit that carries any reward," said John Maynard Keynes. While Keynes likely offered this bit of wisdom with tongue in cheek, it is true that avoiding taxes and using the savings for charity does carry a real reward. Tax incentives for charity will not make an uncharitable person give. But those who are charitably inclined are shortchanging their philanthropy if they don't take full advantage of the tax incentives Congress offers. Start giving annually—directly to charity, or to your foundation, and begin to appreciate the powerful estate planning opportunities you can realize. In Chapter 3, we look at these opportunities, in the form of Charitable Lead Trust planning, and at the often misunderstood topic of Charitable Remainder Trusts.

CHAPTER 3

Charitable Planning and Taxes

Charitable planning is made complex by the large number of factors to be taken into account. Among these are the current and expected income of the donor, the variety and urgency of the needs in the community, the current and future wealth of the donor, the marital and family status of the donor both now and in the future, and, last, but certainly not least, the current and future tax law.

The topic of this chapter is how to plan rationally in the face of the complexity of, and uncertainty about, the tax law. As we write this, the question seems particularly acute because the tax law is prominent in the news.

Economists have long known that taxes harm the economy by destroying wealth and reducing incentives to produce wealth.[1] And the effects are not small, although for some reason they are hardly ever talked about. For example, Martin Feldstein, a Harvard economist and president emeritus of the National Bureau of Economic Research, has estimated that *each dollar of additional income tax may cost the economy two dollars.*[2] In other words, when Washington says they are going to raise income taxes by a trillion dollars, if

---

[1] For an undergraduate-level explanation, complete with graphs and examples, of how taxes create deadweight losses, see, for example, Harvard economist Greg Mankiw's book, *Principles of Economics.* There is no need to buy the current edition, which is very expensive. Earlier editions are available used for as little as one cent, plus shipping, on Amazon.

[2] See, for example, Feldstein's NBER working paper 5055. The abstract says, in part, "A marginal increase in tax revenue achieved by a proportional rise in all personal income tax rates involves a deadweight loss of nearly two dollars per incremental dollar of revenue." NBER working papers are available online. See www.nber.org/papers/w5055.pdf.

they were honest, they would disclose that they are going to destroy an additional two trillion dollars in potential wealth.

Just as they know that high taxes are harmful, economists have also long known that the damage can be minimized by low, fair, reasonable, and predictable taxes.

Unfortunately for the United States and its taxpayers today, none of these four desiderata apply to current U.S. tax law. Taxes are not low. Most people would say they are not low, not fair, not reasonable, and certainly not very predictable.

In fact, the federal tax laws change virtually every year. Some years are more dramatic than others. Furthermore, even many things that do not actually change are implemented only one year at a time.

Some changes are relatively minor, such as the exact dollar amount allowed for a dependent deduction, while others, such as the statutory rate on income, are extremely important. And changes in the statutory tax rate are not rare. Since the implementation of the income tax in 1913, the top statutory rate has changed no fewer than 37 times! That's an average of more than once every three years.

How should a rational person plan charitable giving in the face of such a constantly changing and unpredictable environment?

While we do not have any absolute answers to offer, we have developed some rules of thumb. Our hope is that if you understand how to think about it, you will be able to make more informed, if not actually better, decisions.

Giving Approach

There are perhaps as many approaches to charitable giving as there are donors. However, most approaches fall into one of several categories. We will examine each category and develop rules that apply to each.

Fixed-Dollar Amount

One simple approach to charitable giving is to give a certain, fixed amount each year. While this might seem like a very non-optimal approach, it is quite common. Examples include giving patterns such as multiyear commitments to give a certain amount a year to a charity, such as a church or a school; membership dues to charitable organizations such as museums or synagogues; and hundreds of other instances in which people choose to support an organization at a specified number of dollars per year.

Consider an example in which a hypothetical donor gives a fixed $20,000 a year, in total, to charity. Is there any tax-related optimization available?

At first, it would seem the answer is no. You give $20,000, and you get to deduct it. End of story.

But actually that is not the end of the story. We have to look at the donor's income level and what else is going on in his tax return to determine whether there is a better way to do it.

For example, suppose the donor has total income of $300,000 a year, and lives in a state such as Texas or Florida that has no income tax. To keep things relatively simple, assume that the donor is married and has two dependents.

Under the current law as this is written, this donor, giving $20,000 on December 31, 2011, and $20,000 on December 31, 2012, would pay a total, over the two years, of $157,386.

The same donor, with the same income, and doing everything else the same, except that he waits one day and makes his first contribution on January 1, 2012, would pay a total federal tax, over the two years, of $152,513. In this case, waiting a day saves him $4,783. If this situation in any way fits you, you've just made a fantastically high rate of return on the cost of this book.

If this donor's situation, and the tax laws, held still, we could say with confidence that the donor should take this approach every year.

But in the real world, things rarely hold still for that long. Our hypothetical donor's financial life is so simple that it is unlike the situations of many real people. For example, most people with an income of $300,000, spouse, and two dependents will also have a mortgage. Let us assume that they have a $400,000 mortgage. With this simple change, he now gains no benefit from bunching the payments into one year.

However, if his income were $400,000, and his mortgage $300,000, it again makes sense to bunch the deductions into one year.

So even with no uncertainty about the tax laws, with any complexity at all to the situation it is not possible to make a blanket statement about what is best.

Fixed-Percentage Gifting

Just as some people give a fixed-dollar amount each year, others give a fixed percentage. There is a very long and illustrious tradition of doing exactly that. Many people read the Bible as prescribing that 10 percent should be given to charity each year. (Others view the tithe prescribed to go to the priests as the equivalent of a tax. Still others view the Bible as specifying a 10 percent income tax, and 10 percent for charity.) The Talmud specifies that people must give a minimum of 10 percent and a maximum of 20 percent. The maximum so as not to impoverish themselves, and also perhaps to make sure that there are members of society who are able to accumulate the capital that is so essential to economic progress.

As of this writing, the Internal Revenue Code (IRC) sets various percentage limits on the maximum amounts that can be deducted for income tax purposes. The rules are somewhat involved, but basically the maximum that can be deducted in any one year is 50 percent of adjusted gross income (AGI). For gifts of noncash assets to public charities, and gifts of cash to private foundations, the limit is 30 percent of AGI. For gifts of appreciated publicly traded stock to private foundations, the limit is 20 percent of AGI.

We can now classify fixed-percentage donors into three groups: those giving less than 20 percent of their AGI to charity each year, those giving between 20 and 50 percent each year, and those giving more than 50 percent each year.

As you might expect, the first group, less than 20 percent, is by far the most common. However, you may be surprised at how many are in the second group—20 to 50 percent. In our careers, we have known a few supremely charitable souls who persistently gave more than 50 percent of their income to charity. In fact, based on our observations, we might conclude that the rabbis of the Talmud were right that it is indeed possible for overly generous people to give away so much that they themselves become the recipients of charity. As we write this, we are thinking of a particular person who at one time was worth $50 million dollars, and gave it all away, to the point that he has now borrowed against his future income, against his house, and against his IRA, and goes looking for charitable contributions. This is a highly respectable and upstanding citizen.

Donors who give more than 20 percent a year are likely to find their deductions limited if they attempt to bunch them, so this is not likely to be a useful strategy for them.

But the fixed-percentage donor who contributes less than 20 percent of this annual income should carefully consider whether gift-bunching makes sense. Sometimes it will make her better off, sometimes worse off, and sometimes it won't make much difference. We strongly urge people in this situation to consult with their tax advisers. It may be quite worthwhile to work up a detailed model of various potential scenarios.

For example, consider a donor with an AGI of $200,000, who gives the biblical 10 percent each year. Suppose this donor is married, and a resident of a state with a 5 percent state income tax, like Utah. This donor's default position would be to pay his $10,000 in state taxes each year as they are due, and make his $20,000 charitable contributions each year. Under this scenario (based on current law, and simple assumptions), each year he will pay a two-year total of $82,616 in federal income taxes, and $20,000 in state income taxes.

However, this donor could also consider (and review with his tax adviser) bunching his charitable contributions into the second year. The model will show that this will actually increase his two-year total of federal taxes by $8. But it will reduce his two-year total of state income taxes by almost $600.

Also of interest here is the possibility of bunching three years' contributions into one year. The donor would do this, for example, by making his contribution "for" 2011 on January 1, 2012, his contribution for 2012 in June, and his contribution for 2013 on December 31, 2012. This three-year bunching will drive his three-year total federal tax up by $404, but he will save almost $1,800 in state taxes over the same period.

However, these rules cannot be applied blindly. For example, suppose we have the same taxpayer/donor. Everything is the same, except that he has the opportunity to take a one-time long-term capital gain of $100,000. Does it matter when he takes it? And does this affect the decision of whether or not to bunch the charitable contributions?

The answer is yes—and no. He should still bunch his deductions into the middle year. But he should not put the $100,000 into this same year. He should take it either before or after the bunching year. The difference is about $2,500 in tax.

Tax Planning Complexity

As you can see, even when there is no uncertainty about tax rates, and no uncertainty about income numbers, the problem of determining the optimum is not simple. And as anyone who's filled out a tax return knows, the scenario is almost never as simple as our examples. Furthermore, even a taxpayer/donor living in a no-tax state like Nevada still has to worry about two tax systems: the regular federal income tax and the alternative minimum tax.

In theory, if you could specify the tax laws, the uncertainty in the laws, and the uncertainty in your income, you could set up a type of optimization problem known as a stochastic programming problem. Don't worry if you don't know what those words mean, because the chances are slim to none that you'll ever need to consider it.

When we started our careers, the complexity of the problems was similar, but many of the problems were unsolvable in a reasonable amount of time given the available computing power. Today, computing power is not the constraint. Unfortunately, the expertise necessary to (a) fully understand the problem and (b) solve it once it is understood are rare and costly.

You've probably heard of the Black-Scholes model for calculating the theoretical price of certain option contracts. Myron Scholes, a former professor of ours at Stanford, won the Nobel Prize in economics largely on the strength of this work. Fischer Black did not win the prize only because of his untimely death from throat cancer two years before the Nobel was awarded to Scholes.

Black was a supremely gifted financial economist, and an analytical wizard. In 1984, he was hired by Goldman Sachs. But Black had very little experience in the areas that Goldman traditionally operated in. He reputedly was paid a very large amount of money. But why was he there?

> Most of the people at Goldman Sachs didn't understand and didn't see how Black could be adding much value, because there were no trading coups or corporate transactions with his name on them. Black was never part of the firm's culture in many other ways. He interacted with several hundred people, but only to the extent that their interests overlapped with his and he was learning from them. Without Rubin's [Robert Rubin, former Treasury Secretary in the Clinton administration, and before that a senior partner at Goldman] sponsorship and guidance, he would no more have become part of the firm than oil mixes with water. A loner, he never could join in the intense collaboration that was so central to Goldman Sachs's operation. He was certainly not a team manager and he had no selling skills and no interest in developing client relationships, particularly outside normal business hours. Worse, using Black with clients could backfire on a salesman because Black always spoke as he thought at a particular moment; he was not predictable.[3]

So what was Black doing there? It seems quite likely that he was working on tax planning. The development of optimal tax planning strategy is probably in most cases an even harder problem than was developing the theoretical value for an option.

In 2009, Goldman Sachs reported a $6.4 billion tax expense. We saw from our extremely simple hypothetical taxpayer that optimization, even in a very simple setting, might reduce a tax bill by several percent. Let us just suppose for the sake of discussion that in Goldman's case (we have no information on the matter beyond what is in their publicly reported numbers) optimal planning reduced that tax bill by 1 percent. That would mean that without

---

[3]Charles D. Ellis, *The Partnership: The Making of Goldman Sachs* (Penguin, 2008), 411.

optimization, the tax bill would have been $6.509 billion, for a difference of about $65 million. For comparison, Goldman's chairman was paid a bonus of $9 million. So if, as seems likely, Goldman has some smart people working on tax optimization, they are probably earning their fees.

Unfortunately, no one can afford to pay someone like Fischer Black (as if there were any other people like Fischer Black) to spend most of their time worrying about their tax bill. On the other hand, chances are good that your situation is not as complex as that of Goldman Sachs.

Guidelines for Analytical Expenditure: Or Is Analysis Worth It?

All our experience with tax planning suggests that there is no substitute for close, detailed analysis of your particular situation. However, experience also suggests that it may be possible to offer some useful guidelines about when it is likely to be worthwhile investing time and money in careful tax planning.

The biggest and most important variable will be your income. As we've seen, the kind of tweaking around the edges that you can find by carefully looking is likely to amount, at most, to a few percent. But the cost of that analysis is not zero. If you do it yourself, it will require a certain amount of expertise, and very probably software. You'll need to learn the software and then spend the time looking at different scenarios.

You could also have a professional, such as your accountant, do it. There are two caveats here. One, not all accountants are equally good at it. Remember, people who are very good at this kind of analysis can save large taxpayers millions of dollars. So, just as you're not likely to find a Jack Nicklaus or Tiger Woods to join your foursome at the club, you're not likely to find a Fischer Black to work on your taxes.

The second point follows from the first. The better the professional, and the more value she can add, the higher will tend to be her price. If your taxes are in the millions, that cost is likely to be worthwhile. If your taxes are lower, it might not pay to hire the most expensive professional.

With these points in mind, we can draw some rough rules of thumb. Let's assume that good planning, as opposed to average planning, can reduce your tax bill by 2 to 4 percent a year. So for every $10,000 of taxes, perhaps good planning can save you $300. If you do the planning yourself, you only have to cover your time, and perhaps the cost of some software. Consumer software varies widely in quality and price. Many tax professionals use professional

quality software programs such as BNA Income Tax Planner. A single user
license currently sells for about $650.

With income tax rates as high as they are, even someone earning relatively
modest amounts of income can find himself with a tax bill of $100,000. And
many professionals and businessmen will find themselves paying far in excess
of that.

So at fairly modest levels of income, say around $200,000, it will probably
pay the average taxpayer to invest a little time and effort into tax planning.

What to Do When Tax Rates Are Uncertain

While tax rates change seemingly constantly (on average about every three
years), the changes are not random. Between the inception of the income tax
in 1913 and 2010, the top tax bracket changed in 37 of those years. Of those
37 changes, 17 were up, and 20 were down. Although there were more drops
by count, the increases have been much bigger than the cuts. The actual top
tax rate is now *five times* the original top rate.

But there is another pattern that you would probably guess at if you
thought about it. Changes in tax rates are not independent of each other over
time. At first, you might think that a tax increase is more likely to be followed
by a tax decrease. But in fact exactly the opposite is the truth. Looking at the
record of income tax rates in the United States over the last century, if the last
change in tax rates was an increase, the next one has a much better than even
chance of also being an increase. The same goes with decreases. Economists
say that rate changes are *serially correlated.* Roughly speaking, purely statistically, the next rate change has about a 60 percent probability of being in the
same direction as the last change.

Of course, this is just a statistical observation. It takes no account of
the size of the changes, nor of the absolute level of marginal tax rates. In
the last century, there have been only two periods of steeply declining income tax rates. Those periods happen to match up quite closely, although
not entirely, with the presidencies of just two men: Calvin Coolidge and
Ronald Reagan.

It is not a coincidence that both Coolidge and Reagan were philosophi-
cally committed to smaller government, free markets, individual liberty, and
low(er) taxes.

Unless you are a careful student of history, you might be under the impression that Coolidge's Republican successor, Herbert Hoover, and Reagan's
Republican successor, George H. W. Bush, were free-market advocates like

their predecessors. But if you look at Hoover's and Bush's tax policies, you will see how wrong this view is.

Hoover pushed for and got the largest increase in the top income tax bracket in the history of this country. Hoover increased the top bracket from 25 percent (it's never been that low since) to a shocking 63 percent. He was then followed by Franklin Roosevelt who got Congress to raise the top bracket four times, up to 94 percent.

But even that wasn't enough for Roosevelt. In fact, Roosevelt issued an Executive Order, Number 9520 on October 3, 1942, which contained in its fine print an income tax of 100 percent on salaries over $25,000! You probably never read this in any history book in school. But it is true.[4] Congress soon repealed it.

After Reagan left office, his immediate successors of both parties raised income tax rates, with George "Read-my-lips" Bush boosting the top rate from 28 percent to 31 percent, and then Bill Clinton raising it to 39.6 percent.

Even the much ballyhooed/maligned (depending on one's point of view) income tax cuts during the first administration of George W. Bush left the top tax bracket a full 25 percent higher than it had been at the end of the Reagan administration (35 percent vs. 28 percent).

As long as there is no Reagan or Coolidge, or a successor to that philosophy, in the White House, the bias of tax rates is strongly up. As we write, Congress continues to wrangle over the future direction of tax rates. The tax law adopted at the 11th hour in the waning days of 2010 in many ways intensified the uncertainty because it is effective for only two years.

Timing of Gain Realization

Occasionally, a donor will have a one-time gain realization event, such as the sale of a business. In the great majority of cases, the timing of such decisions will be driven by business considerations and not taxes. Nevertheless, there may be some tweaking around the edges.

In stable tax rate times, the usual consideration is to attempt to push the gain realization event into the next year, if possible, so that the taxpayer will gain the use of the tax money owed for an additional year. Of course, if taxes are expected to rise, then he will want to do the opposite.

---

[4]The executive order is on the Web at www.presidency.ucsb.edu/ws/index.php?pid=16171. Scroll down to Title II, paragraph 7.

Charitable Remainder Trusts and Deferral

One charitable technique that deserves serious consideration every time a large gain is to be realized is the Charitable Remainder Trust (CRT). In addition to being a charitable vehicle, a CRT is also a tax-deferral vehicle.

When rates are flat or falling, deferring taxes from the present into the future is usually a good idea for the taxpayer. However, when taxes are rising or expected to rise, deferring taxes may be a very costly venture.

Charitable Remainder Trusts, and setting them up, are discussed in Chapter 4.

What to do when you already have a CRT, and taxes are heading up, is discussed in Chapter 18.

Conclusion

As Ben Franklin said, taxes are one of the two certainties of life. You cannot avoid taxes. But with good planning, you can minimize them. Unfortunately, the tax system is so complex that tax planning must be highly individualized. For taxpayers earning even modest amounts, this usually means obtaining the advice of experts.

CHAPTER 4

Planning with Charitable Lead Trusts and Charitable Remainder Trusts

Charitable Lead Trusts (CLTs) and Charitable Remainder Trusts (CRTs) are called "split interest" vehicles because they allow you to do two things: give to charity and leave your children an inheritance. This split personality creates some interesting planning opportunities.

Although some of the basics of CLTs and CRTs are similar, they tend to be used quite differently. Let's look at each individually.

Charitable Lead Trusts

Technically, a CLT is a split-interest trust with a charitable beneficiary and a noncharitable beneficiary. The charitable beneficiary (also known as the "lead" beneficiary) gets periodic (usually annual) payments for the term of the trust, and the noncharitable beneficiary gets whatever is left—the "remainder"—at the end of the term. Typically, a donor will create a CLT with his favorite charity as the lead beneficiary and his children as the remainder beneficiaries.

One of the major reasons to create a CLT is to reduce or eliminate gift and estate taxes. CLTs create opportunities through both the tax laws and straightforward mathematics, leading to interesting and surprising results: Anyone planning to leave money both to charity and to heirs at death will pay estate tax only by default (through bad planning) or through a conscious decision not to reduce their estate tax bill. Put another way, anyone planning to leave money to charity and heirs can, assuming reasonable investment returns, give some calculable amount to their heirs free of estate and gift tax simply by setting up an appropriate CLT. Combining the CLT with a private foundation sweetens the deal even further by keeping the charitable money in the family's control.

In creating a CLT, tremendous flexibility is possible. The CLT can be heavily weighted toward charity, with the gift/estate tax benefits considered a freebie. Or the donor can use the CLT mostly to get the tax break, giving to charity only as much as necessary to get the break.

Before we illustrate the workings of CLTs with an example, keep in mind that tax rates change. As we write today, in 2011, the estate tax is 35 percent. But this law is due to expire at the end of 2012. Congress, whether intentionally or not, has made it extremely difficult to anticipate future tax rates.

During much of the decade of the 2000s it seemed possible that the estate tax would go away, as it did for a single year, in 2010. In fact, many countries, including our nearest neighbors Canada and Mexico, have no estate tax. From today's perspective, however, most professionals appear to believe that the estate tax is likely to be with us for quite a while. We can't predict whether there will continue to be an estate tax, or if so at what rate. But for now, because it makes the numbers easier to follow, we'll assume a 50 percent estate tax rate for the purposes of our example.

On to our story. First, assume a father who does not set up a CLT. He has $1 million and has used up all his estate and gift tax exemptions. If he gives the $1 million to his children outright, he will face gift or estate taxes as high as 50 percent. If he holds onto the $1 million and waits, with the money growing at 9 percent a year, in 20 years he'll have $5.6 million. If he then leaves the $5.6 million in his estate for his kids to inherit, the government will get 50 percent, or $2.8 million, and his kids will get the other 50 percent, another $2.8 million.

Now let's look at the same scenario with a CLT. The father takes the same $1 million and puts it in a CLT for 20 years. There it earns the same 9 percent annually, with a stream of payments to his chosen charity each year. But depending on how the CLT is set up, he will also get an immediate income tax deduction on setting up the trust or smaller deductions each year.

A CLT can be set up as a grantor trust, that is, a special type of trust that for most purposes does not pay income taxes and instead passes through its taxable income to the person who set it up. Or a CLT can be set up as a nongrantor trust; the CLT's income will be taxable at applicable trust rates, offset by charitable contributions.

Determining which type of trust is appropriate will depend heavily on the particular circumstances of the trustor. A grantor CLT gives the grantor an up-front income tax deduction equal to the present value (calculated according to rates set by the IRS) of the gifts later given to charity. Because we are not examining the CLT as a planning vehicle for income tax reduction, for simplicity we will ignore the income tax effects.

Continuing with our example, let's suppose that the father's CLT pays $55,000 (i.e., 5.5 percent of the initial $1 million) to charity each year. Let's also assume that 5.5 percent is the current applicable federal interest rate (under IRC sec. 7520). If we apply IRS discount rules, the amount that will go to the kids in 20 years has a value of about $343,000 today. That's the amount that will be taxed. At 50 percent, the tax will be $171,500. This is a huge bargain. In 20 years, the $1 million will grow to $2.8 million, and the kids will get this with no further tax.

Let's review what has happened. *With* the CLT, the father pays $171,000 in estate and gift taxes, the charity receives $1.1 million, the kids get $2.8 million. The total tax bite is just over 6 percent (because 171,000 divided by 2.8 million is 6.1 percent).

Without the CLT, the father keeps the $1 million, lets it grow for 20 years to $5.6 million, and then gives it to his children. The estate tax, at 50 percent, is $2.8 million, leaving the kids $2.8 million. The charity receives nothing.

Conclusion: The CLT allows the kids to get about the same amount they would have received anyway, but allows the donor also to give $1.1 million to charity.

Why does a CLT make tax sense? The tax-saving power of a CLT comes from the mathematical phenomenon known as the *time value* of money. The idea is that, everything else being equal, a dollar today is worth more than a dollar in the future (because people would rather have money now instead of later and demand to be paid interest if they must wait). Luckily for donors, the tax code recognizes the time value of money and tells us exactly how to calculate the value of the *remainder interest*. The remainder interest is a dollar in the future. And as such, it is worth less than a dollar today. The government is pretty conservative in telling us how to calculate this value. And this works to the advantage of the taxpayer.

Let's look at it another way. The government assumes that people will invest their money and earn something on it. In setting up the rules for CLTs, the government tells us what growth rate to use in our calculations, as we just saw in our example. This growth rate is called the applicable federal rate, or

AFR, and the government bases it on government bond rates. That's a bonus for heirs, because if you assume that most long-term investors in equities can expect to earn returns much higher than the returns on government bonds, the government is passing this extra growth along to heirs completely free of gift or estate taxes.

If a CLT is a home run for planning, combining a CLT with a private foundation is a grand slam. Using its own private foundation as the charitable beneficiary, the donor's family can keep control over the money that must be paid out each year to charity. Be careful: When a CLT has a private foundation as a charitable beneficiary, the donor must not end up in control of the funds given by the CLT. But the donor's children can control the funds.

Another advantage of this combined strategy is that the private founda-tion needs to distribute only 5 percent of its assets each year. This means that the foundation's assets can grow, too. In our original CLT example, if both the CLT assets and the foundation assets grow at that same 9 percent, in year 20 the foundation will have grown to $1.8 million, along with the $2.8 million that goes to the kids outright.

In short, a CLT, when combined with a private foundation, is a very pow-erful charitable and tax planning tool. While the concepts are straightforward enough for nontechnically minded donors, the details are complex enough that donors should seek professional advice in applying them.

Perhaps most striking about this strategy is that, given an AFR, a trust term, and an anticipated rate of return, the effective tax rate is not greatly affected by the level of payments to charity. The table shows how this works in the example discussed previously, with different donations to charity.

CLTs Can Cut the Estate Tax Rate

Annual Payment to Charity	Net to Heirs at End of Trust Term	Effective Tax Rate
8% ($80,000)	$1.5 million	1.4%
7% ($70,000)	$2.0 million	4.0%
6% ($60,000)	$2.5 million	5.6%
5% ($50,000)	$3.0 million	6.6%

Source: Sterling Foundation Management, Estate Planning.

The table above illustrates that for a person willing to commit in advance to dividing his estate between charity and children, the effective tax rate can be brought very low. This result proves true the adage that the estate tax is a voluntary tax. And it is not necessary, as some claim, to leave all your wealth to charity. In our CLT example, which was not aggressive, the total transfer tax was less than 7 percent. The heirs got what they would have received without planning, while charity got money that would otherwise have gone to pay taxes.

So far in this discussion, we've looked at CLTs from the point of view of someone motivated to reduce estate taxes. But it may also make sense to consider a CLT to take advantage of income tax deductions.

Any time a donor intends to leave a significant amount to charity upon his death and the remainder (less taxes) to heirs, a CLT must be considered. The logic is straightforward. A donor who waits until death to make the charitable contribution gets (1) no income tax benefit (except whatever relatively small amount may be usable by the estate in the year of death and (2) an unleveraged estate tax benefit, because the only estate tax benefit is the charitable contribution deduction against the value of the taxable estate. However, by taking the amount that is destined for charity and donating it during a donor's lifetime via a CLT, the donor can potentially save an enormous amount in taxes.

This can be illustrated by revisiting our earlier example. Suppose our hypothetical father has determined to leave 25 percent of his estate to charity upon his death in 20 years. In our base case, without the CLT, he would have a pretax, precharity estate of $5.6 million. After giving 25 percent, or $1.4 million, to charity, his remaining taxable estate is $4.2 million. Of this, after estate taxes, his children get 50 percent (at current rates), or $2.1 million. If, however, he uses a CLT, his children get over $2.8 million, while charity gets a total of $1.1 million over the 20 years. If he uses his private foundation as the charitable beneficiary in combination with the CLT, the foundation ends up with $1.8 million in 20 years, even though the foundation has given nearly $700,000 to charity during the father's life. Thus, using a CLT and a private foundation, instead of waiting until death, generates nearly $700,000 more for the children and $1.1 million more for charity.

Charitable Remainder Trusts

While CLTs help cut estate and gift taxes, charitable remainder trusts (CRTs) are primarily income tax planning vehicles. Charity-minded individuals who own appreciated property are often advised to create a CRT because a CRT allows the tax-free sale of appreciated property inside the trust. However, in many cases, they might be better off simply selling the property and using the proceeds to fund a private foundation or other charitable entity. To determine which strategy is better, it helps to understand how CRTs work.

A CRT, like a CLT, is a trust with two beneficiaries. With a CRT, however, the donor and/or the donor's spouse get the annual payments for life or for a specified term, and a charity gets the remainder. There are two primary tax benefits: The donor gets an immediate income tax deduction for the value of the amount donated to charity, and the CRT itself is not subject to income tax. (A CRT is not a very useful estate planning tool, although it is sometimes misperceived as one.)

The amount of the tax deduction is determined by four variables: the value of the assets placed in trust; the present value of the payments the income beneficiary will receive; the interest rate (set monthly by the IRS); and the projected length of the trust, which will be either a set number of years up to 20, or based on life expectancy.

Because a CRT can be used to defer capital gains tax, it is particularly useful for donors who own highly appreciated stock. Suppose a donor owns stock worth $1 million, for which he originally paid $500,000. If he sells the stock, he will pay capital gains taxes of at least $75,000 on the $500,000 gain. This would leave him with $900,000 to invest. If he puts the stock into a CRT instead and the CRT sells the stock, he postpones paying the capital gains tax, and the CRT can reinvest the entire $1 million. In addition, he gets an immediate income tax deduction based on the remainder amount that will go to charity.

Of course, you pay a price for these benefits. Instead of having $900,000, the donor has only the right to receive payments from the CRT. The actual value of these payments may turn out to be more or less than $900,000. These tax benefits are designed to help charity, so the law requires that the remainder beneficiary—the charity—get at least 10 percent of the initial amount. In practice, this limits the amount the donor can receive as annual payments.

There are two types of CRTs. They differ only in how they calculate the cash flows to the donor. The first is a Charitable Remainder Annuity Trust (CRAT), in which the cash flows are fixed at the beginning of the trust and don't change. The second is a Charitable Remainder Unitrust (CRUT), in which the cash flows are set as a percentage of the value of the trust assets. Thus, the cash flows from a CRUT change as the value of the trust's assets change, which means they can grow (as well as shrink). The drawback is that the cash flows are not known in advance. The advantage of a CRAT is just the opposite—the cash flows are known in advance and cannot decline—but the disadvantage is that they cannot grow.

Let's look at an example. Suppose you own $5 million of highly appreciated, publicly traded stock. You've owned it for more than one year. If you put the stock into a CRUT, with 10 percent, or $500,000, going to charity, you get an equivalent tax deduction—$500,000.

Suppose instead that you do not use a CRT. You put the $500,000 into a private foundation, sell the remaining $4.5 million of stock, and reinvest the proceeds. Not only does your contribution generate a $500,000 tax deduction, you avoid paying any tax on that $500,000 gain. Both approaches produce the same up-front income tax deduction, and both will irrevocably set aside assets for charity. However, there are a number of important differences, summarized in the following chart.

Comparison of CRT to Sale and Gift

Issue	Contribute $5 Million of Stock to CRUT	Contribute $500,000 to a Private Foundation and Sell $4.5 Million of Stock (No CRT)
What's the deduction?	$500,000	$500,000
How liquid?	Limited to annual cash flows	Both personal and foundation assets remain completely liquid
Risk that more money than intended will end up going to charity	Risk of not living to life expectancy (if donor dies early, charity will get more and the family less than planned)	None
Any potential for conflict of interest between beneficiaries?	Yes	No
Subject to private foundation rules?	Yes (some)	Yes
Can you defer income taxes for added benefit?	Yes	No
How much flexibility in investing?	Limited by trust rules and by need to protect remainder interest	Almost unlimited

Source: Trusts and Estates, Sterling Foundation Management.

In this example, either a CRUT or a private foundation would produce an income tax deduction of $500,000. However, the CRUT requires the irrevocable commitment of 10 times as much money as the private foundation. With the CRUT, the donor's liquidity is limited to the annual cash flows, which constitute the "retained unitrust" interest. By placing assets into a CRUT, the donor basically gives up liquidity. Furthermore, the charity does not have access to the CRUT assets, either. The CRUT assets are tied up for the term of the trust. Only at the conclusion does the remainder amount become available for charity. Selling stock and then using the proceeds to fund a foundation, on the other hand, leaves the donor with fully liquid assets.

Because a CRUT is a split-interest trust, the trustee owes a fiduciary duty not only to the donor, but also to the charitable remainder beneficiary. At times, the donor's interest and the charity's may conflict. This is particularly likely in cases in which the charity's interest is threatened by poor investment returns. This conflict of interest, combined with the trustee's fiduciary obligations, can cause a trustee to behave in a manner that is not to the donor's liking. For donors who have been led to think of the CRUT as "theirs," this can be a nasty surprise.

The one clear advantage of the CRUT is that it defers income taxes. The question then becomes: When does the value of this deferral outweigh the other considerations?

It depends on a number of factors. But in some cases the answer is never. This is because the deferral value depends heavily upon the ratio of the property's cost basis to its current value. The lower this ratio, the more valuable deferral is; the higher the ratio, the less valuable the deferral. For basis ratios greater than about 0.45:1 (that is, when the basis is more than 45 percent of the current value), the deferral of tax on the gain may never make up for the fact that the donor only gets cash flows and never gets the principal.

If the basis ratio is below 45 percent and the donor can wait long enough, he can eventually realize more value from the CRT alternative than from the private foundation alternative. But this waiting period can be long. For example, assume 8 percent returns over the long run on invested assets, a 20 percent effective income tax rate for the donor, and a lifetime CRUT (that is, one whose term is defined as the life of the donor). This table shows how long would be needed to wait for the accumulated cash flows (distributed to the donor and reinvested) to exceed the amount the donor would have accumulated by selling his appreciated stock and reinvesting the net proceeds.

Years Needed to Break Even with a CRUT

Age	Basis as Percentage of Current Value			
	10%	20%	30%	40%
35	32	34	36	43
45	25	28	31	Never
55	18	21	Never	Never
65	12	14	Never	Never
75	6	7	Never	Never
85	4	5	Never	Never

Source: Trusts and Estates, Sterling Foundation Management.

Several patterns quickly emerge. First, the younger the donor, the longer he has to wait to break even. Second, whatever the donor's age, the break-even period is almost as long as his life expectancy. For example, at age 35, life expectancy is an additional 42 years, and a donor will have to wait 34 years to break even if the basis ratio is 20 percent (or 43 years if it's 40 percent).

At older ages, notably above 65, the break-even periods are much shorter. However, the corresponding annual payment rates are also high.

Even when the deferral benefits exceed the costs, there is no simple right answer as to whether to use a CRUT. The answer depends on the donor's willingness to wait for the deferral benefits to add up, expectations about future tax rates, and his or her level of concern over the other negatives associated with a CRUT.

When a CRUT is used, it may be advisable to name a private foundation as the charitable beneficiary (unless the CRT is funded with appreciated property other than publicly traded stock). This option is often overlooked but may be the best way to maintain flexibility as to the ultimate recipients of the charitable interest. Too often, donors set up a CRUT, name a public charity as the charitable beneficiary, and then, long before the CRUT term is over, regret their choice of charity. Naming your own private foundation as the charity eliminates this problem. It also makes it possible to keep the assets in the family's control and thus build a legacy after the donor is gone. But even if you don't name a private foundation, it is easy to retain the flexibility to change the charitable beneficiary.

Flexibility and Irrevocability

In the past, one of the biggest barriers to setting up a CRT or CLT has been the fact that such trusts are and must be irrevocable. That requirement has not changed.

Irrevocability means that a donor who puts, say, $2 million into a 5 percent CRT has given up the liquidity of that money permanently. He does have the cash flow stream, but that is not the same as access to the principal.

However, in the past decade, a market has developed for the income streams of CRTs. The possibility of selling a CRT income stream means that even though the trust is irrevocable, and the gift to charity irrevocable, the donor is not necessarily stuck with an income stream for the rest of his life. He may be able to turn it back into a lump sum via a sale. See Chapter 18 for more detail.

CHAPTER 5

Foundations and Children

Nearly a hundred years ago, Andrew Carnegie observed that leaving enormous sums to one's children was "most injudicious" because "great sums bequeathed often work more for the injury than for the good of the recipients." He also declared that the "thoughtful man" would say, "I would as soon leave to my son a curse as the almighty dollar." Although many individuals don't subscribe to Carnegie's beliefs, Bill Gates certainly does. "One thing is for sure," the Microsoft founder told *Forbes*, "I won't leave a lot of money to my heirs because I don't think it would be good for them."

In their best-selling book, *The Millionaire Next Door*, Thomas J. Stanley and William Danko confirm Carnegie's and Gates's misgivings. After years of studying wealthy families, Stanley and Danko found that "the more dollars adult children receive [from their parents], the fewer dollars they accumulate, while those who are given fewer dollars accumulate more. This is a statistically proven relationship."

Most parents want to leave their children better off than they were themselves. This is noble and understandable, and wealthy parents are fortunate because they can realize this desire. However, like Carnegie and Gates, many also realize that there can be downsides to a large inheritance. Parents worry that "making it too easy" will undermine their children's discipline or give them a false sense of entitlement. They worry that the children will become preoccupied with the external trappings of wealth, at the expense of cultivating the very traits that helped the parents achieve success in the first place.

Affluenza

Practitioners who counsel wealthy families use the word *affluenza* to describe just these kinds of psychological problems. Affluenza isn't an official psychological diagnosis, but the list of symptoms is long and clear: low self-esteem, addictive or compulsive behavior, guilt, shame, fear, rampant materialism, an unwillingness to delay gratification or tolerate setbacks, and an inability to establish lasting friendships or to find a worthy purpose in life.

"Parents need to prepare children for the opportunities and pressures presented by wealth," says Dr. Ronit Lami, a London-based therapist. "Children develop problems around inherited wealth because they are not prepared to handle it." Psychologists offer an array of suggestions, including proper discipline, structured schooling, and exposure to different ways of life. Philanthropy as a tool for preventing affluenza is unique in that it incorporates discipline, education, and exposure to different environments, while encouraging children to help others and contribute to society.

Charitable or philanthropic activities, Dr. Lami says, are a vital way to inoculate children against affluenza. As she put it in *Private Client Magazine:*

> Parents who emphasize offering assistance to those in need will reinforce learning by modeling and will contribute to their children's increased value of themselves as leaders and contributors to society rather than "a trust benefit person."

Few people would argue that parents should leave no money to their children. Rather, the question is, how much? It is entertaining to view the wide range of answers to the question "how much is enough?" Famed investor Warren Buffett has offered the oft-quoted wisdom that parents should leave children "enough that they can do anything, but not so much that they can do nothing." Buffett is reported to have given each of his children $5 million. Gates is reportedly planning to leave about 1 percent of his money to his children. (That doesn't sound like much until you realize that his wealth is around $53 billion.) Families at less exalted heights, of course, have similar dilemmas. We spoke with a successful insurance agent who didn't want to spoil his kids, so he planned to leave them only $2 million each, and a money manager who was limiting his kids to $12 million.

Affluenza? Really?

As popular as the idea of affluenza may be, that does not mean it is real in the sense of being caused by money. There are many people who exhibit many or all of the traits associated with affluenza, except those that directly require money. Affluenza may be perceived as far more prevalent than it really is because of the media's love for a juicy story. Paris Hilton makes the evening news. But you probably haven't heard of Evan and Daren Metropoulos, or their billionaire father. That's because they aren't colorful screw-ups. Plodding, unspectacular success doesn't make headlines, doesn't sell advertising, and just isn't considered that interesting to the public.

But plodding, unspectacular success is probably how you made your money, and it's probably what you wish for your kids.

In the end, we believe that the "how much" question is best decided within the family. Parents know their own children better than anyone else and thus have the best idea as to what the right amount should be.

The more important question for our discussion is how to prepare children to handle their wealth. Probably the best way is for them to develop their powers of self-discipline, hard work, and clear thinking. But that's just about what you'd want them to do if you didn't have great wealth. So wealth really isn't the issue.

Giving away money isn't a terribly difficult task to do poorly. Getting children involved in charitable activities is probably a good idea on its own, but it isn't a substitute for them to develop the habits of self-discipline and hard work.

Still, a foundation may be a useful tool to bring children into your philanthropic activity. By using a private foundation as their primary charitable vehicle, parents need not choose between their philanthropic goals and their children's inheritance. They can serve both. In fact, as explained in Chapter 2, the powerful tax advantages of a family foundation often mean that a family can give more to charity than they otherwise would and still have more for themselves and their heirs.

Whichever way an estate is divided between foundation and heirs, it is important that parents explain well enough in advance what their intentions are. If children are not old enough, parents might consider writing a carefully worded explanation of their thinking. This way, hurt feelings and dashed expectations are avoided. As Myra Salzer, founder of the Wealth Conservancy, a group that advises the suddenly wealthy, told the *Wall Street Journal,* "I haven't ever seen an heir who was resentful because they didn't get more. But I have seen them get angry because what they did get was unexpected."

In our work, we see three main advantages for families that create foundations: They bring families closer together; they are excellent ways to transmit family values; and they provide valuable skills for children (or grandchildren) that will help them as they grow up, go to college, and develop their careers.

Bringing Families Closer

Karen Maru File, a professor of marketing at the University of Connecticut, surveyed a group of philanthropists who had established their own foundations. Sixty-two percent said the foundation had brought their family closer together.

The reason is simple: A foundation offers a safe yet significant environment in which family members can come to understand one another better and develop a shared sense of values and mission. Most families never develop an explicit mission beyond the goals that everyday life imposes: earning a living, educating the kids, and taking a vacation now and then.

A private foundation facilitates the development of something more explicit and ambitious—a real mission. And the task of using one's money to do good in the world offers a natural venue for the discussions, storytelling, debate, philosophizing, and shared problem solving that can bring families closer together.

Transmitting Values

Not only can parents or grandparents leave money to heirs, they can leave something that can't be taxed, dissipated, or lost to bad investments. The clichés are true: Actions speak louder than words, and example is often the best teacher.

As Lynn Asinof wrote in the *Wall Street Journal:* "If your real goal is to transmit your values as well as your wealth, you can't wait until you're dead." Setting the right example for children can tremendously affect their behavior. Theresa Odendahl, the author of *Charity Begins at Home: Generosity and Self-Interest among the Philanthropic Elite,* heard this view from one philanthropist she interviewed: Philanthropy "was a philosophy that I learned, as many of us do, from our families. My father particularly was involved in the community, both from a tradition of donation and of service. I continue that. I think in a larger measure all of us have had that history. ... We have followed our parents and grandparents."

Similarly, the values transmitted to your children will prepare them to live their own lives, carry out their visions of success—and carry on the family's philanthropic vision after you are gone.

Providing Valuable Skills

A family foundation enables children of all ages to develop important life skills. Our firm, Sterling Foundation Management, has developed a structured way for parents to involve their children in their philanthropy. We call it the Vision, Values, and Family Program. Emphasizing hands-on involvement, the program provides an excellent framework for encouraging charitable behavior and developing a family's own tradition of philanthropy.

The concept is simple: The foundation helps the children develop and implement a series of increasingly ambitious philanthropic projects, based on age and skill levels. The founder and the foundation provide guidance, support, and resources to ensure an interesting, fun, and rewarding experience for the child, who takes an appropriate amount of responsibility for various aspects of the project, such as identifying a goal or problem that should be solved, generating possible solutions, selecting an approach, and implementing a plan. Children can then see their work yield actual results. Charitable giving becomes not some abstract concept, but a hands-on, real-world process.

One important teaching venue is the foundation board meeting. Properly used, a foundation board meeting can become a valuable learning experience for all involved. For example, a board might meet to decide what grants to make, and in what amounts. Even children too young to be on the board can attend and be included in meetings. If the participants have prepared well, enlightening discussion will result.

"When [children] get on the board of a foundation, they learn about cash flow and how to invest," said one financial adviser quoted in *Barron's*. "It becomes a hands-on experiment."

Often successful business founders want to see their children become more sophisticated in handling money and business affairs. And a foundation can be used to train children in some of the basics. By working through the foundation instead of the business, the founder avoids the risk of alienating nonfamily employees.

Consider the case of Hewlett-Packard cofounder William Hewlett and his eldest son, Walter B. Hewlett. The younger Hewlett earned a degree in physics from Harvard in 1966. That same year, William Hewlett created the William and Flora Hewlett Foundation. His son Walter, under no economic pressure to earn a living, went on to spend the next 12 years at Stanford studying subjects ranging from engineering (he earned a Masters) to music (Doctorate), but also paid close attention to his father's activities and pursued his own philanthropic interests actively.

Bill Hewlett had great confidence in his son Walter. Upon his father's death in 2001, Walter took over the chairmanship of the Hewlett Foundation, which was then one of the largest shareholders in HP. Operating for the first time out of the shadow of his father, Walter, then 57, and also serving on HP's board, was quickly thrust into one of the most difficult business situations in which a foundation head is likely to find himself: at the center of the controversy over the proposed merger between HP and Compaq Computer.

Walter Hewlett opposed the merger, which was favored by HP's management. Hewlett raised a number of objections, and came very close to defeating the proposal. In the end, many of Hewlett's concerns were addressed, and the merger went through. Some analysts credit Hewlett's opposition with forcing the company to prepare a much more thorough merger plan than it originally had, and therefore give much credit for the early merger success, ironically, to Walter Hewlett.

Doug, a successful businessman in Southern California, is at the beginning of his story, but is following a similar path. After leaving the Navy, where he was a dentist, Doug turned to real estate development, and over the course of 30 years has built a $25 million empire in the self-storage industry. Doug has seen his friends' children make a mess of thriving businesses, and he is determined to make sure that this doesn't happen when he turns his business over to his own son Tom.

Doug and his wife are using their foundation as a low-risk training ground for Tom, now in his early twenties. Doug has dedicated a fraction of his cash flow each year to the foundation, with the intention of building a large foundation over time. He has made Tom a board member, with the understanding that Tom's responsibility and authority will increase provided he demonstrates an interest and a willingness to learn.

Doug's main philanthropic interest is education, and he gives a great deal of money to help support his alma mater in California. But Doug and his wife have set aside about 20 percent of the foundation's expenditures each year for Tom to use as he sees fit. Tom gets a chance to operate on his own, without jeopardizing the business or the foundation, and his parents have the opportunity to evaluate their son's performance and growth. It's too early to tell whether Tom, now in graduate school in England, will join his father in the real estate business. But if he does, it won't be the first time they have worked together, or the first time Tom has had significant financial responsibility.

The skills that children and grandchildren can acquire in foundations may have an even more immediate payoff: The experience can make them outstanding candidates for elite colleges. As college admissions grow ever more competitive, young people who get involved in the administration of a family foundation can demonstrate a distinctive drive to be involved, a willingness to reach out beyond themselves, the ability to solve problems, and the perseverance to implement solutions. These are qualities universities see little of, even in the most elite pools of applicants. Top colleges are deluged with applications from bright kids with good grades—but not from kids who have administered grants, shaped a new nonprofit program, or helped build community services. This distinction is particularly useful if your kids rank low on the "diversity" scale that is an important part of elite college admissions today.

Many parents find that involvement in a foundation can give teenagers a sense of purpose, especially for those who initially lack direction or who tend to be self-absorbed. Donors often tell us that their foundations have fostered greater maturity and depth of character in their kids, qualities they don't see in kids who are not involved in philanthropy.

For older children already embarked on a career, the approach is different. One benefit of foundation involvement at this stage is networking. There are few more effective methods of networking than helping people with projects close to their heart, backed up by the ability to help finance them. Of course, for this to work most effectively, there must be a sincere desire to help.

Conclusion

People want to give their children more than just material wealth. They want to give them the tools necessary to live happy, productive, meaningful lives. There is, of course, no sure way of doing this, no magic bullet. But more and more, thoughtful people are putting into practice Helen Keller's wisdom that "True happiness is not attained through self-gratification, but through fidelity to a worthy purpose." Their private foundations are an important place to develop such fidelity.

CHAPTER 6

Benefits of Giving While You're Still Alive

Philanthropy is an endeavor that seems particularly ripe for procrastination. After all, it is a very rare person who, upon waking every morning, feels a compelling urgency to get up and give money away.

"People with the resources to have their own foundation tend to be very busy, active sorts, and while they want to proceed with their philanthropic planning, it's not always at the top of the list. I've seen people think about it for years before acting. Some never pull the trigger," observes Andy Bewley, an advisor in Aptos, California. But while there may be good reasons to postpone funding a foundation until death, tax planning is not often one of them. "Good tax planning," involving the use of lifetime gifts to a private foundation, "can double the amount a donor has available for charity, and still leave more for the children," says Barry Bondroff, CPA, a partner in the Baltimore accounting firm Gorfine, Schiller & Gardyn.

In addition to the financial benefits, there are other advantages as well. Three major potential benefits of beginning a philanthropic program such as a private foundation during a donor's lifetime are personal satisfaction, the ability to shape a legacy, and the ability to exert control both during and after life.

Personal Satisfaction

One reason donors start foundations when they are still alive is that they enjoy the gratitude people express to them for their generosity. Donors who wait until they die to make contributions won't see the effects of their generous gifts and certainly won't be able to acknowledge the thanks from those they helped.

Of course, receiving kudos is not the only reason for making donations while still alive, but it can be an enjoyable one, even though it is rarely mentioned out loud, or in public, by donors.

Many donors start foundations during their lifetimes so that they, along with their charitable causes, may enjoy the positive changes brought about by their giving. For example, Michael Milken, a famous name in finance in the 1980s, set up the Milken Family Foundation in 1982. His father suffered from melanoma, and he from prostate cancer. This led to Milken's multi-hundred million dollar commitment to fighting cancer.

Fortune magazine has called him *The Man Who Changed Medicine* for his efforts. The magazine reports:

> Milken has, in fact, turned the cancer establishment upside down. In the time it normally takes a big pharmaceutical company to bring a single new drug to market, Milken has managed to raise the profile of prostate cancer significantly, increase funding dramatically to fight the disease, spur innovative research, attract new people to the field, get myriad drugs into clinical trials, and, dare we say, speed up science. Milken's philanthropy, the Prostate Cancer Foundation, has raised $210 million from its founding in 1993 through 2003, making it the world's largest private sponsor of prostate cancer research. That all-fronts effort, say numerous experts interviewed by *Fortune*, has been a significant factor in reducing deaths and suffering from the disease.

Create a Legacy

Some people care about being remembered after death and some people don't. But, if being remembered is important to you, as it is for many donors, starting a foundation early gives you a chance to explore a rewarding second career as a philanthropist and to create a legacy.

Here's a trivia question for a cocktail party: What do John D. Rockefeller, Andrew Carnegie, and Julius Rosenwald have in common? If you don't know, you're not alone. In the 1930s, Rosenwald, Rockefeller, and Carnegie were the "Big Three" of philanthropy. Rosenwald was a philanthropist on the same scale as Rockefeller and Carnegie. So what happened to Rosenwald? His foundation spent itself out of existence, as he wished, and now it is not making any contributions to anything. But while virtually everyone recognizes the names of Rockefeller and Carnegie, few people today have ever heard of Julius Rosenwald.

Rosenwald required that his foundation spend itself out of existence within a relatively short period following his death, which occurred in 1932.

Rosenwald most likely chose to eliminate the existence of his foundation because he didn't trust those who would be running it after he died. He once said, "It is easier to make $1 million honestly than to give it away wisely." Rosenwald's foundation spent all its money rapidly. Concentrating on the education of poor black children, mainly in the South, the foundation built many schools. For example, in Prince Georges County, Maryland, it built 23 schools. Just nine still survive.

In addition to forgoing a legacy, another problem with Rosenwald's method of giving the foundation an expiration date is the perverse incentive it creates to spend the dollars quickly, but not necessarily in the smartest way. If you've got to shovel money out the door, it is tough to do it well.

John M. Olin, the head of a family chemical and munitions manufacturing business, who died in 1982, avoided the problem by giving his directors flexibility. The John M. Olin Foundation was scheduled by Olin to go out of business in the 1990s, at about the time those trustees who best knew his philanthropic ideals were aging and retiring. The plan was to give away all the money and close the doors. But Olin's will didn't force them to spend recklessly. The will allowed for flexibility when deciding on an appropriate date to close the foundation's doors, thereby enabling the trustees to use discrimination and care when making donations. During the 1990s bull market, faced with the "problem" of soaring investment returns, which made giving away all the money even more difficult, the directors chose to stay in business longer rather than throw huge sums of money at institutions that might not be prepared to use them wisely. The John M. Olin Foundation finally made its last grant in 2005, and closed its doors that year, just as John M. Olin had intended.

While some foundations seek to spend themselves out of existence, the more common course—and in the long run the more prudent and beneficial course for both donors and charities—is to spend only the required 5 percent of assets each year. Because long-term investment returns tend to be above 5 percent, this allows both assets and annual giving to grow. Note that because of the mathematics of investment returns, and the effects of inflation, if a foundation does not grow, it is doomed to give less and less, after inflation, every year, until it finally vanishes. (For more on this topic, see the discussion in Chapter 10 on spending policy.)

The Problem with Waiting

We've already explained in Chapter 2 how a donor can greatly increase the benefits to himself, his charities, and his family by creating a foundation while he is alive. These benefits include the opportunity to establish a track record that allows heirs and successors to work with the donor and learn firsthand how he approaches philanthropy.

Those who know the donor during his lifetime will know how the donor wants the foundation to perform when he is no longer able to guide it himself. Then, after the donor's death, the successors can use the track record to guide the continuation of the foundation.

A donor who fails to develop a sufficient pattern of giving during his lifetime is faced with the challenge of developing an explicit and appropriate mission for his foundation, one that is specific enough to be a guideline for family members or trustees, but flexible enough to allow for social and economic changes that could potentially conflict with the founder's mission.

Donors' missions range from specific to vague. James B. Duke, who earned his fortune through the American Tobacco Company and Duke Power, is perhaps best known for the university that now bears his name. The university is only one of the many institutions he helped create by being tremendously specific. He created a foundation and funded it with shares of Duke Power that could not be sold without unanimous consent of the trustees. He went on to specify how the foundation's income should be distributed: 32 percent to Duke University, 32 percent to hospitals in the Carolinas, all the way on down to a requirement that the foundation spend 2 percent on supporting retired preachers and their families.

Other philanthropists, such as John D. MacArthur, who earned his fortune in the insurance industry, left minimal guidance. When he died in 1978, he left his foundation no instructions other than the legal requirements that the money be used for qualified exempt purposes.

When the donor leaves no clear no pattern of lifetime giving, even instructions he leaves, such as in a will, can be too vague, and his intentions easily misconstrued. But being overly specific creates the risk that conditions will change enough after a donor's death to make his directions impractical. Some philanthropists believe they can avoid such problems by having their foundations spend their money within one generation after the founders' death. For other founders, this is unacceptable, especially if they want the foundation to exist in perpetuity and continue to do good for many generations to come.

From the Grave: Control—But Not Too Much

Sometimes, in the early stages of thinking about their new foundations, founders will be concerned about specifying exactly what their foundations should and should not do, particularly after they are gone. However, this is one of those initially attractive ideas that can turn out to be a mistake.

Often founders do not realize the limited framework of their assumptions when they specify rigid missions for their foundations. It is impossible to accurately predict a century's worth—or more—of social and economic trends and technological innovations. Yet some founders build a highly detailed plan for their foundation without due regard for the unforeseeability of the future. A donor today, for example, could plan to have his foundation help find a cure for a specific debilitating disease. But once that cure is found, due to the rigidity of the founder's plan, there is no longer an outlet for the foundation's largesse.

Consider, for example, the case of Bryan Mullanphy, mayor of St. Louis in the late 1840s. In the early 1800s, many homesteaders heading west in their covered wagons became stranded in Missouri, without enough money to return home or to continue westward. A St. Louis resident, Mullanphy established an endowment in 1850 to help worthy travelers in covered wagons continue west. Failing to anticipate that technology might make the covered wagon obsolete, Mullanphy didn't see that he was creating a problem. As the number of covered wagons declined, opportunities to carry out the foundation's mission also declined. With grants down, the endowment grew. Eventually, Mullanphy's will was challenged. It became necessary to spend a great deal of money on legal proceedings before the court finally ruled that the money could be spent to help all types of travelers in St. Louis.

Or, consider the case of Stephen Girard. In 1831 he endowed an orphanage in Philadelphia and named it Girard College. He specified that the orphanage was to take in white boys aged 6 to 10 who could produce birth certificates as well as parents' marriage certificates, to prove they were not illegitimate. The boys would live at the College until they were 14 to 18 years old.

By the end of the twentieth century, not only was the number of orphans declining (as health care improved and life spans increased), but adoption and foster care were also taking the place of orphanages. Furthermore, Girard's instructions excluded girls, children born to single mothers, and nonwhites—leaving few takers for the 300 places in the orphanage. Of course, finally, in 1968, the U.S. Supreme Court amended the will to strike the "poor, white, male orphan" provision. But Girard College was unable to adapt to societal changes for the 138 years that the original will was in effect.

These examples illustrate some pitfalls of overly specific instructions for charity. But what of the other extreme—simply telling your trustees to do good things with your money, as Rockefeller did when he directed his foundation to "promote the well-being of mankind throughout the world"?

What about Too Little Direction?

There are a number of famous philanthropists who left vague instructions upon their deaths. The subsequent successes or failures of their foundations can be attributed to one factor: whether or not they also left an extensive track record of their philanthropic involvement.

John D. Rockefeller, Sr.'s instructions about the "well-being of mankind" must be among the most general instructions ever left. Yet his successors were hardly in the dark. The elder Rockefeller, having devoted so much of his life to active philanthropy, left an extensive track record. It seems certain that Rockefeller would, on the whole, be pleased with the great accomplishments his foundation has achieved since his death.

The same may not be said of John D. MacArthur and Henry Ford, both of whom left major fortunes in foundations to be administered after their deaths. MacArthur and Ford left very little in the way of either lifetime examples or of clear instructions. As a result, their foundations have at times been accused of funding programs actually antithetical to their founders' interests and desires. Some people in the philanthropy business—especially those on the conservative end of the political spectrum—have seized on these and other examples as evidence of a need for philanthropists to take stronger steps to preserve "donor intent." But sometimes there is very little evidence of what the donor wanted, beyond the obvious tax benefits.

For example, when Henry Ford created the Ford Foundation, he made clear that he had no interest in philanthropy; the foundation was simply a way to avoid estate tax and retain family control of the Ford Motor Company. After he died, the first trustees of the Ford Foundation searched for some guidance from the donor, but in vain. And because he had no track record, conflicts between the foundation's trustees and Ford family members eventually ensued. The Ford Foundation sold the last of its Ford Motor Company stock in 1974, and in 1977, Henry Ford II resigned from the Ford family foundation, accusing it of demonstrating an antibusiness bias through the projects it funded. Today there is little connection between the Ford Foundation and either the automobile company or the family.

In another example, Neal Freeman, an advisor to the wealthy and a strong advocate of respect for donor intent, has complained that the only thing uniting the recipients of the MacArthur Foundation "genius grants" is that the "selection of each would have embarrassed John D. MacArthur." Whether that's true is impossible to know with certainty, because MacArthur's philanthropic guidance to his foundation directors consisted of these words: "I made the money. You guys will have to figure out what to do with it." Since

MacArthur was not involved in charitable activities while he was alive, he left no trail of grants to guide the foundation's trustees. So while MacArthur was a political conservative during his lifetime, there is no evidence on which to build a persuasive case that he intended his foundation to somehow please conservatives. MacArthur most likely misplaced confidence in the initial board of the foundation—which, according to Neal Freeman, "consisted primarily of Chicago social ornaments"—assuming that they would somehow discover his intentions for the foundation. But, says Freeman, forming assumptions about MacArthur's intentions, based on painfully little evidence, proved to be a daunting task for the trustees.

William E. Simon, a well-known conservative who was secretary of the treasury in the Nixon administration, served briefly on the foundation's board. He found the experience on the MacArthur board "the most frustrating of his life," according to Freeman, because as a conservative aware of MacArthur's conservative views, he was unable to bring the board to the position that the foundation should advance conservative views. (Simon also served on the board of the John M. Olin Foundation and found it a far more congenial experience.) MacArthur preferred to concentrate almost entirely on business during his lifetime. But his failure to develop a philanthropic tradition himself means that the current mission of the MacArthur Foundation does not reflect its founder's beliefs.

William Simon was himself an important philanthropist, and his own actions shed light on the difficulty of gauging the philanthropic desires of someone without direct evidence. In addition to serving as treasury secretary, Simon was a very successful businessman. His son, William E. Simon, Jr., credits him with developing the leveraged buyout. He gave away an estimated $30 million during his lifetime and in 1998 announced his intention to devote his fortune, estimated at about $350 million at his death in 2000, to various charities, including AIDS hospices and education for low-income groups. How many people, knowing that Simon was without doubt a staunch political conservative, would, if placed on the board of the William E. Simon Foundation and given no guidance as to Simon's preferences, have allocated funds to AIDS hospices and education for the poor?

Between the Scylla of being too restrictive and the Charybdis of being too vague, how is a donor to specify what his foundation should do after he dies? That depends largely on a donor's goals and wishes. If a donor's mission is vague, he should make sure that his philanthropic goals are specified during his lifetime, either by developing a track record or by spelling out a few general principles in the founding documents and appointing his children or trusted (and younger) friends as directors. But if a donor's mission is quite specific—say, to secure greater recognition for Lithuanian church architecture, enable disabled sculptors to go to art school, or provide scholarships for Armenian-Americans to attend a law enforcement academy—the donor needs to find directors who share their passion or at the very least can be trusted to carry out those wishes.

A potential alternative for some people is a "field of interest fund" with a community foundation. A field of interest fund is created by a community foundation with the goal of attracting funds from donors who want to fund a particular area, but don't want to give away all the money immediately and don't want the burdens—or benefits—of control. For example, the New York Community Trust offers such funds in the areas of drug-abuse prevention, teen pregnancy prevention, and helping poor young artists, among others. They do the work of selecting recipients, according to their views of what is most beneficial, given a donor's guidelines. The gifts can bear the name of the original donor. "The advantage of a field-of-interest fund is that it keeps up with the times," says the Community Trust. "The arts will always depend on private philanthropy, and we'll always have to be concerned about our young people. But today's youth problems weren't around forty years ago, and neither were the many exciting young arts groups that have sprung up all over the City. Rather than locking your charitable contribution into a few specific charities, a field-of-interest fund will always be able to meet contemporary needs."

Who Gets Control?

It is extremely important that a donor consider her relationship with her family or with her trustees when deciding how specific her foundation's mission should be. For example, if the family has a close, harmonious relationship and the donor trusts her children's (or grandchildren's) judgment, she may simply want to appoint them as directors, with no restrictions on what they may do after her death. This approach avoids the pitfalls of overrestriction, since any constraints will not only bind children, but could also bind generations to come.

However, if a donor's family is not close, or if the children don't get along with each other, or the donor has no children or other close relatives and does not intend to disburse the foundation's money before death, then the donor will need to give more thought to who successors will be.

Sometimes the choice is not that difficult. Claude R. Lambe, a dedicated philanthropist and conservative from Kansas who died in 1981 leaving no children, did have a trustworthy friend who was and is a prominent philanthropist in his own right. The friend, industrialist Charles G. Koch, Chairman of Koch Industries, the largest or second-largest privately held company in the United States according to *Forbes* magazine, shared his libertarian beliefs and was a generation younger. Some 20 years after Lambe's death, Koch, along with his wife and some business associates, continues to run Lambe's foundation. Because Koch and Lambe had similar philosophies and knew each other well, Koch doesn't need to waste time wondering what Lambe would have wanted to do with his foundation's money. Lambe, for his part, obtained the executive services of one of America's greatest entrepreneurs for his foundation.

When choosing a foundation's successors, a common assumption is that good business associates will be good foundation board members. Randy Richardson, who spent 20 years as president of the Smith Richardson Foundation (created out of the Vicks VapoRub fortune), a major supporter of higher education and a variety of think tanks, warns against making this assumption. He offered the following advice in *Philanthropy* magazine. "You doubtless have bright business associates. Resist the urge to decorate your beginning board with such folk unless they share your objectives and match your enthusiasm for whatever philanthropic endeavor you choose. There are many business executives whose conduct on charity boards betrays an apparent belief that activities outside business do not merit the full use of their brains. These men and women frequently join a foundation board for the sole purpose of having it fund their favorite charities, thereby enhancing their reputation as fund raisers."

Conclusion

The best approach, whether leaving a foundation in the hands of family or of trustees, is to take an active role in philanthropy while still alive and leave the funds relatively unrestricted after death. This gives the foundation's directors flexibility to respond to changing conditions, while they are always guided by the example set by the founder.

It is always a good idea for founders to state their missions clearly and to spell out values and principles. The trick is to be specific about the vision, and yet flexible about how to achieve it, so that the successors can carry that vision forward despite changes in society and technology.

We cannot overemphasize the value of donors creating a coherent body of precedents by giving during their lifetime. This is the key to sustaining the foundation's mission after the founder's death. There are too many instances in which individuals have waited until their death to create their foundations, only to leave family members and descendants wondering how they should use the money to best honor the beloved deceased. How can the successors know for sure? They can't, unless there were prior actions behind the words.

An established pattern of philanthropy during a donor's lifetime becomes a guide for his family. There is no better way to assure a foundation's future than starting a foundation now, building a solid history of giving, and involving family or others—or both—so that they are prepared for their eventual role in advancing the foundation's mission and goals.

This will not only develop patterns of behavior to guide heirs after a founder is gone, but it will also build good working relationships among the successors. These steps will ensure that a foundation's legacy is one of which the family—and especially the founder—can be proud.

CHAPTER 7

Effective Foundations: The Business of Philanthropy

The most effective foundations are those that take advantage of the best strategies, methods, and tools. A foundation is like a business, and many of the ideas in this chapter are standard business ideas—applied to the foundation world. The chapter looks at a variety of such approaches.

Not every point in this chapter will fit all foundations. But the areas discussed here can offer profound benefits if properly handled, or cause great trouble if ignored. One foundation, for example, may flounder because it lacks a clear mission, while another might effectively double in size with the right use of grant leverage. Our aim is to cover a number of the most common strategies and let founders and advisers decide which are relevant.

The Mission Revisited

In most cases, effectiveness starts with a clearly defined goal. History has shown that the greatness of a foundation—as measured by its impact on the world—is determined by the founder's (or in some cases, a board's) sense of mission. Some donors start a foundation knowing exactly want they want to do. Interestingly, though, many founders have only a vague sense of their philanthropic goals until well after the foundation has been created. A positive transformation seems to take place when a foundation is created. Perhaps it is the process of making a commitment, or the sharpened focus on philanthropy, or perhaps it is simply that people learn by doing. Whatever the reason, founders often find that their philanthropic vision and ability to act on it grow most rapidly after they have created a foundation.

This is one reason why the most effective foundations tend to be those created during the founder's life. A founder who puts the imprint of his or her personal passion on a foundation while he or she is still alive will leave it as a lasting legacy, as we discussed in Chapter 5.

Finding a Focus

Talk about "mission" and "mission statements" has become so commonplace—even among for-profit institutions—that the terms may have become hackneyed. In essence, a foundation's mission is an explicit, even emphatic, statement of philanthropic goals. It represents the founder's and the board's vision, taking the form of a problem to be solved, a cause to be advanced, or a vision for the world that, if achieved, would make the founder feel that his time, effort, and money had been well spent.

Trying to focus one's vision can be a daunting task. Some new philanthropists try to start by "seeing what's out there"—that is, surveying the world of existing charities to see what they might want to support. But "out there" is a huge universe; there are more than 1,000,000 tax-exempt charitable organizations in the United States, and another 30,000 or more are created each year.

There is a simple exercise for those who think they don't have any idea which way to go. All they have to do is to pick up a daily newspaper and read through it. They will see a number of things in the news that either excite, upset, or inspire them. These are areas for further focus, and chances are good that at least some of them will be appropriate areas for philanthropic action.

Most people have a general idea where their interests lie, possibly related to their professions; someone who makes personal computers, for example, may choose to provide computers to underprivileged schoolchildren. Often a founder will decide to work on a problem that has affected his own life, such as a disease, medical condition, or drug or alcohol addiction. For example, Tom Dunbar, a Louisville, Kentucky, businessman, created the Evan T. J. Dunbar Neuroblastoma Foundation in memory of his son Evan, who died at age six after a long battle with cancer. Dunbar's dual aims are to make sure that pediatricians are well informed so that they can spot these types of cancers early, when they're more treatable, and to encourage the search for drugs, which, due to the small market, are not always commercially viable.

Another common situation is a founder who remembers an event that changed her view of the world, and who wants to create similar opportunities for others. For example, one client of ours set up a program in entrepreneurship to help disadvantaged youths get a head start in running their own businesses.

Putting It on Paper

Many founders keep their mission statements largely in their own heads. But even if a founder spends his life as a "living example," such an ephemeral "statement" is of limited value in creating a legacy that will endure. Especially if successors face conflict or uncertainty, they will find it helpful to have the mission in writing.

For some founders, a detailed, carefully thought-out mission statement will be an immediate priority, sometimes even before the foundation is set up. Consider the case of the Liberty Fund foundation. It was founded by Pierre Goodrich, the scion of a wealthy and influential Indiana family. Goodrich was so absorbed by the task of defining his foundation's mission that he ended up writing an entire book to instruct his successors on the details of his vision and his foundation's mission.

For over a generation, since Goodrich's death in 1973, his foundation has continued to carry out his carefully crafted mission. Goodrich wanted to work for "the preservation, restoration and development of individual liberty through investigation, research and educational activity." Goodrich had read widely and wanted to promote the reading and discussion of great works, from Aeschylus to economics. Following his wishes, the foundation has for years sponsored conferences around the world for scholars and intellectuals to meet and discuss ideas pertaining to liberty and has published approximately 20 books a year in areas deemed by the board and staff to be relevant to the mission.

For most foundations, a less formal mission statement will suffice. Nevertheless, at some point it will be beneficial for almost any foundation to develop a clear and easily understood statement to guide activities and funding decisions over time. In the *CPA Journal*, Christopher Bart, who does research on mission statements, describes a good one as follows: It "captures an organization's unique and enduring reason for being, and energizes stakeholders to pursue common goals. It also enables a focused allocation of organizational resources because it compels a firm to address some tough questions: What is our business? Why do we exist? What are we trying to accomplish?"

Jeffrey Abrahams, author of *The Mission Statement Book* (see Resources), offers some famous examples of good mission statements.

Perhaps the very first mission statement, he suggests, is: "Be fruitful and multiply." Most readers will be as familiar with another example: "We the people of the United States, in order to form a more perfect union, establish justice, assure domestic tranquility, provide for the common defense, promote the general welfare and secure the blessings of liberty, to ourselves and our posterity, do ordain and establish this constitution for the United States of America." This, of course, is the preamble to the U.S. Constitution.

Getting Started

The central philanthropic task of every foundation is to decide how its money can make a difference. Just because a foundation has vast sums is no guarantee that it will be an effective presence in the world. Andrew Carnegie, perhaps the most generous philanthropist of all time, wrote, "One of the chief obstacles which the philanthropist meets in his efforts to do real and permanent good in this world, is the practice of indiscriminate giving." (Carnegie believed in targeting the source of a problem, rather than the symptoms. As a result, he and his foundation have always focused on education.) Helping to avoid that kind of indiscriminate giving will be probably the most critical aim of the mission statement. The first challenge for a new foundation, or for one that is reevaluating its mission, is to decide whether to give in one area or related areas or to spread the giving across diverse causes. While some donors find it rewarding to give smaller amounts of money to a variety of causes, most experienced philanthropists find that focusing on a few areas, or just one, is the most effective.

Effective philanthropists tend to have clearly defined goals. For example, when Siebel Systems founder Thomas Siebel learned about the hazards and havoc caused by the illicit use of the drug Methamphetamine, commonly known as *Meth*, he determined to do something about it. But heeding (whether explicitly or not) Carnegie's warning against indiscriminate giving, Siebel decided to tackle the problem in one state: Montana. He set up the Meth Project Foundation. An extensive ad campaign, including 1,764 billboards, 50,000 radio ads, and 61,000 TV ads, and more than 100,000 print impressions, over the course of four years, appears to have had impressive results. Montana reports that teen meth use had declined by 63 percent and adult use declined by 72 percent.

Another high-tech executive who applied his knowledge to charitable purposes is Andrew Rasiej, who founded a thriving tech company in 1997 called Digital Club Network. The Network ties together nearly 30 of the nation's best venues for live rock music. In 1997, when Rasiej visited Washington Irving High School in Manhattan, he found that it had no Internet connection. Andrew Rasiej enlisted help from professional acquaintances from New York City's "Silicon Alley" to volunteer their time to wire the school to the Internet. The 150 people who responded to this call inspired Rasiej to launch a nonprofit called MOUSE (Making Opportunities for Upgrading Schools in Education). Rasiej stated, "The new [tech] industry has to discover and learn how to make an educational system for the new era. It's time to start rethinking what education is." MOUSE is currently operating in 32 public schools across New York City's five boroughs, providing an average of 24 hours of weekly technical assistance for each school.

Mario Lemieux, owner of the Pittsburgh Penguins hockey team, has focused his giving on two medical issues that are unrelated to each other but that have affected him and his family. He has been afflicted with Hodgkin's disease (cancer of the lymph nodes), and his son, Austin, was born two-and-a-half months prematurely. The purpose of the Mario Lemieux Foundation is to fund research on cancer and on premature birth. It donated $5 million to establish the Mario Lemieux Centers for Patient Care and Research at the University of Pittsburgh Medical Center, and it created the Austin Lemieux Neonatal Research Project, which supports research at the Division of Neonatology and Developmental Biology at Magee-Women's Hospital in Pittsburgh.

Know Your Charities

Just as a savvy investor would never buy stock in companies simply because they solicited him, a foundation shouldn't write checks to whatever charities come knocking. Certainly a blue-chip reputation counts—as much as it would on Wall Street. But a foundation must find out how a given charity operates, if it has a good track record, and how its mission fits in with that of the foundation. Keep in mind that the charity's own reports are no more adequate than simply using a company's annual report to evaluate it as an investment. This is true especially, of course, for larger commitments of money. Donors should approach their research on charities accordingly—ask questions, verify information, and build an understanding.

Potential donors may be surprised, too, to find that the most familiar charities don't do exactly what would be expected. Consider the largest charity in the United States, the Salvation Army, with estimated total revenues of almost $3 billion in 2010. Most people think of the Salvation Army as a charity that runs thrift shops and sets up bell-ringing solicitors to collect for the poor at Christmastime. In fact, it is a church—an evangelical Christian denomination with more than 1 million members in 107 countries. Members who have signed the church's Articles of War are considered "soldiers," and must eschew alcohol, tobacco, gambling, pornography, and the occult, leading "a life that is clean in thought, word and deed." The funds it collects help support clergy members who are on call 24 hours a day, and who follow detailed rules on everything from how to save a soul to how to court a prospective spouse. The Salvation Army has a solid reputation and has done incalculable good for millions of people. We are using it as an example only to show that being able to recognize a "name" is not the same as knowing the details about that charity, including its mission, what it stands for, and how exactly it would use a donor's money.

Financial and philanthropic publications such as *Worth* magazine and the *Chronicle of Philanthropy* often issue lists—usually in December—of charities they consider efficient, based on simple formulas concerning the payment of overhead, salaries, and other expenses. These rankings can be a useful beginning for one's research, but should not be the end.

Also keep in mind that celebrity endorsements are no guarantee of a charity's effectiveness. In fact, a celebrity appearance at a charity event can sometimes cost the charity more money than the event raises—as much as $50,000 *per event* for first-class travel, accommodations, limousines, equipment rental, musicians, and technicians—and that doesn't even include the speaking or appearance fee, which might add additional tens of thousands of dollars to the cost.

If you really care about being effective, not just feeling good, you need to look beyond—and behind—well-known names. Good people and groups come in all shapes and sizes, from nationally known to completely unheralded. Some of the most effective groups are small, local organizations that to someone not familiar with their operations might look dicey. When two rather rough-looking young men came to the home of one of the authors to pick up some used furniture for a Los Angeles drug rehab center, People in Progress, they explained that they were now driving the donation-collection truck as part of their rehab program. People in Progress, although it receives important government funding, is an example of an organization that benefits from and relies "on volunteers whose chief qualification may be that they themselves have only recently overcome the problems they're now helping others to face," as Michael S. Joyce wrote in *Philanthropy.*

After you've come up with a short list of potential recipients, it is helpful to look into the available public records, starting with Form 990s—the tax returns filed by nonprofit groups, which are available to the public for inspection. (Many 990s can be found online at www.guidestar.org.)

Here are some questions you should try to answer:

- How much does the group spend directly on its programs, as opposed to expenses or overhead?
- How much are top executives paid, and how does that compare with salaries of executives of similar organizations?
- How dependent is the charity on donations, and how much income does it have from other sources (endowment or sales, for example)?

While this information will help, financial statements and tax returns don't tell the whole story. Try to read behind the numbers. For example, while no one wants to support a charity that pays its staff exorbitant salaries, $20,000 for a full-time CEO might cause one to wonder if he's any good, or if there's more—or less—going on than meets the eye. It can take time and hard work to dig up a true picture of a group and develop a sense for what feels right. Less experienced donors, especially, might consider using a professional foundation management service, which can save a lot of that time and money in checking out appropriate organizations.

When you've narrowed down your list to a few good prospects, it is time to call the charities themselves and talk to management. This may sound awkward, and not many donors actually do it. But it is one of the most valuable things you can do. You can learn a great deal of factual information about the charity and get a feel for how the people running the organization actually think about things and how they approach their mission. Based on this, you can then decide whether you want to enter into a donor-recipient relationship with them.

If the organization is local, or if you are contemplating donating a large amount, visiting the organization would be appropriate. Keep in mind, though, that when you visit, you are imposing a cost on the charity in terms of the time taken away from their regular activities. So visit only if you are really serious about supporting the group. In addition, the charity may be able to supply the names of one or two long-term or major donors as references. These donors will be in a unique position to give additional insight into the organization.

Governing for Effectiveness

Governance is just what it sounds like: the formal and informal rules by which a foundation makes decisions. There is a wide range of governance structures that might work for a given foundation. During the founder's life, it is easy—and tempting—to keep things informal. However, for long-term planning and consistency, a more formal structure is often advisable.

Structure starts with a board, charged with implementing the founder's vision and the foundation's mission. All board members and candidates should be fully apprised of that vision and how it relates to their work. Legally, a foundation's board can be limited to just one member: the founder himself. But in our experience, most founders want to bring others into the enterprise—particularly if they want to begin establishing a legacy—hence the importance of a governance structure. We'll consider here the primary questions. These include defining the chairperson's roles and selecting the chairperson, establishing board committees, duties of board members, and selecting and recruiting board members.

The board of a foundation consists of the people—directors in the case of a corporation and trustees in the case of a trust—who have ultimate responsibility and authority for the foundation's actions. Depending on the laws of the state, a board may consist of as few as one to three individuals, with no upper limit. Boards are generally required to hold meetings a minimum of once a year, although many meet more often.

The Board Chairperson: Roles and Responsibilities

Selection of a chair will be influenced by any number of factors, including family dynamics, seniority, and the knowledge, motivation, and availability of various candidates. Smaller boards—which are common to many family foundations—may want to rotate the post, providing each board member with experience and an opportunity to lead. The main disadvantage: Many founders won't be comfortable with anyone other than themselves in the leading role.

Board members should establish the chairperson's roles and responsibilities. Typically, the job will include building consensus, managing dissent, executing decisions, planning for succession, and encouraging participation by younger members.

The issue of consensus is especially important and can significantly affect the direction of the foundation and its ability to act. Sometimes, of course, it will be difficult or even impossible to achieve consensus. In these situations, the chairperson's ability to manage dissent constructively becomes critical. In the worst cases (rare in early years, more frequent in later generations), the board can become deadlocked, making continuing operations almost impossible. Even in these worst-case scenarios, however, it may be possible to break up the foundation into several smaller foundations, and thereby break the deadlock.

For example, consider the Wallace Genetic Foundation, created in 1959 by president Franklin Roosevelt's former secretary of agriculture, Henry Wallace. Functioning very smoothly during Wallace's life, it was split into three separate foundations in 1996 by Wallace's three children, allowing each to pursue his own agenda without family friction.

Succession is another key area for the chair to manage. In most cases, the founders' successors are their children or grandchildren. When this isn't the case—or when there are several possible candidates among the offspring—succession issues will demand the full attention of the chair and the board.

Board Committees

The more ambitious the foundation, and the larger its board, the more likely it is that you'll need committees to get things done. If many family members are on the board, for example, an executive committee should be established to make decisions and act between meetings of the full board. If a few members have a particular interest or expertise in some area—the city symphony, for example, or a particular human rights issue—a committee devoted to that area can be more effective than the full board.

Directors

In the early years of a foundation, the group of directors gathered by the founder is probably sufficient to handle most issues. But over time, there is perhaps no issue more important for existing directors than finding, recruiting, and evaluating new directors. Whether or not recruitment is to stay within the family—and especially if it is to go outside—there are a number of important issues. These start with the impact of the board structure on the selection of directors. For example, a board consisting of mostly family members may have a harder time attracting nonfamily members than one with a majority of nonfamily members. Other issues include the terms of board membership, identifying potential candidates to serve on the board, selling points to present to potential candidates to persuade them to serve, and evaluating new members before making them permanent members. Here are some key questions the board will need to address:

- **How will you find qualified candidates?** As is the case with hiring for any venture, finding appropriate candidates is critical. It's common for directors to consider professional advisers such as attorneys, accountants, and investment professionals. Depending on the board's relationship with these advisers, they may make good candidates. But in our view, it's most critical to freshly evaluate even candidates you know well, looking for such factors as integrity, trustworthiness, and shared values.

- **In seeking new board members, remember that you may need to sell them on the job.** It takes time and energy to be a board member, and foundation board memberships are rarely lucrative. High-quality candidates probably won't be attracted by any fees; it will be the board's job to show candidates how their membership will help them further their own phil-anthropic ideals or generate valuable contacts for them in the community. Board members have many motives, and part of the recruitment process is determining what opportunity will appeal to the desired candidates.
- **Should nonfamily board members be in the minority?** This and other questions of structure and power on the board will be most important to directors from outside the family. If those members will be a minority, for example, it may be harder to recruit them, or they may be less engaged once they have joined.
- **Should members have a specified term?** When a board of family members brings on its first nonfamily member, it might be particularly appropriate to create a specified term—perhaps one to three years—for that new member and all future board members. There's one big advantage to specified terms: If the board decides it needs to remove a member, but does not want to challenge a sitting director, it can simply wait for his term to expire.
- **Should you subject new members to formal evaluations?** It may make sense to decide on a specific evaluation period for new members and to tell them explicitly that they will be on the board on a trial basis. An easy way to do this is to make the evaluation period coincide with the first term of a new board member.

Although nonprofit board members are generally shielded from many of the concerns common to for-profit company board members, it's prudent to factor liabilities into the equation when you design a board. Among the issues to be considered are the directors' fiduciary duties; the duty of care, skill, and diligence in administering the foundation; and the need to comply with various tax and employment laws that come up when a foundation has employees.

Many states have laws that insulate unpaid nonprofit board members from most liabilities (as long as the directors don't commit fraud or other criminal behavior). However, these laws should not be viewed as a license to be negligent. And it is worth bearing in mind that while nonprofit direc-tors have limited liability, that does not necessarily prevent a lawsuit. For this reason, some foundations choose to purchase directors and officers liability insurance for extra peace of mind.

Approaches to Grant Making

Grant making is the technical term for giving the foundation's money to charities, and it is the central activity of most foundations. It is the job of the founder and/or board to develop an effective approach to grant making, and, ultimately, to make these decisions.

Our experience in this area suggests that both careful analysis and trial-and-error approaches are useful. As professional advisers working with foundations, we encourage founders to approach the topic with an open mind and a willingness to experiment. Following is a brief discussion of two of the most common approaches.

Evaluating Unsolicited Grant Requests

A traditional approach to grant making is to sit back and wait for requests to come in. This passive approach probably works best for established foundations that are well known, whose missions are clear, and that receive a large volume of high-quality grant requests.

But most foundations cannot and should not rely on this approach, because they will get a virtually random hodgepodge of unsolicited requests, most of which are unlikely to be related to the foundation's mission. Many foundations, particularly the least effective, lack any systematic approach to evaluating requests. There are probably as many approaches to evaluating unsolicited grant requests as there are foundations. However, the most effective foundations develop a set of criteria that fit its goals and values, then evaluate grant requests explicitly against these criteria.

Actively Soliciting Grant Requests

Other foundations establish a program to actively seek grant requests that meet their criteria. These criteria range from simple to complex. At the one end of the spectrum is a foundation that grants scholarships, such as the Buffett Foundation (created by billionaire investor Warren Buffett), which limits its funding to disadvantaged students in Buffett's home state of Nebraska.

Somewhat broader but more complex criteria are set by the SFC Charitable Foundation, created by Buffett's distant cousin, the singer Jimmy Buffett (SFC stands for "Singing for Change"). SFC seeks to make grants to small, well-run charities that work in the areas of children and families, the environment, and disenfranchised groups.

At the far end of the spectrum are organizations such as the James McDonnell Foundation, founded in 1950 by aviation pioneer James McDonnell (as in McDonnell Douglas), which focuses on science and technology. In 2000, it announced the criteria for its 21st Century Science Initiative, identifying three areas: "Bridging Mind, Brain and Matter"; "Studying Complex Systems"; and "Brain Cancer Research." The criteria describe in general terms what they mean by these topics and the types of research they would like to fund.

You Get What You Negotiate

For years, negotiation guru Chester Karras has been advertising his highly successful seminars by telling readers that "in business as in life, you don't get what you deserve, you get what you negotiate." Well, the same is true when looking for the best grant-making opportunities. If a foundation does not receive the grant proposals it hopes for, it may be time to create them.

One way is to approach potential grantees to ask about projects that could achieve the foundation's goals. For example, when the Bond Foundation in Lutherville, Maryland, wanted to fund a program to encourage literature students to study philosophy, it proposed and helped fund the creation of such a program with one of its grantees, the New York–based Atlas Society. Since philosophy tends to be a rather difficult sell to most people, Atlas offers a gentle introduction to students, with an emphasis on applications of philosophy in literature, movies, and popular culture. While still appealing to a relatively narrow group of students, the Atlas Society aims to bring philosophical thought to many people who would otherwise never be exposed.

When a foundation works to create new programs, it's often useful to build the initiative on top of existing elements, usually by finding a partner. For example, one foundation wished to create a program to teach congressional interns how to use economics in policy analysis. Instead of trying to design and build the program from scratch, the foundation teamed up with the economics department at George Mason University in suburban Washington, DC. This fit in nicely with the mission of the economics department as well as the funding charity and worked well for everybody. By selecting the right partner, the foundation got built-in educational capability, geographic proximity, and access to facilities. All that was needed was a curriculum and a program to reach the interns.

Sophisticated donors realize that overhead is a part of every organization's budget. In most cases, then, some of the money they donate will go, directly or indirectly, toward overhead. However, that amount is not written in stone. The overhead charged by most research institutions—universities, hospitals, research organizations—reflects the fact that most such research is funded by the federal government. Even private universities derive a major portion of their budgets from the federal government, and much of that budget comes in the form of overhead charges applied against research grants.

We regularly negotiate on behalf of clients to reduce the amount of a grant that goes to overhead and increase what can go to the program our clients wish to support. For example, when the Bruce and Giovanna Ames Foundation made a grant for cancer research by Stanford University professor Philip Hanawalt, the university initially sought to impose its standard 57 percent overhead charge. Out of each $100,000, Stanford planned to take $57,000, leaving Hanawalt's program with $43,000. We were able to negotiate the overhead piece down to 6 percent, more than doubling the money made available for Hanawalt's research.

Stand on the Shoulders of Others

Isaac Newton, in commenting on his own stupendous achievements, observed modestly, "If I have seen farther than others, it is because I was standing on the shoulders of giants." If such a towering intellect felt comfortable building on other's work, surely we lesser mortals should, too. An excellent place for new foundations to begin developing their grant-making process is to research the best practices of others with similar goals. Such practices might be found in the foundation community, the public charity world, in universities, or in the private sector. They may also be found domestically or internationally.

In business, gaining access to best practices can be hard, if not impossible, because many of the best businesses rightly consider their practices to be valuable proprietary information. Fortunately, your nonprofit "competitors" are usually not only willing but also eager to help. It may be useful to think of scientific experiment protocol as a model. In science, an experimental procedure is tested against a known, or control, procedure. Researchers evaluating the efficacy of a drug, for example, will design a study to compare the effects of the drug to the effects of a placebo. Once an effective drug is found, it becomes the control, and future drugs will be compared not merely against the placebo but also against the established drug.

Developing an effective set of charitable programs can be similar. In our experience, it usually takes quite a bit of trial-and-error to identify a set of core programs that the foundation will support. A new foundation should expect a period of several years during which it will work to identify and fully implement programs. Once these are established, they become the control or base case, and the effort to generate improved results then can build.

Of course, it's a good idea to remember that the "best practice" can always be improved on. Working with our clients and partners, and drawing on the combination of their experience, ideas, and insight, and ours, we can develop a "better practice." How that is done depends on the field. In more established fields where the best practices appear to be very solid, donors should emulate them. Certainly there is no foolproof method of knowing whether a best practice is, in fact, best. But it's the part of the donor's job, and challenge, to do the due diligence to make a best guess, and act accordingly.

Outside Experts Can Make the Difference

The philanthropic landscape is diverse. Whether the area is education, science, the arts, medicine, the environment, or any other field, there are people with far more specific knowledge than most donors will have. Unless you choose an arena in which you are already an expert, you should find experts to give you guidance.

Our approach is to identify five or six experts in, say, lung cancer research, and then ask those experts to name three or four additional researchers who are experts. We contact those names, and repeat the process.

Having identified a good list of experts, we are then in a position to call on them in a number of different ways: as peer reviewers of proposals; as advisers; as sources to help find programs and funders in the same area; as idea sources for innovative new programs, to help us brainstorm; and, finally, as evaluators of completed projects. In most cases, because we are interested in the work to which they have devoted their lives, they are more than happy to cooperate, and often at no charge or with a simple offset of expenses.

Types of Support: Periodic versus Endowment, General versus Program

One important decision for a donor is whether to give endowment or periodic support to a given charity. Endowment support means giving all the money at once. Periodic support consists of smaller gifts spread out over time. As we explained in Chapter 1, we generally recommend periodic support because it gives a donor more control. Once a donor gives endowment money to a charity, the charity is in control. If the donor's charitable goals change, or if the charity's goals change, the donor has already committed the money and has lost the opportunity to make sure his intentions are being matched by those of the charity.

Many charities argue that periodic support is not in their best interest, because they plan their charitable programs far into the future, and it is difficult for a charity to build long-term programs without long-term support. Fortunately, an easy solution exists. If a donor wants to support long-term programs, a donor (or the foundation's manager, acting as the donor's representative) can reach an understanding with the charity that the foundation will give support over the long term, provided that the charity continues to fulfill the charitable agreement as worked out by both parties. This way, the charity gets its long-term support, while the donor is assured that the charity will not change its mission or activities (or if it does, the donor has recourse).

Another decision is whether to give general support or program support. Program support is support of the charity's specific programs. Here the results are often visible and decisive. It's easy to feel that money is doing good when it is being used for something tangible and dramatic, such as buying blankets that go directly to children made homeless by sudden flooding. General support, also known as overhead or operating support, is unglamorous and unexciting, yet it is essential to every charity. All charities have overhead, and money for its own operations is usually the most difficult to raise. When a donor gives money to a charity in response to a general appeal, that money will go for general support unless the donor specifies otherwise.

It's hard to see specific results of these donations and therefore hard to evaluate their effectiveness. And it's harder to get an emotional reward from paying for overhead, such as the telephone bill. But without the telephone to make logistical arrangements, those blankets would not get to the needy kids.

Because general support is usually more difficult to raise, a dollar of general support can be more valuable to a charity than a dollar of program support. Unless the charity does a good job of donor relations, which at its best means educating donors about the charity's activities and accomplishments, a donor may feel as if his or her money is producing no visible results. If you have confidence in a charity, and don't have a specific program that you want to support there, giving general support is an excellent way to help the charity pursue its mission.

It is received wisdom in the philanthropic community that a good charity is one that spends very little of its budget on fund-raising. As a consequence, most charities try to keep down their fund-raising costs and would rarely think of raising money specifically to be used *for* fund-raising. But for an enterprising donor and the charities he supports, this can create an opportunity. For example, a donor may put up the risk capital to launch an experimental fund-raising campaign aimed at a previously untapped group of potential donors.

Is Measurement Worthwhile?

The issue of measuring philanthropy is one that arouses passions from both skeptics and advocates.

The skeptic's view was colorfully demonstrated by author Edward Schwartz a generation ago in his ironic *Letter to Mr. Thomas Jefferson:*

> "Life, liberty and the pursuit of happiness" seem to be the goals of your pro-posal. These are not measurable goals. If you were to say that "among these is the ability to sustain an average life expectancy in six of the thirteen colonies of at least thirty-five years, and to enable all newspapers in the colonies to print news without outside interference, and to raise the average income of the next colonists by 10 percent in the next ten years," these would be measurable goals.

Those who see the benefits are equally forceful. Mark Kramer, a professor at Harvard Business School writing in the *Chronicle of Philanthropy,* represents this position well. There's a difference between thinking you know what's hap-pening and having actual measures of what you're achieving.

> The foundation may look to see if the money was spent as intended. The board may feel good when it gets a report that tells how important the grant was, though such reports are usually thinly disguised preludes to further requests for money. The grant maker might even hire an outside evaluator to decide if the grant "worked" and what lessons can be learned for next time. But how often do foundations look to see if the services were delivered as cost-effectively as they were at other organizations with similar missions?
> The problem with non-profit management lies right there—in the foundation's failure to link financial support to performance. What grant makers and individual donors most often support is charisma. And they mistake leadership for management.
> If, instead, foundations focused their grant making on well-managed charities and didn't contribute to poorly managed ones, they would begin to exert forces that parallel a competitive market and push non-profit groups toward better performance in their delivery of services. This [would] re-dound to everyone's benefit, because as charities become more efficient, they begin to have greater impact, and both the charities' and the foundations' limited resources can go further in tackling society's problems.

Historically, donors have not been very forceful in seeking or demanding measures of effectiveness. Corporations that donate money probably face the most pressure to do so, because they have shareholders to answer to. Yet even among corporations, fewer than half (44 percent) do any measuring of their philanthropy's impact, according to Myra Alperson, author of *Building the Corporate Community Development Team,* a book published by The Conference Board. "I use the term social investment," says Alperson, "to describe how corporations should view their giving. And since it's an investment, it follows that it should have a return."

Pressure may build on corporate donors to measure and publicly justify to their stockholders their corporate philanthropy, in light of recent scandals. For example, it was reported in 2002 that Citicorp chairman Sanford Weill had donated $1 million of stockholders' money to Manhattan's exclusive 92nd Street Y nursery school, allegedly in part to help get places in the school for the twin children of former star stock analyst Jack Grubman. Allegedly, Weill wanted Grubman to change his rating on the stock of AT&T, an investment banking client of the firm. (The *New York Post* ran the story with the headline "Jack Grubs Slots for Tots.") It was the kind of PR a corporation hates to see associated with its charitable giving programs.

But what about foundations? Do individuals who create foundations need to worry about measurements? An investment metaphor applies here as well. Few people with the wealth to establish a foundation would invest much of that wealth without some idea what a successful investment would look like. Their yardstick might be a hurdle rate, a number of years to payback, a target rate of annual return, or something similar.

When it comes to philanthropic giving, it's considerably harder to measure results. Nevertheless, it is important for donors to ask themselves, "How will I determine whether and when my philanthropic goals are being achieved?" Keep this in mind when evaluating charities and programs, and pose the question to their officers.

Many major donors want more than mere assurances of progress from the beneficiaries of their largesse. That's in part because, historically, charities and foundations have too often been willing to engage in what Jed Emerson, senior fellow at the Hewlett Foundation, calls the "dance of deceit." This, according to Emerson, occurs when foundations state goals but don't do much to ensure that the grants actually support the goals. The charities learn to "contort themselves to accommodate the stated funding interests of the foundation" and then simply assure the foundation that it is supporting the foundation's goals, when, in reality, the "charity pursues its own work in whatever way it sees fit."

"Like any other customer, donors want a modicum of service for their money," says Fleming Meeks, assistant managing editor of *Barron's*. "I think people today want to see more specific results and to hold organizations accountable," observes Chicago-area donor Chuck Frank, who supports the Sierra Club and local causes. "They're unwilling to say, 'Here, take my money and I hope you do well.' Giving now is much more specific, with strings attached." In deciding what strings should apply, it can be useful for a donor to get input from an outsider who isn't emotionally invested in the outcome and will do real analysis.

Progress toward some goals is relatively easy to measure. For example, if a donor is supporting his city's opera company, it's easy to determine whether the shows did go on. Even certain social service outcomes are quantifiable. "Things like literacy rates or immunizations you can measure quite well," notes Dorothy Ridings, president of the Council on Foundations, a clearinghouse for much foundation information (see Resources).

However, other charitable endeavors are often harder to evaluate. "Some of the most intractable social problems are the hardest to get a handle on in terms of success," says Ridings. "When I see this enthusiasm for measurable outcomes, I just hope donors are realistic and won't be disappointed when they can't 'end poverty.'" The chances are that you will not be able to end poverty—just as Andrew Carnegie, with all of his money, was unable to achieve world peace. But in these cases, the problem is the choice of goals, not the attempt to measure results.

Faced with the difficulty of measuring charitable achievements, too many donors simply give up. But giving up is not the responsible course.

Many in the charitable community, especially those raising money, have a general dislike of measurement. Good stories sell better than statistics. In fund-raising, measurement yields fairly dry results that don't work as well as human stories. For example, Covenant House, a New York–based charity that helps runaway and abused children, has raised millions of dollars over the years by using poignant tear-jerking stories about individual kids in their fund-raising and almost never mentioning a statistic. (Incidentally, Covenant House has had to overcome terrible publicity from a scandal involving its founder.) We're not suggesting that the work of Covenant House doesn't achieve real results. But a lot of charities like to follow this same pattern in their public relations. The last thing a typical fund-raiser wants is carefully derived statistics that contradict the human appeal story or show that the good was done at exorbitant cost.

Another concern we hear is that measuring will cause the wrong things to be done. Peter B. Goldberg, president of the Alliance for Children and

Families, does not want measures to "drive you to do only what you can measure instead of measuring what you should be doing." Yet a donor who cares about effectiveness must insist on some type of measures, even if these are only subjective impressions of people he trusts.

Emmett D. Carson, president of the Minneapolis Foundation, makes a trenchant point about the difficulties of measurement. "I can't count social attitudes or race relations," he told the *New York Times*. "The toughest work is the [least] countable."

Yet this is not a repudiation of the importance of measurement, but instead an affirmation that it *is* important. After all, if the goals being supported are the most important, then effectively advancing them is also important. And it's the charities themselves that are often in the best position to measure and track effectiveness. As donors evaluate charities, they should pay attention to the charities' own attitudes toward measurement. The best charities will welcome questions about their success, will have thought long and hard about the issues, and will give informed answers. If a charity tries to steer a donor clear of measurement issues, that's a signal to donors to think twice before supporting it.

Many donors view measurement as too difficult, so by default their process of making funding decisions boils down to funding "whatever we did last year." Instead of a redoubled effort at devising intelligent measurement, they essentially throw up their hands. For example, philanthropy researcher Odendahl cites a donor who says, "We usually, if everything works out all right, will probably give the same thing next year, or slightly increase it, or if something happens that lowers our opinion of that particular charity, we'll decrease it. It's really very, very subjective. At this point, I don't know how to make it anything else." This donor doesn't have high expectations. He would probably find pleasant company in the anonymous foundation president quoted by Hewlett Senior Fellow Jed Emerson, who said, "Foundations are like the cadaver at a family wake—their presence is essential, but not very much is expected of them." One purpose of this book is to change that sort of perception and to make foundations vital agents of transformation in our culture.

The only way for a donor to "succeed" at everything is to take no risks: Stick only with proven winners and hope the world doesn't change. The donor who simply funds the local opera, for example, may be able to say that everything she touched was a success. If she ventures into unexplored territory, the chances are that she may have some failures, or that she won't succeed in exactly the way she envisioned. But failures, of course, are learning experiences.

The most important factor is the donor's own temperament; if she wants to play it safe, she should play it safe. If she can handle the ups and downs of experimentation, she can take more risks. Keep in mind this observation offered to philanthropists by adviser Andy Bewley: "Don't focus on the failures. If you can be half as successful in philanthropy as in business, you'll still be doing great things for the community, the country, and posterity."

Establishing Measures

Establishing measures is not easy, but it is not impossible, either. Consider the battle against cancer. Waged on many fronts, over many decades, the battle continues to consume huge resources. But is it being won? Fortunately, we don't have to answer this big question. Better questions are whether a particular program is achieving its goals and how its performance stacks up against similar programs. Is a breast-cancer screening program reaching the number of women it's supposed to? Is a children's cancer relief fund helping the number of kids it promises to? If there is another program pursuing a similar mission (chances are good that there is), how do the programs compare in cost and effectiveness?

At least one grant maker, the Edna McConnell Clark Foundation, looks intensively at prospective grantees in an effort to answer these sorts of questions. Before a grant is made, the foundation investigates potential recipients, focusing on seven factors: mission, social impact, financial health, management capacity, operational viability, evaluation processes, and technological capability. The foundation has developed a "theory behind evaluations," which informs their own evaluation efforts and is intended to serve as a model for the foundation community (see Resources).

The Roberts Foundation is also devising a way to measure seemingly intangible results. The foundation was started in 1986 by George and Leanne Roberts. (George Roberts was one of the founders of the extremely successful investment firm Kolberg, Kravis and Roberts.) In 1997, it started the Roberts Enterprise Development Fund, which is spending millions of dollars to measure social outcomes. The Development Fund supports 23 nonprofit businesses in the San Francisco Bay area that employ homeless people, recovering drug addicts, and people with mental illness. To measure results, the fund looks at data from each agency—debt, grants received, and other income—and gathers "soft" information from employees by surveying them every six months on such factors as housing status and drug use. The benefits to clients and to society (in the form of tax dollars generated by wages and the reduced cost of social services) are set against an organization's costs, producing a ratio that the Development Fund calls the "social return on investment."

For example, Einstein's Cafe, opened in 1997 in San Francisco's Sunset district, gives homeless youths the opportunity to learn the food service industry and acquire marketable skills. The fund reports that in 1999 the cafe generated $12,389 of public savings per employee and $1,023 in new tax revenues. Employees' annual income rose by an average of $6,823. Things don't always work out as planned, though. Einstein's Cafe closed and no longer provides these opportunities.

This kind of measure may not work in every situation, but it represents a useful and powerful way of thinking about measurement. Keep in mind that grant makers taking these approaches face a fairly steep learning curve. However, over time, the foundation will gain expertise and become far more effective.

Provide Feedback

Public charities, from the local church to the American Red Cross, typically have boards or presidents that have formal, legal control over the charity's actions and make key decisions about what it does and how—about measurements, fund-raising, and other issues. However, this does not mean that a donor has no voice.

While many, perhaps most, charities do not actively solicit input from donors, donors can have valuable insights. It is donors' responsibility to make sure that they communicate their ideas. If a donor gives $100 a year to the Red Cross, he can't expect its officials to spend hours listening to his critique on how they should do their jobs. But if a donor gives $10,000 a year to a local church or temple, its leaders will probably be quite interested in his opinion—especially if he's done his homework and respects the many pressures under which they operate.

Whenever a donor cuts off significant support for a charity, he will be doing the charity a service if he explains why. Charities typically don't know enough about their donors and what motivates them, so any information a donor (or ex-donor) provides can be valuable.

Give Wisdom in Addition to Wealth

Successful individuals contemplating charitable donations often focus on what their money can do. But many charities need not only money but also wisdom and experience. Donors can do well by donating the skills and know-how that got them where they are.

"When you go and fund somebody, typically they say, 'All I need is money,'" notes philanthropist Mario Morino, who created his wealth in the software industry and now heads the Morino Institute. "But often they need a lot more than money and sometimes they don't even need the money, they need management or other help—everything from training to deploying and managing technology."

When two former America Online presidents—Bob Pittman and Barry Shuler, and their wives—pledged $30 million to a new building being planned by the Corcoran Gallery of Art and the School of Art and Design in Washington, DC, one said, "The cash is one component of the gift. The other is our commitment to working with [the museum director] and his team, and thinking through how the Internet and technology are going to transform the art and media world."

Nonprofits especially tend to need management expertise. Probably because they don't face the market discipline of profit-and-loss statements or the wrath of unhappy shareholders (as we've seen, some pride themselves on focusing on the intangible and avoiding the strictures of measurement and accountability), many charities have not developed strong management structures. "Far too many nonprofits believe that good intentions are sufficient," management expert Peter Drucker told *Barron's*: "They lack the discipline—the imposed discipline of the bottom line." Comparing business and charitable management, Drucker concluded, "Nonprofits today [i.e., 2000] are probably pretty much where American business was in the late 1940s, [when there were] a few outstandingly effective, well-managed companies, and the great bulk of them [were] at a very low level. In the business world, the average has risen dramatically. Yet the vast majority of nonprofits are not so much badly managed as not managed at all."

Many managers of nonprofit groups are less-than-competent managers. They may be highly competent in their fields, but then, many excellent doctors make poor hospital managers, and many excellent teachers make poor school administrators. What exacerbates this problem is that too many donors and nonprofit directors are willing to tolerate incompetence and inefficiency. Even donors who care deeply about the missions they support often rationalize about the effectiveness of organizations they support. They feel that something is better than nothing, and they therefore underwrite an inefficient operation. Adviser Andy Bewley explains, "While I'd never expect a donor to say this in public, for fear of encouraging inefficiency, I think in their heart of hearts many realize that if they give one thousand dollars and only one hundred dollars goes to help homeless kids and the rest is wasted, that one hundred dollars is still doing more good than the one thousand dollars would staying in their bank account." He goes on to stress that it is even better if a donor is able and willing to help the organization become more efficient.

Give Strategically

In the excitement of the dot-com era, the notion of contributing business expertise along with dollars came to be associated with the terms *venture philanthropy* or *social entrepreneurship*. While philanthropic thought and practice has been evolving over the years, these terms can be traced to a 1997 *Harvard Business Review* article, "Virtuous Capital: What Foundations Can Learn from Venture Capitalists," and *venture philanthropy* has recently received a lot of publicity. (Research for the *HBR* article was funded by the Rockefeller and Pew Foundations.) The article focused on "the organizational issues that could make or break the nonprofit," urging charities to strengthen their management.

Venture philanthropy "combines the passion of a social mission with an image of business-like discipline, innovation, and determination," says Stanford Business School professor J. Gregory Dees. While the current fashion is to view venture philanthropy as new, Dees's formulation is virtually identical to that expressed by Rockefeller nearly a century ago. Rockefeller demanded that the administrators of his charitable enterprises "have the exactitude of scientists, the sound economy of businessmen, and the passion of preachers." Although we can't prove it, it is easy to speculate that the resurgence of interest in venture philanthropy is related to the resurgence of entrepreneurship, which occurred with a vengeance in the late 1990s. The economic environment of the 1990s had many parallels to the environment that produced the great fortunes and philanthropists of the Gilded Age. Paul Shoemaker, a former Microsoft executive who runs Seattle's Social Venture Partners, elaborates: "In our case, [venture philanthropy] means long-term, sustained relationships with non-profits; imparting business skills and expertise as well as money; a focus on giving general operating grants; and trying to be invested. These organizations need more than money; they need human and financial capital. Each part is necessary but insufficient [on its own]."

Steve Kirsch, founder of Internet firm Infoseek, put $70 million into the Steve and Michelle Kirsch Foundation during the late 1990s. With the collapse of Internet stocks, the foundation shrank to just about half that by mid-2001. Kirsch attempted to reorient the foundation to be more in line with the reduced circumstances. Kirsch sought to be very hands-on, personally reviewing many proposals. He looked for "Market opportunities, areas not being funded by traditional sources. For instance...three-year grants to accomplished scientists; older researchers find it hard to get funding for a new field of study." He wanted to do more than "just write checks." And he did.

Then tragedy struck, when Kirsch was diagnosed with a rare form of cancer called Waldenstrom's Macroglobulinemia. Again, the foundation was rocked. After "extensive deliberation" the board decided in 2007 to cease being a private foundation, let all its staff go, and function as a supporting organization for research into the rare blood disease. As the Yiddish proverb says, *Mentsch tracht, Gott lacht*. "Man plans, God laughs."

Like Carnegie, Rockefeller, and others before him, Kirsch also wants to be sure that his donations strike at the root cause of problems. "Rather than feeding homeless people, I'm more interested in preventing the problem in the first place."

There is "a lot of talk about reinventing how giving works," notes Stacy Palmer, editor of the *Chronicle of Philanthropy*. "That same conversation was going on at the beginning of the 20th century." The early industrialists brought an aggressive, hands-on approach to giving and carefully chose the causes they supported—just like the new high-tech donors. The dot-com philanthropists "are actually looking to Carnegie in many ways," Palmer says. "Whether they know it or not, he's a role model."

While some nonprofit managers view this sort of hands-on, aggressive approach as meddling, others welcome it. "Everyone I've spoken to with a venture philanthropist on board views it as a godsend," says Albert Ruesga, director of New Ventures in Philanthropy, a program of the Regional Association of Grantmakers. "To have someone who cares enough about the organization to stick with it and give time as well as money, I'd cry tears of joy."

Some venture philanthropists structure their giving the way they would structure a business venture: They give seed capital and see which area sprouts the most promising results. When Bill Coleman, chairman of San Jose, California software maker BEA Systems, gave $250 million to the University of Colorado for research on mental disabilities, he started by giving the school smaller amounts to survey the research fields and figure out how his larger gift would have the greatest impact. He also negotiated with the university to have the new Coleman Institute for Cognitive Disabilities—rather than the entire university—retain ownership of any new developments, so that it can plow royalties or other earnings back into research, instead of having that money disbursed (and dispersed) to unrelated university projects.

Even if a donor doesn't have specialized business expertise, she can be actively engaged. Lois B. Pope is neither a doctor nor a business executive, but a former actress who inherited her money from Generoso Pope Jr., the late publisher of the *National Enquirer.* She donated $10 million to help pay for the Lois Pope LIFE Center at the University of Miami School of Medicine, which will house the Miami Project to Cure Paralysis. Mrs. Pope will have office space in the new building and says she doesn't hesitate to ask questions of university officials or other recipients of her grants. "Involvement by donors is always very important," she says.

"Mrs. Pope is a giving person, but at the same time she wants to make sure that the money she is donating is well spent," says W. Dalton Dietrich, scientific director of the Project. "That's why she asks so many questions. We speak quite frequently about the science we are doing."

Whether a donor sees himself as a venture philanthropist or a traditional philanthropist, conversations with recipient organizations are important—not just to make the best use of the donor's money, but also to ensure the continued vitality of the nonprofit sector. Like other sectors of the economy, the nonprofit sector is subject to market forces. Although the demand for nonprofit services, and the capital to provide them, create unique dynamics, the principles of adaptation and survival still apply. As a result, the actions of venture philanthropists, and those who think like them, are inspiring the nonprofit sector to evolve in the direction of greater efficiency, greater effectiveness, and hence, greater relevance.

Today, you don't hear the term *venture philanthropy* very much. But the ideas and techniques of effective philanthropy continue to be developed and refined, whatever the name.

One enormous difference, however, between the philanthropic world and venture-capital world (or any part of the for-profit world) is that the bottom line continues to be very elusive and hard to measure in many charitable pursuits. So it seems likely that aggressive philanthropists will continue to come up with new approaches, and new names for old approaches, in their ongoing effort to solve difficult, real-world problems.

Exercise of Leverage

Leverage is key in the nonprofit world. By leverage, we mean getting a single dollar of a donor's money to do the work of more than a dollar, preferably two or three or more. If a grant can help attract more money to a cause, a foundation can multiply its effectiveness. Various approaches can ensure that a gift to a charity is leveraged as effectively as possible. It is not uncommon for a dollar of a donation to result in two, three, or even four times as much money being put toward the foundation's mission. This is one of the ways the most sophisticated charitable foundations achieve maximum results.

Leverage can be applied in a number of ways. For example, a client of ours recently wanted to make a significant grant to a charity that assists philosophy students. We learned that the charity, which receives important support from a large number of members, was experiencing a drop in membership. Drawing from experience with similar situations, we recommended that our client make his grant in the form of a matching grant to encourage lapsed members to reactivate. He did, and membership levels recovered.

The timing of gifts can be an important part of leverage. As in politics, early money sometimes speaks loudest, allowing small seed grants to grow into major self-supporting programs. Disbursed at the right time, thousands of dollars can create millions of dollars of new programs. It is also important to know when to delay a grant, perhaps because of technology issues, expected government policy changes, additional funding, or other factors. For example, three Pittsburgh foundations—Grable, Heinz, and the Pittsburgh Foundation—announced in 2002 that they were temporarily suspending grants to Pittsburgh schools scheduled to total $3.8 million because they were so dissatisfied with the state of the schools. The action got the attention of Pittsburgh's mayor, city council, and school board. Max King, spokesman for the Heinz Foundation, explained that the foundations were taking action now to influence the $485-million-budget district. "Why wait until the situation is hopeless?" he says.

Experts can help a donor and her foundation choose the most leveraged place to invest. In the medical field, for example, a donor must choose between pure research, applied research, short-term maintenance solutions, caregiving, and curative processes. By working with experts in the field, professional foundation managers can help a donor determine the best place to make a difference.

Make Foreign Donations Deductible

A personal donation to a charity is tax deductible only if the charity has been recognized by the IRS as a qualified tax-exempt organization. For charities in the United States, this does not present a problem. However, there are a great many foreign charities that do good work but are not recognized by the IRS because they have not applied for such status. Most charities in places like India, Asia, Africa, and South America have much more pressing uses for their scarce resources than to use them applying to the IRS for tax-exempt status. (Note that contributions to charitable organizations in Canada, Mexico, and Israel that are similar to charitable organizations in the United States are deductible under the applicable income tax treaties with those countries; see Publication 526 for more details.)

Whether it's creating scholarships for university students in Argentina or funding medical clinics in India or scientific research in France, a private foundation can provide tremendous financial leverage—with proper professional advice—by making otherwise nondeductible gifts deductible. If a donor would like to support a foreign charity, he can do it with tax-deductible dollars by using his private foundation.

The idea of making foreign donations is simple, but the procedure is fairly complex and technical. Before making the donation, the foundation must follow the due-diligence procedure required by the IRS. This is another area where experienced foundation professionals can add value. It will usually be more cost-effective to seek help from professionals who are familiar with IRS regulations and procedures and who can readily complete the due diligence for the foundation.

Use Public Relations Effectively

Proper, effective use of publicity can greatly aid a foundation in achieving its goals. For example, the Mark McGwire Foundation used the St. Louis Cardinals player's fame during his late 1990s home-run derbies to increase awareness about child abuse and to raise money to fight it.

Most foundations do not have a world-famous athlete to help get their message out. However, there are many creative ways for foundations to use publicity. The Susan G. Komen Foundation, sponsor of the Race for the Cure, has been able to raise millions of dollars for breast cancer research through well-placed publicity. This kind of strategy requires articulating a cogent message, targeting the audience, generating an appropriate "hook," and getting the message to the appropriate media.

Foundation managers with experience in publicity in the for-profit world can offer valuable insight and have relationships with public relations experts who are experienced in the nonprofit arena.

Conversely, there are times when foundations wish to avoid publicity. Perhaps they are pursuing an experimental line of activity that they don't want to commit to publicly. Or maybe the founder has a desire to support a cause but doesn't want his name associated with the support.

Whether a foundation needs to take advantage of the opportunities publicity can offer, or avoid it altogether, professional managers or consultants can help the foundation's board reason through the alternatives and develop methods to reach the desired results.

Create Financial Leverage through Tax-Exempt Financing

In certain circumstances, such as when a foundation is making a large grant to finance the construction of buildings for a grantee organization, it may be possible to leverage the value of the grant by obtaining tax-exempt financing. This is a complex undertaking, involving many specialties, and it requires professional assistance. Given the right circumstances, however, tax-exempt financing can be feasible for surprisingly small amounts of money, in some cases less than $10 million. While a full discussion of tax-exempt financing is beyond the scope of this book, any foundation contemplating the financing of construction for grantees should be aware of it before making such grants and make arrangements well ahead of time with the help of professionals.

Let Your Foundation Do the Dirty Work

There are certain aspects of being an effective philanthropist that can be personally unpleasant or uncomfortable. Examples of these are rejecting grant applications and engaging in tough negotiations with charities.

Many wealthy people find there are more good causes than they have money to support. Often those who have done well for themselves, especially those who have a reputation for being generous, receive many unwanted requests for funds. It is sometimes uncomfortable to say no to such requests. Yet good business sense dictates that no must often be said. A foundation should focus on the founder's mission and not allow itself to be used as the Community Chest.

Facing such pressure, many founders are pleased to have a professional say no for them, politely and respectfully. The best way is to tell those who request money (often friends of the donor) that their charity is great (if it is) but does not fit within the current foundation guidelines. A foundation manager can let the persons know that their work is respected but that the foundation has other priorities.

Delicate negotiations with charities are an area in which it can be particularly helpful to have that third party. For example, if a donor wants to gain a formal role in an organization for himself or his children—as a board member, for example—this can be awkward to pursue himself. A representative acting on his behalf can easily, comfortably, and confidentially explore the possibilities for such positions. A professional who brings experience and credibility in the nonprofit world will find it easier to make inquiries and may also be able to negotiate successfully in situations in which it would be difficult for a donor to do that directly.

Similarly, a donor might wish to be on advisory panels of public charities. Often it works more smoothly to have a representative prepare a nonprofit vita for the donor and act as a "broker," discussing the donor's strengths and interests with charities. This way, the representative acting on the donor's behalf can find the best place for the donor to use his knowledge to advance the mission of a specific nonprofit. A representative can also research the time commitment needed, the other members, and the reputation of the board or panel, so that a donor can make sure it is worth his time and energy. When there is no fit, the representative can save the relationship between the charity and donor by sparing the donor's ego.

Conclusion

This chapter has touched on many of the issues involved in maximizing the effectiveness of a donor's philanthropic efforts. If there is one point we wish readers to take away, it is that giving away money and making that money perform is hard work. If a foundation doesn't get that work done somehow—whether the directors do it or it is delegated to professionals—that foundation is wasting a portion, perhaps a large portion, of every dollar it does give away. Thus, it is imperative that founders and directors explore their options and employ those methods that will make their charitable giving as effective as possible.

CHAPTER 8

The Road to Hell:[1] Beware of Unintended Consequences

Charity always has been and always will be a double-edged sword. On the one hand, it can be an effective way to solve real-world problems and help people in need. On the other hand, the giver has a responsibility that all too often, is forgotten. That responsibility is the same as applies to a doctor: Do no harm. Unfortunately, a distressingly large fraction of aid and charity does harm, albeit inadvertently.

A thousand years ago, the Jewish physician and renowned Torah scholar Moses Maimonides spelled out a hierarchy of charitable giving. As a doctor, Maimonides was no doubt aware of the admonition "Do no harm," and he incorporated it in his thinking about the hierarchy. At the top of the ladder, the most exalted kind of charity, Maimonides put charity that helps the recipient grow out of the need for charity. In other words, don't give a man a fish, teach him how to fish.

Maimonides was ahead of his time. Perhaps drawing on the ancient Hippocratic insight, he realized that charitable giving can have secondary consequences. Only in the twentieth century have some economists come to

---

[1]See also the book, *The Road to Hell: The Ravaging Effects of Foreign Aid and International Charity*, which tells the story of how foreign aid, both government and private, contributed to the collapse, war, and tyranny in Somalia. The author, Michael Maren, advances the argument that major international charities, including CARE and Save the Children, are aware that they may be doing more harm than good, but persist anyway.

understand the profoundly important effects of what have come to be called "unintended consequences."

An unintended consequence, as the name suggests, refers to the results of a program that were not intended. Usually, it refers to adverse results.

For example, the push during the mid-2000s to develop "sustainable bio-fuels" has had a catastrophic effect on hundreds of millions of the world's poorest people. How?

By securing subsidies from the governments of many Western nations, including the United States and many European countries, the "sustainable fuels" lobby greatly increased the demand for fuel feedstocks. Most of the main crops that are diverted into fuel are also food for people. These crops include corn, sugar, soybeans, palm oil, and cassava. In other words, a substantial fraction of the world's food crops can and are being used to make fuels.

Unfortunately for people who need to eat, this massive increase in demand from fuel producers has caused the price of many staple foods to skyrocket. The United Nations Food and Agricultural Organization (FAO) compiles an index of food prices, which emphasizes agricultural commodities. The overall index more than doubled over the past decade, from 90 at the end of 2000 to 205 in November 2010. The price of some bio-fuel target crops, such as sugar, rose even more sharply. The oils and fats category rose by more than 250 percent during the period, and sugar by more than 220 percent.

The impact on the world's poor has been devastating. There are hundreds of millions of people (no one knows exactly how many), mostly in Asia, Africa, and South America, for whom the bio-fuel insanity has meant hunger and an increased risk of starvation.

But that's not the limit of the damage. High prices for many tropical crops, such as sugarcane and palm oil, have meant more land brought into production to grow those crops for export. That has accelerated slash-and-burn cultivation of the rain forests in Brazil, largely for sugar, and south-east Asia, where much palm oil is grown.

Meanwhile, what is the benefit from all this destruction? According to the best estimates we are able to obtain from industry sources, there is *zero net gain in energy*, at least from corn ethanol! That's right. When all the inputs are counted, including the energy required to plow, fertilize, harvest, transport, and refine corn into ethanol, the resulting ethanol has no more energy than the various petroleum fuels that went into its production.

The problem is not limited to industries like bio-fuel seeking economic gains through lobbying. The problem of unintended consequences also afflicts programs that are intended to help people directly.

Food Aid

One may often hear statements such as "There's enough food in the world that no one should be hungry." The implication often is that if we simply distributed the food where it was needed, no one would be hungry. This kind of one-stage-only thinking leads to programs such as food aid to poor countries.

In a typical food aid program (as opposed to very short-term, highly targeted disaster relief), bulk foodstuffs are shipped into a target country for distribution by local authorities. All too often, these programs not only fail to relieve hunger, but also actually make the problem worse.

There are two main ways that programs like food aid can cause unintended and undesirable consequences. The first is by destroying local food production, and the second is enrichment and further empowerment of corrupt officials.

Food aid is usually delivered for free to the recipient country. Even if the local officials responsible don't seek to line their own pockets by selling the food, the food can still hurt in the long run. What happens when lots of free or low-cost food suddenly becomes available? Obviously, the local price of food drops. That means that the hardworking local farmers either cannot sell their crops or sell them at a loss. If the local farmers are losing money, they will decrease, not increase, production, thus making the food shortage even worse in the future.

Alternatively, if corruption is the order of the day, many of the more talented people will be drawn to so-called public service so they can gain more access to free food and profit by selling it. It is almost impossible for a country to pull itself out of poverty if there is a high level of government corruption. Thus, to the extent that food aid aids and comforts these corrupt governments, it worsens, and doesn't improve, the long-run prospects for the average person in the country. Indeed, tragically, this has been the fate of many sub-Saharan African countries since they gained their independence. Although there have been notable exceptions, such as Botswana, the rule has been corrupt government and bad policies. Food aid has not helped.

The United Nations (U.N.) is typically a backer of such schemes. However, the U.N. has admitted that sometimes food aid does more harm than good. Even the U.N. Food and Agriculture Organization (FAO) has realized there is a problem. Cornell University economist Christopher Barrett wrote in a 2006 paper, "The available evidence suggests that harmful effects are most likely to occur when food aid arrives or is purchased at the wrong time

[and] ... when food aid distribution is not well targeted to the most food insecure households.... ."[2] These results imply the need for caution.

Yet, aid can have even worse consequences. Oxford University economists Paul Collier and Anke Hoeffler looked at a global data set covering the 40-year period from 1960 to 1999. They found that development aid encouraged arms races and probably wars.

While at first blush this may be surprising, a bit of reflection shows how it can occur, and indeed is likely to occur.

A government may desire both development and military spending. In the absence of aid, that government will have to allocate its resources between the two goals. However, if that government receives aid that is restricted to development, this aid will subsidize military expenditures. Note that this military subsidy will occur even if the recipient government is scrupulously honest and spends the development aid 100 percent on donor-approved development programs and projects. By providing the development aid, the donor has freed up cash that the recipient formerly would have spent on development.

The problem arises because the giver of aid expects the recipient to behave as the giver wants. But the recipient, whether individual or country, has its own goals. Consider a welfare mother who desires to purchase both regular foods and cigarettes. If she receives food stamps, which can only be spent on government-approved foods, she can use the food stamps to buy her food, thereby preserving her scarce cash. She now has cash, which she can use to buy tobacco. In a very real and very direct way, the food stamps have subsidized the purchase of tobacco. Without food stamps, she would have purchased fewer or no cigarettes. With them, she puffs contentedly away.

It is impossible to provide aid in one area without affecting other things. The same type of problem plagues student aid programs, rent subsidy programs, indeed, any type of "directed" aid or welfare.

Collier and Hoeffler find, based on their extensive data set covering 40 years, that the effect is not just theoretical. Development aid, they conclude, has practically the same effect that targeted military aid would have. Their conclusion should be extremely sobering to anyone making a broad claim that aid is always good. In what for academic writing is very strong terminology, they say, "There appears to be no regional public good effect offsetting the public bad arising from a neighbourhood arms race."[3]

---

[2] ESA Working Paper No. 06–05, www.fao.org/es/esa, *Food Aid's Intended and Unintended Consequences*. May 2006.

[3] "Unintended Consequences: Does Aid Promote Arms Races?" (with Paul Collier), *Oxford Bulletin of Economics and Statistics* 69 (2007): 1–28.

Zambian economist Dambisa Moyo puts it even more bluntly: "Aid has been, and continues to be, an unmitigated political, economic, and humanitarian disaster for most parts of the developing world." In her book, *Dead Aid: Why Aid Is Not Working and How There Is a Better Way for Africa*, she examines the facts and impacts of aid, and finds it has been very damaging. She asks, "Has more than US$1 trillion in development assistance over the last several decades made African people better off?" The answer is as unambiguous as it might be surprising: "No. In fact, across the globe, recipients of this aid are worse off; much worse off. Aid has helped make the poor poorer, and growth slower."[4]

Private Charity and Unintended Consequences

The problem of unintended consequences afflicts private charitable giving just as it does government programs. A major difference, though, is that you, as a donor or an adviser, can much more easily exert influence on a charity. We will discuss various approaches to exerting influence later in this chapter. But first, we will look as some real-world cases of unintended philanthropic harm.

The Bill and Melinda Gates Foundation reaped an unwanted surfeit of publicity regarding the unintended consequences of its anti-AIDS program in Africa. The Gates Foundation since early in the 2000s has made a major effort to limit and treat AIDS in Africa.

In 2007, the *Los Angeles Times* ran a major investigative piece that presented arguments and evidence that the Gates Foundation's AIDS program was having dire and widespread repercussions in the very communities it was designed to help. In December of that year, the *Times* published a 4,500-word article under the provocative headline:

UNINTENDED VICTIMS OF GATES FOUNDATION GENEROSITY.

The article, in typical journalistic style, led off with a tear-evoking story of a baby who had died in a primitive African hospital.

How, you might ask, could Gates's money have caused that? The *Times* reporters, Charles Piller and Doug Smith, argue that the Gates aid to fight AIDS flooding into Africa has distorted the incentives in the health-care system. Because the Gates money is targeted specifically at AIDS, it has the unintended effect of driving up the relative value of AIDS-related resources. This in turn has attracted doctors, nurses, and other providers to AIDS-related

---

[4] *Dead Aid* (Douglas & Mcintyre Ltd., 2010), xix.

care. Unfortunately, this has left a serious hole in the supply of services for non-AIDS medical issues, because many health-care resources—such as doctors and nurses, not to mention common hospital and care-related items—are also necessary for the treatment of a wide variety of problems.

In other words, Gates's money pulls resources—especially doctors and nurses—away from what may be the most pressing life and death issues and toward AIDS.

Piller and Smith reasonably point out that saving the lives of AIDS patients is not such a great thing if it comes at the expense of the lives of other, non-AIDS patients. And it may indeed be a bad thing if it causes more deaths than it prevents. Yet that is, in essence, what they say is happening. They cite a number of experts with experience in the field who raise serious questions as to the real impact of well-intentioned charitable aid. For example:

> Dr. Peter Poore, a pediatrician who has worked in Africa for three decades, is a former Global Fund board member and consultant to GAVI (formerly the Global Alliance for Vaccines and Immunization). He says they and other donors provide crucial help but overstate the impact of their programs. "They can also do dangerous things," he said. "They can be very disruptive to health systems—the very things they claim they are trying to improve."

And

> Joe McCannon, vice president of the Institute for Healthcare Improvement, a U.S.-based nongovernmental aid organization, or NGO, with operations in Africa, said, "You have to ask: 'Net, are we having a positive effect?' It's a haunting question."

People who have devoted their lives to helping the very poor, such as Poore and McCannon, do not say such things about the world's largest private donor lightly. If anything, it is likely that they deliberately understate what they really believe: namely, that the well-intentioned help is probably doing more harm than good.

Another provocative view is voiced by the man whom *Forbes* magazine calls the world's richest man—Mexican telecom tycoon Carlos Slim Helu. Slim publicly chided Gates for trying to help people via philanthropy. Slim said that Gates giving his wealth to charity "Is an interesting idea … but it won't solve any problems."[5] Instead, he said, Gates should help people by creating jobs. Microsoft employed about 88,000 people worldwide as of June 2010.

---

[5]http://blogs.forbes.com/meghabahree/2010/10/29/carlos-slim-disses-gates-and -buffettspledges-to-give-away-their-billions/.

The lesson of history is unambiguous that sustained economic growth is the only real solution to poverty and its attendant dangers and misery. And in that sense, Slim may well be right. At the same time, Slim himself has a foundation and gives significant amounts of money to charitable causes.

Fungible Money and Inadvertent Funding of Terrorism

The word *fungible* is one that most people rarely come across. But you need to understand the concept if you want to ensure that your philanthropic activity does not create unintended consequences.

A commodity is fungible if any unit of it is just as good as any other unit. For example, a one-ounce bar of .995 gold is pretty much the same as any other. They are interchangeable, or fungible. Money is the ultimate fungible commodity because every dollar is just as good as every other dollar.

This fungibility of money also means that it is very difficult to restrict grants to specific purposes, without also funding other purposes of the recipient. We have already seen this principle at work in the study of development funding by Collier and Hoeffler. They found that development aid has the main effect of funding military expansion.

This effect also means that many attempts to provide humanitarian aid to states that sponsor terrorism in fact fund terrorism. The mechanism is straightforward. Every state has limited resources. It must allocate those resources among competing ends. In the case of states sponsoring terrorism, terrorism is one of those competing ends.

In this way, the U.S. government inadvertently funds terrorism. According to a speech given by U.S. Secretary of State Hillary Clinton[6] in November 2010, the United States gave $600 million to the Palestinian Authority. In her speech, Clinton went out of her way to emphasize that "Strict safeguards are in place to ensure the money will be used responsibly. The United States, the World Bank, and the International Monetary Fund all carefully monitor the use of donor funds and we have great confidence in Prime Minister Fayyad and his ability to provide accountability and transparency."

Yet surely Secretary Clinton knows that just a few months earlier her own State Department said that the Palestinian Authority supports terrorism. In April 2010, the Palestinian Authority named a street in Ramallah after a notorious terrorist. And not just any street. On that very street a Palestinian Authority Presidential Compound is under construction. It is almost as if the United States renamed Washington, DC's Pennsylvania Avenue—site of the White House—after the founder of the Ku Klux Klan.

---

[6]http://blogs.state.gov/index.php/site/entry/clinton_budget_palestinian_authority/.

Responding to the street naming in Ramallah, Phillip Crowley, a spokesman for the U.S. State Department said, "We also strongly condemn the glorification of terrorists. Honoring terrorists who have murdered innocent civilians, either by official statements or by the dedication of public places, hurts peace efforts and must end. We will continue to hold Palestinian leaders accountable for incitement."[7]

But the United States and Europe, by funding the Palestinian Authority, are directly and indirectly funding terrorism. Palestinian Authority president Abbas told the Algerian newspaper *Al-Shuruk* that well over half of the Palestinian Authority's budget goes to Gaza, which is controlled by the avowedly terrorist organization Hamas.[8]

Thus, despite Hillary Clinton's words, the United States (and Europe) are indirectly funding known and avowed terrorist organizations.

Private Individuals

Private individuals and foundations can also find themselves "inadvertently" funding terrorism. For example, former basketball star Hakeem Olajuwon found himself in hot water in 2005 when it was revealed that the "humanitarian" aid he had been providing via a mosque that he had established was going to support terrorism. The mosque had given more than $80,000 to an organization called the Islamic African Relief Agency. The U.S. government shut down the ostensible charity, stating that it had supplied money to Osama bin Laden and Al Qaeda. Olajuwon's mosque also supported another supposed charity that the United States shut down for raising money for Hamas.

Olajuwon claimed that he had no knowledge that the organizations were directly funding terrorism. You now understand that by funding such organizations, he would likely have been funding terrorism indirectly even if the actual dollars he was giving didn't go directly to terrorist activity.[9]

The Income Effect and Indirect Funding

It is hard to accept that a well-intentioned gift might end up funding terrorism. But even if your gift doesn't go directly to something you don't like, you might end up funding it indirectly.

---

[7]www.state.gov/r/pa/prs/dpb/2010/04/139894.htm.

[8]www.israelnationalnews.com/News/News.aspx/140963.

[9]www.nytimes.com/2005/02/16/s...l/16Hakeem.html.

So let's look at the phenomenon in less emotionally loaded terms. Economists describe this phenomenon as the income effect. Here's how it works.

Suppose that you, as a consumer, consume only two goods: coffee and tea. Let's say you like them both equally, and their prices per unit in the market are the same, say, $1 a cup. Your budget of $4 per day permits you to consume two cups of coffee and two cups of tea each day.

Now suppose some well-meaning coffee lover favors you with a grant of $2 a day. But he restricts the grant so that you can spend it only on coffee. What do you do?

Look at your new situation, and decide. You still like coffee and tea equally. You'd like to consume them in equal amounts. Now your income is $6 per day. So you will want to buy three cups of coffee and three cups of tea. You can comply 100 percent with the terms of your restricted coffee grant, and yet still increase your tea consumption as a direct result.

Your coffee benefactor wants to increase your consumption of coffee. He has done so. But he has also increased your consumption of tea.

In almost exactly this same way, all sorts of restricted grant funding in fact goes to fund all sorts of undesired and unintended activities. From Hillary Clinton's State Department funding terrorism to people inadvertently funding abortion or anti-abortion, restricted grants can be a chimera. If you're not careful, you may end up funding something irrelevant to, or even directly opposed to, your intentions.

So what can you do?

How to Give Restricted Grants

If you wish to support an organization, find out what it does. Find out how it spends its money. You can learn this from a variety of sources. The organization may publish financial statements, annual reports, program reports, and a variety of other materials either in print or on the Web. In addition, every public charity (except some religious organizations) must make its annual tax form 990 available to anyone who asks. Most are also available online, for example through the web site guidestar.org.

Look through the expenditures. If the organization is spending its money on programs, and not funding other organizations, then you can look at those programs. If there's nothing there that bothers you or offends you, then you may be pretty safe in funding the organization. However, keep in mind that even if you intend to fund only one activity, by way of restricted funding, you may still be subsidizing other activities of the organization. Remember how the coffee grant ended up subsidizing not only coffee consumption but tea consumption as well.

If you do choose to make a restricted grant, you might also wish to require as a condition of the grant that the recipient organization must maintain its prior level of funding for your project(s), in addition to the restricted money you are granting.

However, be aware that even if you do add this spending maintenance requirement, your grant may end up simply displacing future growth of spending on your favored area, at least to some extent.

If you are serious about directing your funding in a targeted manner, you may even wish to have some expert help in researching your target recipient charities, and perhaps also expert help in drafting restricted grant agreements.

Finally, you may just have to accept that to promote coffee drinking, you're going to have to also, at least somewhat, promote tea drinking. Just make sure you're not supporting something that you're actively against.

Poverty—Again

A great deal of charitable effort is aimed at alleviating conditions such as hunger, preventable disease, substandard housing, and lack of education.

At bottom, most of these are different manifestations of a single underlying problem: poverty.

Until a few hundred years ago, poverty was the common lot of 99 percent of mankind. Only with the Industrial Revolution did that change. The developed world did not emerge from poverty as a result of aid or philanthropy from outside. It developed and grew rich precisely because people were free to make decisions for themselves; to decide on which goods were most valuable; when, where, and in what quantities.[10]

Economists and others who study the problem have known for decades that the world's hunger problem is in fact almost exclusively a poverty problem. As the Chinese have shown so brilliantly over the past 20 years, economic growth is the only real way to alleviate hunger permanently.

Similarly, the shortage of health care, whether in America or anywhere in the world, is not a health-care problem. It is a poverty problem: Some people simply don't produce enough to be able to trade what they do produce for what they want or need.

---

[10]See, for example, Greg Clark's excellent *A Farewell to Alms: A Brief Economic History of the World* (Princeton University Press, 2007).

In America and the rest of the developed world, there is very little, if any, poverty of the Third-World kind. No one in America lives on a dollar a day. In the United States, the "poor" routinely own cars and color televisions, are overweight, and may even own a home. The poor of a place like Bangladesh or Malawi would think they had died and gone to heaven (or perhaps Nirvana) if they were to suddenly attain the standard of living that the U.S. government defines as marking the poverty line.

In the long run, we are optimistic that, given good government policy, and God's help, the entire world can enjoy the benefits of economic growth, which is the only way that the "bottom billion" will ever escape poverty.

And so perhaps one of the most important things that philanthropists can do, if they wish to alleviate the suffering that poverty induces, is to avoid making it worse, and to help poor people help themselves.

CHAPTER 9

Developing an Appropriate Foundation Investment Policy

The field of investment is vast, and we make no attempt here to cover it all. The point of this chapter is to highlight some of the key investment issues that deserve special attention in the context of a private foundation. Above all, private foundations (like other charitable endowments) should have their own carefully thought-out investment policies.

This chapter outlines a more comprehensive view of investment policy than many foundations today adopt. We cover more than just investment issues, including day-to-day cash management, long-term projections of sources and uses of cash, detailed quantitative measures of risk, development and application of risk models, development of a target asset allocation, and systematic portfolio rebalancing to capture the "rebalancing bonus."

This set of tasks is outside the normal scope of most investment managers. Most foundation directors will want to assume responsibility for these issues, either directly or by obtaining expert help from appropriately trained consultants for these specific issues.

What to Include in an Investment Policy

An investment policy is a statement of guidelines by which a foundation plans to invest its assets. At a minimum, the policy should take into account the following:

- Anticipated life of the foundation.
- Anticipated cash flow into the foundation.
- The rule on jeopardizing investments.
- The rule on unrelated business income.
- The tax-exempt status of the foundation.
- The foundation's attitude toward risk.
- Anticipated cash flows out.

The ideal investment policy will take a carefully considered approach to a foundation's goals. This chapter suggests some of the best tools for making appropriate investment choices.

Anticipated Life of the Foundation

Since most foundations are created with the expectation that they will have perpetual life, their investment policies should aim to produce returns that can sustain their spending and cover inflation. For example, the Rockefeller Foundation, founded in 1913, was funded in installments over several years with a total of $250 million, which equals about $3.2 billion in year 2010 dollars. The foundation's very successful investment policy has enabled it to spend an estimated $14.5 billion (in 2010 dollars) since its founding and end the year 2009 with an endowment of more than $3 billion.

Foundations with a finite life—a plan to spend down their assets within a specific period of time—can pursue a policy with lower expected risk, and therefore lower expected returns. The John M. Olin Foundation, for example, during the process of spending down its assets, had a significantly larger allocation to fixed-income securities than did the Rockefeller Foundation, because fixed income offers lower risks—as well as lower return—than investments such as equities.

Anticipated Cash Flows into the Foundation

It is common for the founder of a private foundation to view the foundation's assets in concert with his overall portfolio. While the foundation's assets are not legally on the founder's personal balance sheet, personal concern for them may be logically and economically appropriate during the founder's lifetime.

The reason this is logical is that many donors who create and fund foundations during their lifetime will continue to fund the foundation in the coming years. The extent of this future funding is usually dependent upon the founder's future wealth and income. Since a founder's future wealth and income depend to some extent on the performance of his investments, it follows that the future funding of the foundation will also depend on the future performance of the founder's personal portfolio.

This economic relationship between the founder's personal portfolio and his likely future contributions to his foundation means that the foundation can be evaluated and invested in the larger context of the founder's overall portfolio. This adds another degree of flexibility in terms of investing.

When there is an expected long-term series of cash flows into the foundation from the founder, foundation directors and investment managers can logically think and plan in terms of a large overall portfolio (that is, the founder's personal assets plus the foundation assets) divided into a tax-exempt account and a taxable account. In such a case, it may make sense to put investments that would otherwise bear heavy tax burdens into the foundation, in which they are not taxable, and to leave lower-taxed items in the founder's personal account. For example, it may make sense to have taxable fixed-income, high-yield strategies, high-dividend strategies, and high-turnover strategies (which tend to produce short-term capital gains) disproportionately represented in the foundation.

Jeopardizing Investments

The Internal Revenue Code prohibits private foundations from making "jeopardizing investments." While such investments are not clearly defined, the rule is analogous to the "prudent man" rules; common law requires that trustees manage assets in accordance with what a prudent man would be expected to do. Generally speaking, a portfolio will comply with the rules if it is well diversified, does not use debt, and limits itself to conventional investments in stocks, bonds, and cash.

The application of these rules can sometimes be surprising, though. Under certain conditions other investments may be permitted, including options, futures, private equity, hedge funds, real estate, and venture capital. For instance, the IRS has ruled that a managed futures trading program could be viewed as adding diversification to an overall portfolio, because it has little or no correlation with other asset classes, such as the stock market. (The foundation in this case proposed to allocate 10 percent to the managed futures program.) On the other hand, debt should not be *directly* employed in private foundation accounts. Obvious things like mortgaged real estate or margin trading should be avoided. Note that this prohibition also rules out the use of debt as a cash-management tool (that is, short-term borrowing to make distributions).

Keep in mind, too, the lesson learned anew in the tech-stock bubble and in the Enron and WorldCom episodes: Some investments might comply with the jeopardy investment rules (see Chapter 11) but still pose a risk to a foundation's long-term future. For example, many people who create foundations make their initial donations in the form of stock in their company. There is nothing wrong with that (as long as they obey the excess business holdings rule explained in Chapter 11), but they need to think about what could happen to their foundation if the business takes a downturn.

The issue is not a new one. In the second half of the twentieth century, scientific genius Edwin Land's Polaroid Corp. reaped huge profits from his inventions of Polaroid cameras and other advances in photography and color television. But he kept all the assets of his foundation in Polaroid stock. After Polaroid stock plummeted in the 1970s, he had to shut down his foundation.

More recently, a number of new foundations were created with high-flying tech stocks before that market crashed in 2000. Many of the foundations that were not diversified saw their assets crumble by 50 to 95 percent, and in some cases they effectively disappeared. For example, the well-respected David and Lucille Packard Foundation announced in late 2002 that it was cutting its staff nearly in half and dropping its giving plans by over 50 percent as compared to 2001 because of the steep drop in its endowment's value caused by the more than 60 percent drop in the value of its very large holdings of HP stock.

This sad story was repeated again as many foundations found themselves grievously exposed to the market collapse of 2008–2009. Even some of the oldest and most well-established charities, such as Harvard, that were exposed to aggressive investment strategies saw their assets or endowments cut by a third or more.

Unrelated Business Income

All charities, whether public or private, must be aware of the rules on unrelated business income (UBI). As the name implies, unrelated business income is income from a business that is unrelated to the exempt purpose of the charity. This income will generate a tax, called the unrelated business income tax (UBIT), which foundations must avoid.

The problem arises when foundation investment managers, from time to time, are tempted by the opportunity to own directly an operating business such as a pizza parlor (for example, if a business owner considers giving one of his stores to his foundation). Under certain conditions this can be feasible. An ownership interest in a C corporation (that is, a regular corporation like the vast majority of publicly traded companies) will not typically generate

UBI. So while generally a business may not be owned directly, exceptions are generally made for companies organized as C corporations.

There is a broad exception to the UBI rules that allows foundations to own a variety of portfolio-type investments. Generally, such permitted investments include stocks, bonds, money market instruments, cash, mutual funds, and, depending on the specifics, a variety of other alternative investments. Thanks to these broad exceptions, it is unlikely that a foundation that is careful to avoid debt and owns only portfolio-type assets will ever run into a UBIT situation.

The Tax-Exempt Status of the Foundation

Private foundations are exempt from income taxes. They pay no income tax on investment income, whether in the form of interest, dividends, capital gains, or any other income. While there is a 2 percent excise tax (not technically an income tax) on net investment income (not net assets), it is so small as to be immaterial in most investment decisions. (Nonetheless, even this small tax should be noted, because with proper management, it can sometimes be reduced.)

The foundation's tax-exempt status means that it doesn't need to engage in all the usual efforts to defer, play down, or otherwise manipulate taxable income. The investment manager can straightforwardly seek high-yielding investments, unabashedly collect dividends, and take profits or hold onto temporary losses, all without worrying about taxes. This should be explicitly recognized in the investment policy, for example, by directly stating that income can be pursued without regard to income taxes.

The Foundation's Attitude toward Risk

The whole point of an investment policy is to have a carefully thought-out, coherent approach to managing investment risks that cannot be avoided. Most important, of course, is the most basic risk of all—not having enough money to accomplish your goals.

We believe there are several issues foundations should take into account:

- Losing so much in assets that the foundation cannot accomplish its goals or is forced out of business.
- Gradual, long-term shrinkage of foundation assets, in real (inflation-adjusted) terms.
- Fluctuations in assets big enough to affect the stability of grant programs.

In addition, many foundation directors and investment professionals view the possibility of underperformance relative to established benchmarks as a risk worth taking into account. This is the investment world's version of the bandwagon thinking embodied in the adage "nobody ever got fired for buying IBM." In an investment environment in which real (inflation-adjusted) interest rates are low (which is most of the time), there is no such thing as a risk-free investment policy for a foundation, unless that foundation plans to spend itself out of existence over a relatively short period of time.

Investment risk was once viewed as a simple and obvious concept, but it is now seen as having many facets. For most people, risk is simply the possibility of losing money. Financial academicians have developed a number of sophisticated measures of risk, such as "beta" and standard deviation. Essentially, these academic measures define risk not as the probability of losing money, but as the volatility of a portfolio.

Recently, a number of practitioners have pointed out serious flaws with the academic measures of risk. One of the most important of these criticisms, and one that is relevant to foundation investing, is that the academic measures do not directly address the most basic risk, the risk of not having enough money to accomplish your goals.

- **No riskless option.** Most important to remember is that foundations must distribute 5 percent of assets annually, and that 5 percent is significantly in excess of the risk-free rates available on short- or intermediate-term government bonds. If inflation is expected to run typically at just 2 percent per year over the long run (it averaged slightly higher during the twentieth century), then a foundation must earn an average of about 7 percent (the required 5 percent, plus 2 percent in inflation) just to stay even.
- **Quantitative risk model.** The future is, by definition, unknown. The best we can do is make an informed guess as to risks and tradeoffs, or—more technically—to develop a model that quantifies the risks as much as possible, along with possible outcomes. There are several approaches to creating such a model.

One of the best is to use historical data and assume that what has happened in the past can happen again, if not in exactly the same way. However, it is beyond the scope of this book to describe how to build and use such a model. Here's one example. The Monte Carlo analysis—which you can create with the help of an expert in financial modeling—helps investors answer questions like: "If we spend X, and invest in asset Y, what is the probability that we will experience a loss of Z percent of assets over one year, five years, ten years, and twenty years?" By simulating various scenarios, it is possible for foundation directors to evaluate a spectrum of what-if questions, giving them better insight into a spectrum of specific risks and trade-offs. Of course, such a model is only as good as the data that is put into it. And it's not a substitute for subjective human analysis of risk. It's not an oracle of truth, but a useful tool.

Anticipated Cash Flows Out

As we have noted, foundations must spend 5 percent of their average net assets each year. (While a foundation can make distributions in kind, this has little benefit and imposes costs for both foundation and recipient.) The first step in developing a foundation's cash management policy is to project both incoming contributions and outflows of cash in the form of grants and other spending.

• **Cash management.** Contributions from a living founder commonly take the form of annual contributions (often driven by the founder's income tax situation) and bequests on the death of the founder or a spouse. Particular attention should be paid to expected regular annual additions. If these regular annual additions can be relied upon, they may serve as the core of the cash flow necessary to fund the foundation's grants, meaning that grants won't have to be funded from investment assets.

Furthermore, in the early years of a growing foundation, this stream of expected future cash inflows might well exceed in present-value terms the actual value of the foundation. For example, consider a foundation that is started with $1 million and expects to receive $500,000 a year for the next 10 years. The value of this stream of $500,000 inflows is much greater than the $1 million the foundation already has. In such a case, a more aggressive investment policy may be appropriate, because the risk taken with the $1 million will not affect the $5 million in cash the foundation will be receiving over the next 10 years.

The average foundation spends just above the 5 percent annual disbursement required by law; most perpetual-life foundations distribute just the amount required.

• **The effect of fluctuating investment returns.** The central cash management issue for foundations is how to handle the fluctuation of investment returns while accomplishing philanthropic goals and complying with the 5 percent rule. Such planning requires decisions about philanthropic priorities, tolerance of risk, desire for preservation and growth of the real (inflation-adjusted) size of the foundation, and the time horizon (either finite or perpetual life) of the foundation.

Especially in a low interest rate environment, cash management is an important, if often overlooked, issue. Without a deliberate policy, foundations can end up losing money by holding on to cash for too long, or by not holding enough cash at the right time. The first kind of loss is easy to understand. The foundation holds more cash than it needs, missing opportunities to earn higher returns. If the differential between expected returns on cash and the rest of the portfolio is 5 percent per year, this loss can easily be in the range of 0.25 to 0.50 percent per year.

The other kind of loss is more subtle but just as real. Essentially, the foundation finds itself forced into a policy of "selling low." That is, it systematically sells relatively more assets when investment markets are low and fewer assets when the markets are high. Here's an example. Imagine that in year 1, a foundation has assets of $1 million. The 5 percent rule means that it must distribute $50,000. In year 2, let's say the assets are at $1.1 million, so the foundation will have to distribute $55,000. But in year 3, suppose that just as that check is to be written, the market is down, so that the assets are again worth only $1 million. Now the $55,000 that the foundation must give away represents 5.5 percent of the foundation's assets. In this way, the foundation is forced to systematically sell relatively more assets when the market is down.

Over time, this can create a meaningful drag on performance. Our analysis suggests that for a foundation with perpetual life (and, consequently, a portfolio heavily weighted with equities), this drag can amount to 0.25 percent to 0.50 percent per year (coincidentally, the same amount of loss incurred by holding too much cash).

• **Grant planning.** Since investment results are not predictable, there is no perfect way to plan grant expenditures. But there are some tools. The central problem is clear: Generally, it is desirable to keep grant support stable. But fluctuating investment markets create pressure to vary grant levels. The goal of a long-term grant plan is to find the best balance between maintaining effective program support and not spending too much in years in which the portfolio value is down.

In up years, grant support must automatically rise, because the 5 percent distribution requirement makes no allowance for exceptionally good years.

However, once grant support has been increased as the result of a good year, there may appear to be good reasons to keep it at such increased levels even in a bad year.

Unfortunately, the mathematics of investment returns means that if foundations keep their spending up even in down years (and thereby spend significantly more than 5 percent), they may find themselves forced into a pattern of an ever-shrinking asset base. This pattern may eventually force the foundation out of existence. Keeping grant support up in years in which investment returns are negative is an option that should be adopted only after careful evaluation of the long-term effects.

How big a problem this is will depend on a number of factors, especially the expected long-run return on the portfolio and the volatility of those returns. Each situation needs to be analyzed individually.

Fortunately, there is another answer to this dilemma. The solution is to develop a program of core grants and variable grants. Base the core program on a spending level that the foundation can maintain without cutting into capital, even in bad years. Create a variable grant program of additional grants made as returns and asset values dictate.

Developing and implementing this dual program involves financial modeling (to determine the appropriate levels of core grants, which may change over time). It also means developing trust and understanding with grantee organizations, so that both kinds of grants can be effective.

Conclusion

An appropriate investment policy can be a crucial component of a foundation's long-term approach to its mission. When an investment policy takes account of a foundation's goals, its likely future cash inflows, and available investment alternatives, and is carefully integrated with the foundation's grant-making program, the foundation can capture as much as 1 to 2 percent per year of additional return. Over the life of a foundation, this is an amount that simply cannot be ignored by fiduciaries. They will embrace it as a valuable means of accomplishing the foundation's mission.

CHAPTER 10

Developing and Implementing a Foundation Asset Allocation Policy

As we saw in the previous chapter, the main goal of a foundation's investment policy is to ensure that it has the resources to achieve its mission. Since most foundations have perpetual lives, this discussion assumes that situation.

The first requirement for translating an investment policy into action is an asset allocation policy, a statement of how to allocate the portfolio among a number of defined asset classes. We can clarify the issues involved by reviewing some lessons from the world of tax-exempt corporate pension plans.

Differences between Corporation and Foundation Investment Plans

Many donors and investment professionals are familiar with these pension plans, but there are a few key differences when a foundation is involved. First, while pension plans often have long time horizons, that span is usually finite, while foundation time horizons are unlimited. Second, defined-benefit pension plans can go back to the sponsoring corporation for more funds if necessary. Very few foundations have that option. Third, and perhaps most importantly, a strict set of accounting rules forces pension plan administrators to make sure that pension plan assets are sufficient, on an actuarial basis, to pay its obligations. There are no such rules imposed on foundations.

Perpetual Life

Perpetual life as an investing concept is new to most people. Although corporations theoretically have perpetual life, in practice, most do not. However, foundations that are well managed can and do last for many generations. A number of the oldest foundations, including Rockefeller and Carnegie, are now stronger than ever. Perpetual life means that even small errors in planning, if they are continued and compounded over the years, can have catastrophic results. For example, a 1 percent shortfall in assets in a single year or even several years is no big deal. But a 1 percent shortfall in assets for a hundred years would be terminal.

No Corporate Sponsor

For a pension plan, the corporate sponsor is the immediate guarantor that the plan will have sufficient funds. The Employee Retirement Income Security Act (ERISA) rules require that the corporation make more contributions to the plan if assets get too low. This guarantee has the effect of lowering the overall risk level of the plan (where risk is defined as the probability that it won't meet its obligations). In addition, the federal Pension Benefit Guarantee Corporation serves as an ultimate guarantor of the liabilities of these pension plans.

Paradoxically, this lower overall risk means that the plan's investment managers may be comfortable taking more risk when it comes to making investments in the markets. They can invest a greater percentage of assets in equities, for example, which have higher risk levels but, over the long run, tend to have higher returns. That, in turn, can *reduce* the risk that the pension plan could run out of money.

Required Pension Accounting

Pension accounting is the bane of many an aspiring accountant, but it is arguably the savior of many a retiree. The Financial Accounting Standards Board (FASB) is the organization that sets the accounting standards for qualified corporate pension plans. FASB has issued a set of rules for how corporations must account for their pension obligations and how they must treat current expenses related to funding those obligations.

The rules require a corporation to make a reasonable estimate of the pension payments it will have to make over the entire future life of the plan. The present value of these payments, known as the *benefit obligation*, must be measured against the current market value of the plan's assets. If the market value of the assets is greater than the obligation, the plan is said to be *overfunded.* If the market value is less, the plan is *underfunded*, and the corporation must add money.

While these rules are not perfect, they do force corporations to be more aware of the financial condition of their pension plans. And the requirement to contribute extra cash when required makes it harder for companies to incur pension liabilities far in excess of their ability to pay them.

No such accounting requirements exist for private foundations. They may spend themselves into oblivion before they even notice their problems. We have identified below seven blind spots that can lead to this kind of disaster.

The Seven Deadly Sins of Foundation Asset Allocation Policy

For foundations, most bad decisions on asset allocation come from one or more common errors:

1. Failing to adequately diversify.
2. Holding too much cash.
3. Ignoring inflation.
4. Overemphasizing liquidity.
5. Misunderstanding risk.
6. Overemphasizing income-producing investments.
7. Not taking advantage of professional help.

Failing to Adequately Diversify

Almost everybody knows that diversification is good strategy for an investment portfolio. It may seem obvious, especially in the post-Enron, post–Internet bubble era, that it is a bad idea to keep most of a foundation's assets invested in a single company. However, too many founders create their foundations with just the founder's stock and let the foundation continue to hold this stock. Think dot-com. Think financial stocks. In recent years, a number of foundations and their founders have come to grief because they held on to a single stock even as it plummeted. Even old and venerable companies like General Motors and Citibank can be and have been brought low. A number of foundations have been wiped out, and many more have seen their assets drop by as much as 90 percent.

The cure, easy to state, can be hard emotionally for a founder: Have the foundation sell its stock as soon as possible and adopt a diversified portfolio.

Holding Too Much Cash

For many investors, cash represents comfort and security. After all, cash *seems* never to go down in value (especially if you commit the third deadly sin, ignoring inflation). But holding too much cash is very costly because the returns of such vehicles as money market funds are always low. In most cases, if a foundation has good cash management, holding 1 percent in cash should be plenty. Holding more than 1 percent cash means that the foundation will forfeit higher returns, with no offsetting benefit.

Ignoring Inflation

Inflation is easy to overlook. Most investors know, intellectually, that they should consider inflation when making long-term plans. But too often, they don't act on this knowledge. When it comes to foundation strategy, it is literally suicide (albeit a slow suicide) to let this happen.

It is a mathematical fact: Inflation at an apparently benign 3 percent a year (approximately its average over the last century) causes a dollar to lose *half* of its value in 24 years. Over 100 years, that benign 3 percent will cause a dollar to lose 95 percent of its value. (See the table below.) Here's what this means in practice: If a foundation allocates its assets conservatively and earns 5 percent a year, and inflation runs at 3 percent, over a century that foundation will have seen the purchasing power of its grants (which would remain stable in nominal dollars) decline by 95 percent. In other words, if the foundation's grants in the year 2000 would buy $100,000 of goods and services, by 2100 the foundation's grants would buy just $5,000 worth of goods and services. That's what we mean by slow suicide.

Effect of 3% Inflation

Year	Value	Year	Value	Year	Value
1	100.00	34	36.60	68	12.99
2	97.00	36	34.44	70	12.23
3	94.09	37	33.40	71	11.86
4	91.27	38	32.40	72	11.50

Year	Value	Year	Value	Year	Value
5	88.53	39	31.43	73	11.16
6	85.87	40	30.49	74	10.82
7	83.30	41	29.57	75	10.50
8	80.80	42	28.68	76	10.18
9	78.37	43	27.82	77	9.88
10	76.02	44	26.99	78	9.58
11	73.74	45	26.18	79	9.29
12	71.53	46	25.39	80	9.02
13	69.38	47	24.63	81	8.74
14	67.30	48	23.89	82	8.48
15	65.28	49	23.18	83	8.23
16	63.33	50	22.48	84	7.98
17	61.43	51	21.81	85	7.74
18	59.58	52	21.15	86	7.51
19	57.80	53	20.52	87	7.28
20	56.06	54	19.90	88	7.07
21	54.38	55	19.31	89	6.85
22	52.75	56	18.73	90	6.65
23	51.17	57	18.16	91	6.45
24	49.63	58	17.62	92	6.26
25	48.14	59	17.09	93	6.07
26	46.70	60	16.58	94	5.89
27	45.30	61	16.08	95	5.71
28	43.94	62	15.60	96	5.54
29	42.62	63	15.13	97	5.37
30	41.34	64	14.68	98	5.21
31	40.10	65	14.24	99	5.05
32	38.90	66	13.81	100	4.90
33	37.73	67	13.39		

If we assume inflation of 3 percent and a requirement that the foundation disburse 5 percent a year, a perpetual life foundation must adopt a strategy that will return at least 8 percent to avoid shrinking in real terms.

For more on the inflation threat, see Chapter 12.

Overemphasizing Liquidity

Foundations with perpetual time horizons need very little liquidity. On average, they will spend about 5 percent of their assets each year and don't need access to much more. Yet the typical foundation today has few if any investments that are not liquid within days. They are ignoring a whole array of potential moneymakers, including private-equity limited partnerships, income-producing real estate, hedge funds, timber, equipment leasing, and venture capital.

Misunderstanding Risk

Risk has many meanings. In investing, it usually refers to the volatility of an investment or portfolio. Individuals typically view risk as the possibility of losing money, and many of us are what economists call "risk-averse." Accordingly, foundation founders often believe that a perpetual life entity needs to avoid risk. This is true to some extent. But when applied too broadly, it leads to trouble.

For example, when a foundation focuses on avoiding volatility or minimizing loss, it will generally hold too much cash, cash equivalents, and fixed-income securities. It will be unlikely to earn enough to stay ahead of inflation and meet its 5 percent distribution requirement. When interest rates are low, as in recent years, these problems become obvious. When rates are higher, the problem is still there, but harder to spot.

For a foundation, the risk that matters the most is not having enough resources to achieve its mission. The only effective way to assess this risk is with fairly sophisticated financial models. We discuss some approaches to assessment later in this chapter.

Overemphasizing Income-Producing Investments

Because of the 5 percent rule, foundations naturally tend to invest their assets to produce exactly that much income. It may be natural, but it's often not smart. With some exceptions, most assets that produce a steady 5 percent are fixed-income investments such as bonds. Again, too heavy a reliance on bonds makes it very difficult, over time, to keep up with inflation and meet the 5 percent rule.

An appropriate cash management strategy can make it feasible for a foundation to rely on asset sales to produce at least part of the cash flow it needs. This opens up a large universe of assets that might not produce much income while they sit in the portfolio, but deliver higher returns when they are sold. A basic example is the stock of large companies. Few yield 5 percent in dividends, but historically, over time, the returns from large stocks have significantly exceeded both 5 percent and the returns on bonds.

Not Taking Advantage of Professional Help

Unless a foundation is run by people who happen to be investment professionals, it probably should not take a do-it-yourself approach. Sometimes at our firm, we hear that foundations want to save money by not using professionals. But proper investing is a complex, involved business, even if professionals work to make it look easy.

Helen Modly, a planner with Focus Financial Consultants in Middleburg, Virginia, offered the following analogy. You can write your own will. It is neither illegal nor immoral. But if you own anything you really care about, it is probably stupid to write the will yourself. The amount you can save is tiny compared with what you will probably lose. And, she adds, if you have anything you care about and you do go to a professional, you may find that you need more than a will to secure those treasured possessions.

In most cases, it is penny-wise and pound-foolish to try to save money by skimping on smart counsel.

Developing a Good Asset Allocation Policy

William Sharpe, the Nobel Prize-winning Stanford University professor who developed much of modern financial theory, defines asset allocation as "the allocation of an investor's portfolio among a number of 'major' asset classes." Asset allocation among asset classes that behave differently is the single most important investment consideration, according to a number of academicians and practitioners. These researchers and investors have found that long-term investment performance depends more on asset allocation than on any other single decision. Roger Ibbotson, a leading researcher, even went so far as to report, in the late 1990s in the *Financial Analysts' Journal*, that asset allocation, on average, determines 100 percent of returns obtained by an investor.

The concept here is that the expected risk and expected return of a port-folio are primarily a function of how it spreads money among different asset classes. One approach to developing an asset allocation is to assign expected returns and expected risk (as measured by volatility of returns) to each asset class in a portfolio, compare the risk and return of each class one at a time to those of each other class, and assign a covariance to each pair of returns. (Doing this generates a large number of covariances, because the analysis re-quires one for each pairing of assets.) Apply a mathematical optimization pro-cedure to this data, and you will be able to calculate an efficient portfolio—one with the maximum return for a given level of risk. (This kind of problem is known as quadratic optimization. There is software available, but it can do more harm than good in the hands of someone who doesn't fully understand the ins and outs.)

One important insight that may not be immediately obvious is that you can reduce the overall risk of a portfolio—without reducing its expected return—by including one or more assets that might be deemed risky or even very risky. Large, successful foundations and endowments, such as the Rockefeller Foundation and Harvard University, have lots of higher-risk assets and allocate significant percentages of their portfolios to nontraditional asset classes. For example, the Rockefeller Foundation has significant holdings in real estate and private equity, and Harvard's endowment invests in high-yield bonds, commodities, and absolute return hedge funds.

This chapter cannot address in any depth the wide range of alternatives in all risk categories. But it is advisable to consider as many as possible, including the following:

- Cash.
- Money market instruments.
- High-grade bonds.
- High-yield corporate bonds and emerging-market debt.
- Equities (stocks).
- Real estate.
- Timber.
- Hedge funds.
- Commodity futures.
- Venture capital and private equities.

Cash and Money Market Instruments

We've said that foundations shouldn't hold too much cash or equivalent money market instruments, so exactly how these cash assets are invested should not have a major impact on long-term results. Nevertheless, foundations would do well to consider whether it makes sense to keep cash reserves in risk-free U.S. Treasury Bills, or whether it is better to seek a little extra yield from high-grade corporate or bank paper. This depends on the investor's view and time horizons. Over short periods of time, it may be difficult to justify accepting any risk of default. But remember the effect of compounding: Even 1 percent additional yield (the difference between earning 4 percent and 5 percent on cash balances, for example) means *doubling* your money over 70 years. A dollar invested at 4 percent will grow to about $15 in 70 years, but at 5 percent it will grow to about $30.

When the additional risk of high-grade nongovernment money market instruments is viewed in the overall context of a foundation's allocation policy, pursuing the additional return will often make sense.

High-Grade Bonds

High-grade bonds include corporate bonds, government agency bonds, and high-grade government bonds. Bonds are a staple of most foundation investment policies, but they are often overused. Some foundations have virtually *all* their assets invested in bonds. Over the long run, high-grade bonds are unlikely to generate enough return to both meet the 5 percent distribution requirement and keep up with inflation. In our view, the proper role for bonds is simply to complement other assets, making up about 10 to 20 percent of the portfolio.

Inflation-Protected U.S. Government Bonds (TIPS)

Treasury Inflation-Protected Securities (TIPS) allow investors to see the yield they'll get after inflation. The actual return on TIPS depends on inflation. The bonds have a fixed interest rate, and the principal is adjusted to keep up with inflation. The actual interest paid is based on the adjusted principal value. The adjusted principal is not paid until maturity. Investors are also protected against deflation because the bonds will pay the greater of issue par value or adjusted principal value at maturity.

As we write, the inflation-adjusted return on TIPS is between 3 percent and 4 percent. Obviously, this return by itself is not enough to sustain a foundation meeting the 5 percent rule. Investing in TIPS may still make sense, provided they are part of an overall asset allocation strategy that will produce sufficient returns over the long term.

High-Yield Bonds and Emerging-Market Bonds

High-yield or "junk" bonds can be a useful investment for foundations. The main attraction is the promise of equity-like returns with less risk. The main disadvantage, as with most investments, is that it can be difficult to get a good handle on the actual risk of default. Emerging-market bonds are issued by governments of developing countries. Because they are quite risky, they tend to carry high yields. They have also tended to have highly volatile market prices. Again, they need to be analyzed to determine the specific risk.

Because these investments are so complex, it makes sense to use professional managers for these asset classes.

Equities

Whether U.S. or foreign, small cap, large cap, or any other variety, equities will probably be the mainstay investment of a perpetual-life foundation. But because there is such copious information available about investing in equities, we won't dwell on them here. See the Resources for some of our favorite books.

Real Estate

Real estate constitutes a significant proportion of all the money invested in the United States. But it is often underrepresented in foundation strategies, even though unleveraged real estate has a number of attractive characteristics for foundations. It tends to hold its value despite inflation, it can produce good cash flows, and returns are not highly correlated with equity returns. And different real estate sectors—such as residential income, office buildings, industrial or retail—perform differently in different environments.

Smaller foundations may participate in this market by investing in publicly traded real estate investment trusts (REITs), while larger foundations may invest directly or through professionally managed nonpublic investment vehicles.

Depending on circumstance, real estate may comfortably represent a fairly significant (10 to 20 percent) portion of a foundation's overall asset allocation strategy.

Hedge Funds

The term *hedge fund* covers a very wide variety of strategies, ranging from relatively low-risk, low-return activities like convertible bond arbitrage to very high-risk, very high-potential return methods such as leveraged macro trading of the style that made George Soros famous.

Like the world of equities, the hedge fund universe is too vast and diverse to cover in depth here. But a few notes are in order. Many individual high-net-worth investors have never looked seriously into hedge funds, because such funds have little tax advantage. However, foundations, being tax-exempt entities, can ignore this issue and choose to include one or more hedge funds, or funds of funds, in their asset allocation strategy.

Some hedge funds may offer attractive combinations of return, volatility, and correlation with other asset classes. It is probably meaningless to talk of hedge fund indexes as a useful measure of the hedge fund market, although such indexes do exist. Because the characteristics of individual hedge funds vary so much, foundations must consider each hedge fund separately, rather than lumping them into a single asset class called hedge funds. Foundations also must be careful that any hedge fund investments do not produce unrelated business income subject to taxation. (See Chapter 9.)

Venture Capital

There can be huge returns and huge risks in venture capital investing and private equity. (A note on terminology: Whether a given investment is considered venture capital or private equity largely depends on timing—when a manager decides to invest and where the company is in its growth cycle. It may also be a question of semantics.)

Venture capital is compelling because when it works, the returns are not measured in percentages but in *multiples* of the investment. For example, in the late 1990s, one of the major venture capital funds, run by Matrix Partners in Menlo Park, California, returned 35 times the investors' money in just under two years. Again, this was not 35 percent of, but 35 *times* the investment amount.

Obviously, if such returns were reliably available, everyone would put all their money into venture capital. Such tremendous returns are not the norm, but it is not uncommon for the better venture capitalists to earn their investors returns that average in the high teens or higher. But venture capital returns are highly volatile. And it may be difficult to get a good handle on the correlation of such returns with other asset classes because such correlations are hard to measure and may vary considerably over time.

There are a huge number of different approaches and niches, and it is impossible to summarize them here. The important point is that if a foundation can find an appropriate means for investing a portion of its assets in venture capital, it may be an excellent addition to the mix; 10 percent or even more might be appropriate.

Timber

Even though trees are everywhere, when it comes to investing, it seems that trees are almost nowhere. There are only a few timber companies whose stocks are listed, and most of these are not pure timber plays. Yet timber is a valid asset class with a good and long track record.

Timber is grown and harvested around the world. It is used in construction, in furniture, and to make paper products. One unique feature of timber is that, unlike virtually every other asset class, it grows while in storage. This means that, when prices are too low, a prudently financed timber owner can simply not cut trees. And he need not lose money, because his trees continue to grow. Good timber can add an average 4 to 5 percent or so to its value each year through biological growth.

Timber is not very liquid, and opportunities to invest are somewhat limited. However, returns from timber have tended to be relatively stable, and there is evidence that timber returns have a low correlation with U.S. equity returns, particularly over periods during which equity returns have been poor.

There are also some unique risks in timber investing. Here are just a few examples. For one, there is the (very low) risk of the investment literally burning up, and in most instances fire insurance is not available or is prohibitively expensive. In another twist, the market in the U.S. northwest is periodically subject to bouts of weakness caused by the Canadian government's permitting people to cut trees for free in the western provinces. And although the logs may not enter the U.S. market, Japanese and other Asians are happy to buy the cheap lumber, depressing the market.

Commodity Futures

We can hear it now. "Commodity futures? Are you crazy?" No, we are not crazy. We probably know more than most investors about this widely misunderstood asset class (Dr. Silk wrote his PhD dissertation on the subject of futures markets). But we offer one ironclad rule for foundations thinking about investing in futures: Don't do it yourself. It is estimated that more than 95 percent of nonprofessionals who trade futures lose money. But—less widely known—a small number of experienced professionals who manage money for investors have excellent, long-term track records.

In the proper hands, commodity futures can offer returns averaging as much as 15 percent per year. For example, Dunn Capital Management of Stuart, Florida, a leader in the field, has compiled a 35-year track record of double-digit compounded returns. Dunn's *average* return over the period has been about 15 percent per year; however, this is anything but consistent. It would not be uncommon to see a zero return year followed by a 50 percent year. Volatility is the name of this game.

Even so, a modest asset allocation to managed futures can increase a portfolio's returns *and* decrease the variance of the portfolio. The secret is that the returns from well-managed futures portfolios are uncorrelated with the returns from most other asset classes. An allocation of up to 25 percent can be mathematically optimal, although most people who are not familiar with the asset class will probably feel more comfortable with around 10 percent.

Successful professional futures managers are highly quantitatively driven. Dunn uses computerized trading models developed and honed over many years. If an investor wants to go this route, it would make sense to understand quantitative analysis well or to get help from someone who does.

Should an Asset Allocation Policy Change over Time?

If a foundation's target asset allocation today is 50 percent stocks and 50 percent bonds, should it stay at 50–50 come hell or high water? Opinions vary.

Many investment professionals believe it makes sense to adjust the target allocation as the relative value of stocks and bonds changes. Many major brokerage firms, for example, publish their experts' target allocation between stocks and bonds regularly. The most bullish have higher weighting in stocks, while the most bearish de-emphasize stocks.

The decision of whether to vary the asset allocation policy over time may depend both on how asset classes are defined and whether the foundation can determine when the relative attractiveness of one asset class versus another class changes.

Asset allocation policy should, of course, be adjusted when it seems clear that an asset class is shifting to become either ridiculously expensive or remarkably inexpensive. A view that an asset class is either very expensive or very inexpensive might make it seem reasonable to allow asset allocation policy to vary. How often to adjust it is quite subjective. Even so, it should probably not be changed more than once a year.

Whatever the approach over the long term, it always makes sense to fix targets in the short run. By systematically rebalancing the actual portfolio toward the target allocation, it may be possible to significantly increase the returns.

Capturing the Rebalancing Bonus

Making the initial decisions about how to balance the portfolio can be long and involved. But once this is done, there is an additional benefit, not widely appreciated, called the *rebalancing bonus*.

The rebalancing bonus is the extra return that, over time, can be expected as a result of rebalancing the portfolio to keep the portfolio's assets allocated in accordance with the targets. In effect, the rebalancing bonus is the benefit derived from a policy that forces the foundation to systematically "buy low and sell high."

The rebalancing bonus mechanism is simple. For example, suppose the target asset allocation is 50 percent stocks and 50 percent cash. On day one, once the policy is implemented, the portfolio will be perfectly balanced. Now suppose the stock market drops by 20 percent and the value of the stocks in the portfolio correspondingly drops by 20 percent. The portfolio will now be overweighted in cash (55.55 percent weighting) and underweighted in stocks (a 44.44 percent weighting).

By rebalancing, the portfolio automatically buys more stock at the lower prices. In this example, if the stock market then recovers to its beginning level, instead of being just at breakeven the rebalanced portfolio will show a profit of about 1.25 percent. And rebalancing will force the foundation to take that profit, because the portfolio will then be overweight stocks and underweight cash.

In real-world portfolios, the value of this bonus can be significant. For example, economist William Bernstein has estimated its value at between 1.2 percent and 1.6 percent per year for portfolios with five asset classes. The rebalancing bonus probably deserves more attention than it has received. One reason is that, for taxable accounts, the tax impact of rebalancing can be negative, and these tax costs may outweigh the benefits. However, tax-exempt accounts such as foundations and endowments do not suffer this handicap. For them, rebalancing offers an important and valuable benefit.

There is no single best strategy for rebalancing. It can be done at set intervals, for example, monthly or quarterly, or whenever the asset allocation moves away from its target by a specified percentage. But the bonus is too great to be left to chance. The subject should be dealt with explicitly in the investment policy and should get regular attention. If there is more than one manager involved in managing the assets, rebalancing must be made the responsibility of one person, and she should have access to the necessary information.

Active Management versus Indexing

A final aspect of asset allocation policy is whether to use active management or a passive, indexed-investment approach. One of the hotter debates of recent years for all investors has been the comparative merits of active management and index investing. At the center of the debate is an academic theory that has come to be known as the *efficient market hypothesis*. Adherents believe that securities are rarely or never mispriced on the basis of publicly available information and that, as a consequence, it is difficult or impossible for an investor to consistently beat the market. Under this perspective, trying to predict the investment markets is, to use investment consultant Charles Ellis's term, a *loser's game*. The best approach, they think, is to simply buy "the index."

Many others, including top financial economists such as Robert Shiller, who coined the term *irrational exuberance*, have offered numerous challenges to the efficient market view. One thing, ironically, that makes it tricky to evaluate the efficient market hypothesis is that it often appears to be correct. Even Warren Buffett, whose amazing record of investment performance could be seen as a fatal refutation to the hypothesis, has stated that most of the time it is very hard to find securities that are significantly mispriced. Indeed, few investment professionals would argue with the idea that, even if markets are not perfectly efficient, they come close.

However, "close" leaves lots of room to do better than the indexers, and indeed many investors do beat the indexes, and some manage to do this for years in a row. Indexing is not the simple solution its proponents claim. First, there is the question of which index is the right index. For example, in the U.S. stock market, is it the Dow Jones Industrial Average, the Standard & Poor's 500, or the Wilshire 5000? For an investor, should the chosen index be capitalization weighted, equally weighted, or weighted by some other criteria? There are no clear answers. Moreover, whatever index is chosen implies a bet that the indexer may not even realize he is making. For example, James P. O'Shaughnessy, the best-selling author and Chairman and CEO of O'Shaughnessy Asset Management, LLC, has observed that the S&P 500, which has been widely regarded as the best proxy for the U.S. market, is in fact a large-cap growth-style index, so that an investor who invests in it is actually making a bet on large-cap growth.

Furthermore, indexes are not static, and they are not neutral. They, too, are managed. Stocks are added or deleted, and weightings are changed, usually for reasons that have nothing to do with what would usually be considered investment-related reasons. So the indexed investor is actually buying and selling securities for reasons unrelated to investment considerations.

For some markets, certain indexes simply include every security issued, but the definition of what belongs in that market category in the first place is ultimately arbitrary. While it may make sense for the sponsor of the index to include everything (after all, it makes their job easier), it is hard to see why an investor would want to own a tiny piece of every security that happens to fit the index sponsor's idea of what that market is. For many markets, there is no evidence that indexes are a smart or desirable way to invest. (Of course, for markets such as venture capital, hedge funds, managed futures, and private equity, there is no way to invest in an index, even if one wanted to.)

Investors who do take an active approach often view fees paid to professional managers as a great bargain, provided such management helps the foundation accomplish its goals. Over time, the wisest foundation managers have produced outstanding outcomes by focusing on overall results, not by focusing on costs alone. When additional net benefits can be gained by incurring additional costs, the best managers embrace the opportunity.

We believe that indexing is not the best approach in most cases. Instead, good, active managers should be sought and employed. Many foundations in their search for a good manager focus on these characteristics: a consistent and logical approach, a good track record, a sense of commitment (often indicated if the manager invests his own funds), and the founder's comfort level with the manager.

Who Is Responsible for the Asset Allocation Policy?

Establishing, implementing, and monitoring an appropriate asset allocation policy is one of the key responsibilities of a foundation board. The board may do this on its own or in conjunction with consultants or investment managers.

Board Authority

Many foundation boards, particularly those dominated by a living founder, decide to create the allocation policy on their own. In the best-case scenario, this is a cost-effective option: The board has the requisite skill, knowledge, and time, and does an excellent job. Unfortunately, it is not often the case that skill, knowledge, and time all converge. We were consulted recently by a board that was debating its investment policy. On the board were three professional money managers. Each had a great deal of skill and knowledge, but none had the time to devote to the issue. The result was that each offered an off-the-cuff view, but none was able to do a real analysis or offer a fully integrated policy recommendation. The result was that no action was taken, and the assets in question were kept in cash.

Outside Consultants

When the board is open to input and willing to make use of it, good advice can be invaluable. There are plenty of professional firms that specialize in investment policy and asset allocation, as distinct from the day-to-day running of a portfolio. An advantage of using such outside consultants who do *not* themselves manage money is that they have no ax to grind. A good consultant is conversant with a wide range of asset classes and managers and understands the technical issues we have touched on in this and previous chapters.

That said, many otherwise excellent consultants do not focus on private foundations and may not know their particular concerns or opportunities. Investment managers can be good sources of advice for developing an investment and asset allocation policy, but since most such managers specialize in one or a few asset classes, they may not have a good grasp on the others and may not pay sufficient attention to all the issues that should be considered.

Conclusion

The asset allocation policy decision is very important and over the long run can prove to be the decisive factor in a foundation's continued financial viability. But it's an area many foundations neglect. With the right knowledge, tools, and approach, a foundation can develop and implement an asset allocation policy that will ensure its success in the long run.

CHAPTER 11

Main Themes in Legal Compliance

Ever since Congress levied the first income tax in 1913, it has given Americans exemptions, deductions, credits, and other incentives to encourage charitable giving. It wasn't until 1969, however, at the urging of Congressman Wright Patman of Texas, that Congress created a veritable encyclopedia of rules and regulations governing private foundations. And although there had been regulations before 1969, they had been only loosely enforced.

The 1969 reforms were designed to address perceived abuses of private foundations; Senator Vance Hartke of Indiana described the situation. Before the reforms, he said, "there were many examples of private foundations in this country [doing] an excellent job, but they [were] outnumbered at least five to one by foundations which were failing to serve the public purpose adequately." At the top of the list for reformers was the use of private foundations to avoid taxes; to own businesses (which the reformers thought was unfair to other businesses, because other businesses had to pay income tax); and to funnel money and perks illegally to the founders and their friends, family, and associates.

In addition, Patman, a Texas populist, took the position that private foundations were accumulating too much wealth (one wonders what he'd think today of Harvard's endowment of more than $19 billion) and spending too much money overseas.

Today, tax specialists know the 1969 rules and regulations as IRS Code Sections 4940 to 4946. Few people can claim to be experts in all of them, as they cover hundreds of pages of codes and regulations. As former Senator Hartke told one of the authors of this book: "We eliminated a lot of the abuses, but the IRS really complicated the issues."

Attorneys who create private foundations for their clients typically explain the key aspects of sections 4940 through 4946 to their clients both in conversation and in a several-thousand-word letter. Still, foundation directors and trustees—who aren't usually compliance professionals—will need more help to get through the thicket of rules. Typically, that means professional help from attorneys, accountants, or professional foundation managers. In this chapter, we want to lay out the key elements of a private foundation management system that private foundations can implement to ensure compliance.

The challenge has several dimensions. Some functions are naturally in the domain of lawyers (state filings, annual board meeting minutes, and others), some are naturally in the domain of accountants (bookkeeping and tax returns), and many don't fall naturally in either domain (for example, properly documenting the tax-exempt status of grant recipients or complying with public inspection requirements). This leaves plenty of opportunity for things to fall between the cracks.

Some Compliance Errors May Seem Funny, but They're Not

The list of errors foundations can commit is long. The following table lists a few of these errors and examples of them, as well as the kind of thinking that can lead to such errors.

Category of Violation	Typical Example	Excuse
Treating a taxable expenditure as a donation	Founders paying their nephew's college tuition with foundation funds	"I made a contribution that included the tuition."
Lobbying	Buying a seat at a fund-raising dinner with foundation funds	"It seems like charity to me."
Confusion regarding eligible recipients	Giving to a 501(c)(4) organization (which is a tax-exempt organization but to which contributions by a foundation are not allowed, and to which individual contributions are not deductible)	"But it is a nonprofit."
Excessive compensation to the founder's family or the founder's business's employees	Paying a family member $100,000 for a few hours' work a month in the foundation	"I can't let Junior work in my business!"

Category of Violation	Typical Example	Excuse
Confusion regarding prohibited transactions	Having the foundation pay part of the cost of the family business's office and overhead	"I'm just charging them proportionally. That's fair."
Receiving an improper personal benefit	Buying a trip to Paris at charity auction	"We're planning to discuss charity on the way over to Paris, so I deducted that part of the donation as well."
Jeopardizing investments (rarely seen)	Investing all the foundation's assets in a single wild bet	"But this dot-com is going to strike it rich!"

These examples are a sampling of the more entertaining types of violations (if you're not the one making the mistake). Unfortunately, there is a host of other more subtle and less obvious pitfalls. A well-run foundation must have a thorough and practical system for compliance if it is to adhere to all legal requirements.

A Fail-Safe System

Compliance System Structure: Required Activities and Prohibited Activities

It helps to look at the compliance system with two lists in mind: activities that are required and activities that are prohibited. The most important in each category are listed below:

Required	Prohibited
Annual disbursements	Self-dealing
Grantee status verification	Jeopardizing investments
Tax returns	Taxable expenditures
Annual corporate filings	Excess business holdings
Payment of excise taxes (if any)	Unrelated business income
Documentation of gifts received	
Expenditure responsibility (if applicable)	
Public inspection	

Required Activities

Give It Away

The rule of thumb regarding disbursements is that a foundation must distribute 5 percent of its average net assets each year. (We use just the word assets for the sake of simplicity.) Of course, to meet this requirement, you must know the size of your assets. But that's not as easy as it sounds; there are several interpretations.

One accepted method of determining assets is to calculate the average of assets at the beginning and end of each month in the fiscal year. For example, if a foundation uses the calendar year, it would calculate its assets as follows: Take the foundation's net assets on January 1, add the net assets on February 1, and divide by two. Then take the net assets on February 1, add the net assets on March 1, and divide by two. Repeat each month, then add all the figures together and divide by 12. Using this figure as the assets, you then multiply by 0.05 to get the preliminary required distribution. Certain expenses may be deducted from this number. In addition, any grants from prior years in excess of the required amounts may also be deducted.

After taking those deductions, you have the required annual distribution. This is the minimum amount that must be distributed to qualified charities within 12 months of the close of the fiscal year. If a foundation fails to make such distributions, the IRS can impose a 15 percent penalty excise tax (and the foundation will still need to make the distribution). If the violations continue, the foundation may lose its tax exemption.

Give It to the Right People

Many private foundations fall short when it comes to choosing grantees, often because they don't even know that it can be a problem. This is especially true if the donor is used to making donations as an individual; individual taxpayers don't have the same obligations. Luckily, while fulfilling this requirement may be time-consuming, it's relatively straightforward. Step 1: Ask the recipient for a written statement verifying that it is in good standing with the IRS and a copy of the recipient's most recent IRS determination letter. Step 2: Consult IRS Publication 78—which is published three times a year and updated weekly—to make sure the recipient's status has not been revoked.

Failure to follow these rules can result in a penalty excise tax, to be paid by the foundation, which is equal to 100 percent of the gift, and an additional 50 percent tax to be paid by the individual who approved the donation, out of his own funds, not the foundation's.

Tax Returns

All private foundations must file the tax return form 990-PF. The deadline is May 15 of the year following a given calendar year, or, if the foundation doesn't follow the calendar year, the fifteenth day of the fifth month following the end of the foundation's fiscal year. It's probably wise to get professional help with 990-PFs; proper filing involves completing a tax return that can run upward of 50 pages.

In addition to the 990-PF, foundations that own certain types of assets, such as mortgaged real property, certain partnerships, or certain S corporation interests, may be required to file an additional form—990-T. And it may be necessary to file one or both of these federal tax returns with the attorney general in the state in which the foundation is domiciled.

If the foundation operates as a business as well as a philanthropic venture, it will have to comply with tax-reporting rules relevant for businesses. For example, if the foundation employs a staff, it will have to do the necessary reporting on payroll and benefits. Failure to file these returns can also lead to loss of the tax-exempt status.

Other tax returns may be required for certain types of donated property for which a charitable contribution deduction may be claimed. Examples include Form 1098-C for donated vehicles, Form 8899 for each year (for up to 10 years) that the charity receives net income from donated intellectual property, Form 8282 if donated property valued at more than $5,000 is sold within three years after the donation, and Form 8870 to report premiums paid on donated split dollar life insurance policies.

Annual Corporate Filings

Private foundations organized as not-for-profit corporations are responsible for the usual corporate formalities, just as are for-profit corporations. At a minimum, this requires annual directors meetings, minutes, and the required annual filings with the state of incorporation and any other state where the foundation is qualified to do business.

Excise Taxes

A well-run private foundation can avoid all excise taxes except the tax on net investment income. This tax, levied at 2 percent (reducible in certain cases to 1 percent), isn't much of a tax burden, but it can be a sizable accounting burden. That's because calculating investment income properly requires extensive and long-term records. A foundation must account for every dollar of income and expense, including investment gains and losses. It's necessary, for example, to keep track of the cost basis of every asset received or purchased. If the level of investment activity is at all significant (and even a portfolio of mutual funds can become complex because of dividend reinvestments), this task can become cumbersome.

In most cases, foundations should use an accounting software package, or farm the task out. The alternative is to manually account for the activity, which, while possible, can become burdensome.

Don't Forget to Write a Thank-You Note!

As we said, a foundation has to do more to document gifts it makes than an individual does. And don't forget that the foundation must also account for gifts it *receives* (most often from the founder). Without proper accounting, the donor may not get the expected income tax deduction.

Section 170 of the Internal Revenue Code requires that donors obtain "contemporaneous" written acknowledgement for all donations over $250 in order to get an income tax deduction. "Contemporaneous" in this context means before the date upon which the individual's return is due, or filed if earlier. For example, if you give money to your foundation, and your income tax return is due on April 15 but you file it on March 1, you must have your written acknowledgement by March 1. The foundation should state the amount of the gift and the date it was received, and that no benefits or goods were provided in exchange.

From a "best practices" standpoint, the foundation should respond quickly to donors to acknowledge receipt of their gift. Don H. Twietmeyer, a Partner of the law firm Hiscock & Barclay, recommends that clients write the thank-you note within 24 to 48 hours after receipt of the gift, and to have a Board member call the donor to thank them for the gift within 72 hours (not only for tax purposes, but also to ensure that the donor will remember the charity in the future). "We do this for a hospital foundation board that I sit on, and it provides great feedback to both the donor and the donee," says Twietmeyer.

Expenditure Responsibility

Sometimes a foundation may make a grant to another private foundation. When this occurs, the granting foundation must exercise *expenditure responsibility*. Expenditure responsibility is described in Internal Revenue Code,

Section 4945. It means that the private foundation must, in effect, monitor the recipient to ensure that the gifted funds get spent as the grant intended and not for another purpose that might not be allowable. The foundation must obtain detailed spending reports from the grantee and report to the IRS in detail on those expenditures.

Such grants are very demanding from a compliance view, and foundations should make them only after careful consideration. Here again, noncompliance can be costly. Failure to follow the complicated rules can result in a penalty excise tax equal to 20 percent of the taxable expenditure, and if the transaction is not corrected before the excise tax is assessed or a notice of deficiency regarding the excise tax is mailed, an additional tax equal to 100 percent of the taxable expenditure may be imposed (the 100 percent tax would only apply if the correction did not occur within the applicable time period). Also, there is an excise tax on the foundation manager who knowingly approved the taxable expenditure equal to 5 percent of the taxable expenditure, and if the transaction is not corrected before the excise tax is assessed or a notice of deficiency regarding the excise tax is mailed, an additional tax equal to 50 percent of the taxable expenditure may be imposed if the foundation manager refuses to correct the transaction (the 50 percent tax would only apply if the correction did not occur within the applicable time period). The initial excise tax on the foundation manager is capped at $10,000, and the subsequent additional excise tax on the foundation manager is capped at $20,000.

Public Inspection

Members of the public (grant seekers, for example) are entitled to free copies of certain forms on demand. (The foundation may charge a modest printing fee.) These include the foundation's 990-PF, its exemption application, its form 1023, and any IRS correspondence relating to the exemption application. Failure to provide the documents can lead to penalties of up to $50,000, payable by the individual responsible for the foundation's compliance. These are generally made available by the IRS to one or more organizations that post them on the Internet.

Prohibited Activities

Self-Dealing

Self-dealing (described in IRC, Section 4941) is prohibited, and acts of self-dealing are subject to various levels of excise tax. To make sense of the self-dealing rules requires the concept of *substantial contributors* and *disqualified persons.*

A substantial contributor is a person who has given at least $5,000 to a foundation or who has given more than 2 percent of the total amounts received cumulatively by the foundation.

Generally, disqualified persons are people who are substantial contributors to the foundation, spouses, lineal descendants, or ancestors of such people, foundation managers, and certain people involved in certain kinds of business relationships with a substantial contributor. For example, a 50–50 business partner of a private foundation founder will be a disqualified person with respect to his partner's foundation.

In effect, this means that every foundation founder and the founder's family (spouse, children, and grandchildren, etc.) will be disqualified persons. In addition, any person in business, or in a business partnership, with a founder is likely a disqualified person.

Self-dealing is any transaction (except certain defined exceptions) between a foundation and any of its disqualified persons (Section 4946).

To be on the safe side, scrutinize any proposed transaction with anyone who could possibly be a disqualified person. Assume that any transaction is prohibited until the foundation can demonstrate that it is not.

There are three common exceptions to the prohibited-transaction rules: (1) Disqualified persons are allowed to make no-strings-attached gifts to the foundation. (2) Disqualified persons may make zero-interest loans to the foundation. (3) Disqualified persons may be paid for "reasonable and necessary" work performed for the foundation, provided they are paid reasonable compensation. (Defining "reasonable" can be tricky, and it is wise to consult with a compensation specialist or other expert before implementing a compensation plan for any disqualified person.)

The penalties for self-dealing are especially severe. For example, suppose that Mr. Smith is the founder of the Smith Foundation, and he sells his foundation a piece of real estate at fair market value. This by itself would be self-dealing. The law requires that Smith put the foundation back in the same financial position it was in before the self-dealing, so he would have to refund the full costs incurred by the foundation. The IRS levies an initial penalty tax of 10 percent, to be paid by Smith in his nonfoundation role, and a further 5 percent tax to be paid by him in his role as foundation manager. (These penalties were adjusted upward in 2006, from 5 percent and 2.5 percent, respectively.) If Smith does not properly correct his self-dealing at this point, the IRS can impose another tier of taxes on him as a disqualified person equal to 200 percent of the amount involved, and as a foundation manager equal to

50 percent of the amount involved. (The initial excise tax and the subsequent excise tax on the foundation manager are both capped at $20,000 each; this was adjusted upward in 2006, from $10,000 each.) If Smith were to engage in further self-dealing, he would be subject to a third level of taxes, equal to all of the tax benefits the foundation and Smith have ever received.

Jeopardizing Investments

Section 4944 of the IRC is designed to prevent a private foundation from jeopardizing its principal through excessively risky investments. The rule is not especially stringent and will usually not constrain any reasonably prudent, diversified investment approach. The IRS does not, for example, preclude investments in nontraditional areas such as futures, options, warrants, or hedge funds. Indeed, some of the best-run foundations, such as the Rockefeller Foundation, have significant investments in nontraditional asset classes. But such investments may require special scrutiny, and a plan to make such investments should be evaluated both by an expert in investing and by one familiar with the jeopardizing investment rules before it is adopted. Adequate documentation should be maintained.

The rules are not intended to prevent a foundation from making any risky investments in an overall portfolio. Even significant losses won't get a foundation in trouble if its assets are managed by investment professionals and it has a carefully documented investment policy. The IRS will most likely rule an investment jeopardizing only if the investment was clearly reckless, and after the investment has resulted in a loss. For example, if a foundation invested all of its money in IBM call options, and the options expired worthless, that would be considered a jeopardizing investment.

If the IRS does determine that an investment was a jeopardizing investment, there is a 10 percent excise tax on the foundation and a 10 percent excise tax on the foundation manager who knowingly made the investment. If the investment is not removed from jeopardy before the tax is assessed or a notice of deficiency is mailed, there are additional taxes of 25 percent on the foundation and 5 percent on the foundation manager. The cap on the initial tax imposed on the foundation manager is $10,000, and the cap on the additional tax imposed on the foundation manager is $20,000. If the foundation engages in jeopardizing investments, is put on notice, and still fails to correct the problem by getting out of the jeopardizing investment, the IRS will ultimately terminate the foundation and confiscate its assets by means of taxes.

Taxable Expenditures

Taxable expenditures are another area where an unwary foundation can find itself in trouble without warning, having no idea that it was in dangerous territory. The way to avoid this is to make a distinction between expenses that relate to charitable activities and those that don't. The former can't be taxed; the latter will be. A taxable expenditure is an expense incurred by a foundation that is not for charitable purposes and is not an exception to the taxable expenditure rules. The IRS defines charitable purposes as religious, scientific, literary, educational, or other endeavors. It includes, for example, prevention of cruelty to animals and fostering international sports competition.

Exceptions to the taxable expenditure rules exist, generally, for the expenses ordinary and necessary for the foundation to continue. These include, for example, reasonable administration expenses, employee wages, professional advice and counsel, and investment management services.

The most common problem with taxable expenditures occurs when a foundation makes a grant to a nonqualified recipient. Examples would include the support of prohibited political issues or candidates, a grant made to a 501(c)(4) nonprofit (a tax-exempt organization but one to which contributions are not deductible), or the support of specific individuals without a prior-approved plan to make such support. So, for example, even though a qualified charity might make grants to homeless people, a private foundation that has not submitted a plan for such grants to the IRS and received approval could not make such grants directly. If it did, such grants would be taxable expenditures.

Failure to comply can result in a penalty excise tax equal to 20 percent of the taxable expenditure, and if the transaction is not corrected before the excise tax is assessed or a notice of deficiency regarding the excise tax is mailed, an additional tax equal to 100 percent of the taxable expenditure may be imposed (the 100 percent tax would only apply if the correction did not occur within the applicable time period). Also, there is an excise tax on the foundation manager who knowingly approved the taxable expenditure equal to 5 percent of the taxable expenditure, and if the transaction is not corrected before the excise tax is assessed or a notice of deficiency regarding the excise tax is mailed, an additional tax equal to 50 percent of the taxable expenditure may be imposed if the foundation manager refuses to correct the transaction (the 50 percent tax would only apply if the correction did not occur within the applicable time period). The initial excise tax on the foundation manager is capped at $10,000, and the subsequent additional excise tax on the foundation manager is capped at $20,000.

As a practical matter, the compliance system of a private foundation should flag for prior review any expenditure that is not clearly being made to a qualified charity for a permitted charitable purpose.

Excess Business Holdings

Congress didn't want foundations to own entire businesses, so it included a set of rules designed to prevent this in the 1969 reforms.

A foundation is prohibited under Section 4943 from having "excess business holdings." These rules prohibit a foundation and all of its disqualified people from owning more than 20 percent (35 percent under certain circumstances) of any business enterprise.

These rules are complex, full of qualifications and exceptions. Practically speaking, this issue most often arises when an entrepreneur wants to donate part of his business to his foundation. Unlike many of the other prohibitions, there is generally an opportunity to correct excess business holdings without incurring the types of excise taxes and penalties that the other violations bring. Nevertheless, it would be wise to carefully evaluate any possible excess business holding issues before acquiring the assets in question. Failure to comply can result in an initial tax equal to 10 percent of the value of the excess holdings, and an additional tax equal to 200 percent of the value of the excess holdings is imposed if nothing is done to eliminate the excess holdings before the close of the taxable year.

Unrelated Business Income

As discussed in more detail in Chapter 9, charities must be aware of the rules on unrelated business income (UBI). This income will generate a tax, called the unrelated business income tax (UBIT), which foundations should avoid.

Conclusion

If the regulations before 1969 were too loose, they leave no room now for abuse. If anything, they are now too extensive and too complex. Nevertheless, that is the situation foundations must deal with.

Without a careful compliance program, a foundation is likely to run afoul of one or another of these many rules, exposing itself, its directors, or its trustees to substantial liability. The typical smaller foundation (one without dedicated full-time staff well schooled in compliance issues) may have difficulty meeting the compliance requirements without outside help.

CHAPTER 12

Fraud, Inflation, and Market Risk

Many charities, like many businesses, have a lot of cash. Sometimes this cash is necessary as working capital (e.g., it is cash needed to fund coming programs, to pay employees, to match the cash needs of the business with the cash inflows), and sometimes there is cash not needed for current working capital. In profit-making businesses, this excess cash is either invested with the intention of producing more income in the future, or it is returned to shareholders. In the case of nonprofits, cash over and above the amount needed for working capital becomes part of the charity's endowment.

Endowments for public charities may or may not be a good idea, but they are at the very core of the business of all private foundations. So properly investing their endowments is one of the core functions of private foundations. Investing well is a difficult task. However, foundation managers need to be aware that in addition to the usual dangers of market losses, foundations are sometimes specifically targeted by criminals bent on stealing their money.

The publicity surrounding Bernie Madoff's $50 billion Ponzi scheme serves as a cruel reminder that investors need to concern themselves not merely with issues of return *on* capital, but more fundamentally with the issue of return *of* capital. The same lesson should be taken away for donors and charity managers—Madoff's scandal jeopardized the investments of at least 23 different charities.

To take a well-publicized example, the Elie Wiesel Foundation for Humanity, a charity founded by Holocaust survivor, author, and Nobel Laureate

Elie Wiesel, lost $15.2 million.[1] The Foundation's major projects include helping Darfurian and Sudanese refugees who have fled to Israel.[2] Wiesel's Foundation, although seriously hurt by the Madoff losses, has been able to keep operating, and says it expects to be able to meet its charitable commitments.

When explaining his decision to invest his charity's assets with Madoff, Wiesel said he had been referred by a wealthy old friend. "We checked the people who [had] business with [Madoff], and they were among the best minds on Wall Street, the geniuses of finance ... I am not a genius of finance ... and so it happened."[3] Madoff attracted clients through his impressively consistent record embellished with an air of exclusivity and intrigue. Madoff kept the details of his investment strategies a secret, refusing to divulge to clients exactly where their assets were held, claiming that such an explanation would be much too complicated for the layman. Clients were attracted by a combination of Madoff's long and apparently excellent track record and his reputation.

It is not entirely clear at what point Madoff began his fraudulent activities. It appears likely that for at least part of his career, Madoff ran a legitimate operation. He was involved in the 1960s and 1970s in market making in small companies, and was involved in the development of what eventually became, in 1971, the NASDAQ (National Association of Securities Dealers Automated Quotation system). The NASDAQ has evolved into one of the largest stock markets in the world.

Madoff later became the chairman of the NASD, the National Association of Securities Dealers. NASD had been delegated the authority to provide much of the regulatory oversight by the Securities and Exchange Commission (SEC). So Madoff, in effect, was the head of the organization that was deeply involved in regulating operations like Madoff's.

Madoff used this perceived credibility to market himself, and generate a growing stream of investors. As it got going, Madoff was able to put to use what psychologists call "social proof," also known as the "bandwagon effect." Madoff made it known, or gave the impression, that he had many important, wealthy, and sophisticated clients, and used this perception to gain more.

---

[1] www.nytimes.com/2009/02/27/business/27madoff.html?_r=1.

[2] http://kristof.blogs.nytimes.com/tag/darfur/ (*New York Times* correspondent Nicholas Kristof has followed Darfur, which is in Sudan, for years. He describes the mass murder in Darfur as the result of the Arab government attempting to silence opposition by mass murder. Kristof estimates that the Arab government of Omar al-Bashir has murdered "hundreds of thousands" of black Africans living in the Sudan.)

[3] www.nytimes.com/2009/02/27/business/27madoff.html?_r=1.

Madoff accepted investors across the board—individuals, investment funds, banks, pension funds, and charities and foundations. He may have strategically targeted private foundations because of the 5 percent payoff rule[4]—private foundations must spend at least 5 percent of their assets every year (so, for example, for every $1 billion of assets under management, Madoff need only have (at least) $50 million on hand for withdrawals per year). Since many foundations adhere closely to the 5 percent rule, this was an easy way for Madoff to sustain the life of his Ponzi scheme; having private foundations as clients could lower the average demand for cash withdrawals and therefore keep his scheme in play longer than otherwise possible. It is also possible, and perhaps likely, that Madoff simply took whatever investors he could, since if he were going to steal the money anyway, it didn't really matter where it came from.

One foundation that was extensively involved with Madoff was the Picower Foundation. The Picower Foundation was at one time reported to be the seventh-largest foundation in the United States. It was originally established by Jeffry Picower to fund medical research; it was forced to close entirely due to massive losses with Madoff.[5] There are allegations that Picower knew that Madoff was a fraud, as the Foundation reportedly drew out from Madoff billions more than it put in.[6] Jeffry Picower died shortly after the scandal was revealed. He was found dead at the bottom of a swimming pool. The coroner ruled it a heart attack. Since the death of Jeffry Picower, the Picower estate has agreed to pay out billions that it allegedly received improperly from Madoff. As of this writing, the Picower estate is in discussions with the Madoff bankruptcy estate's trustee to pay the estate about $7.2 billion. Other claimants are objecting.[7] The windup could go on for years.

While most of Madoff's investors were innocent victims, other investment decisions appear suspect. For example, former CFO Sheryl Weinstein of Hadassah, a Jewish volunteer organization, had been having, by her own admission, an adulterous affair with Madoff since the late 1980s.[8] We truly live in a troubled world when a woman has an adulterous affair, plunks her employer's money into a Ponzi scheme run by her adulterous boyfriend, and then has the gall to publish a kiss-and-tell exposé in which she—get this—blames him. According to news reports, by the late 1990s Hadassah

[4]http://money.cnn.com/2008/12/29/news/newsmakers/zuckoff_madoff.fortune/.
[5]www.telegraph.co.uk/finance/financetopics/bernard-madoff/3868882/Bernard-Madoff-One-of-worlds-biggest-charity-foundations-forced-to-shut.html.
[6]www.propublica.org/article/madoff-client-jeffry-picower-netted-5-billion.
[7]www.businessweek.com/news/2011-01-06/madoff-investors-object-to-picower-accord-with-trustee.html.
[8]www.topnews.in/ex-jewish-charity-cfo-had-roaring-affair-ponzi-king-madoff-2201736.

Madoff Investor	Potential Exposure
Carl and Ruth Shapiro Family Foundation	$145 million
Hadassah	$90 million
Wolosoff Foundation	$38 million
Mortimer B. Zuckerman Charitable Remainder Trust (*New York Daily News* owner's charity)	$30 million
Arthur I. and Sydelle F. Meyer Charitable Foundation	$29.2 million
Madoff Family Foundation	$19 million
Los Angeles Jewish Community Foundation	$18 million
America-Israel Cultural Foundation	$15 million
Lautenberg Family Foundation	$12.8 million
United Jewish Endowment Fund	Less than $10 million
Robert I. Lappin Charitable Foundation	$8 million
Chais Family Foundation	$7 million
Jewish Federation of Greater Los Angeles	$6.4 million
Julian J. Levitt Foundation	$6 million
American Friends of Yad Sarah	$1.5 million
Chair Family Foundation	n/a
Fair Food Foundation	n/a
Foundation for Humanity (Elie Wiesel's charity)	$15.2 million
JEHT Foundation	n/a
The Moriah Fund	n/a
MorseLife	n/a
Wunderkinder Foundation (Steven Spielberg's charity)	n/a
Total	**$451.1 million**

had invested $40 million with Madoff; since then they've taken $130 million out of their Madoff account with millions still on his books at the time of the scandal's exposure; now $90 million of their investment is in jeopardy. We have included a list of many of the charities affected by Madoff's scandal.[9]

Though the Madoff scandal was of epic proportions, it in essence took the form of a classic Ponzi scheme, which, unfortunately, is no anomaly in modern times. As the market fell in 2008, many investors, across the board, asked for their money back. Such runs on even a small scale will uproot most Ponzi schemes since they betray the perpetrator's fatal lack of assets. Alas, following the 2008 market crash, many fraudulent schemes have come bubbling up to the surface. And although many or most of these are at their core Ponzi schemes, the veneer comes in a bewildering array of guises.

Stanford Case

Chances are you've never heard of Robert Allen Stanford, alias Sir Robert Allen Stanford, alias Allen Stanford. But he holds the dubious distinction of being the operator of the second-largest alleged Ponzi scheme in history. So why haven't you heard of him? He had the public relations good fortune of having his story driven from the headlines by Bernie Madoff.

In February of 2009, the SEC filed a lawsuit against Stanford International Bank (SIB), Stanford Group Company (SGC) and Stanford Capital Management (SCM)—three out of several dozen companies owned and operated by Robert Allen Stanford.

Stanford, who was knighted in Antigua, the country in which he operated Stanford International Bank (SIB), and six of his colleagues face 21 criminal charges, primarily consisting of defrauding investors out of $8 billion by selling "bogus" certificates of deposits (CDs). The SEC also accused those from Stanford of doctoring financial statements, fabricating historical returns to attract customers, bribing Antigua's Financial Services Regulatory Commission (FSRC) to look the other way, and wrongfully appropriating client investments for personal use and loans without proper disclosure to investors.

The CDs were sold by Stanford's bank in Antigua and brokered through the Stanford Group Company, which was based in Houston, Texas. The bank reportedly attracted 30,000 investors from more than a hundred countries. According to the SEC, Stanford misrepresented that the CDs were "safe, were invested in liquid financial instruments, that the portfolio was monitored by more than 20 analysts and annually audited by Antiguan regulators," none of which was apparently true.

---

[9]http://en.wikipedia.org/wiki/List_of_investors_in_Bernard_L._Madoff_Securities.

The SEC states that the CDs were advertised as offering rates of return as much as four times the industry average.[10] The SEC also claimed that to help woo potential investors, SIB falsely advertised double-digit average rates of return on its investments over the past 15 years[11] and used this as an explanation of how they could afford to pay such high returns for their CDs. To help make sales to potential investors, brokers were told to emphasize that clients' assets would be invested in a globally diversified portfolio of liquid and marketable securities.

The CDs, which were SIB's primary product, were sold through SGC. To aid sales, SIB offered brokers high commissions for the sale of these CDs—SGC received a 3 percent trailing fee from SIB on sales of the CDs. SGC advisers received a 1 percent commission upon sale and were eligible to receive as much as a 1 percent trailing commission throughout the term of the CD. With these high commissions, advisers had strong incentives to push SIB's CDs on potential investors. In 2006 and 2007 alone, SIB paid $502 million in management fees and CD commissions to SGC.

It is worth pausing in this description of the fraud to reflect on what the scheme consisted of. CDs are a very simple investment. A CD is a short-term loan to a bank. Most CDs offer a stated rate of interest, for a stated term. Banks issue CDs because this gives them a source of funds that is not normally subject to overnight withdrawal. Banks then use the money that they raise through CDs and other deposits to make investments. Normally, the overwhelming majority of a bank's investments are in loans. A bank may occasionally invest a small amount of its assets in equities or other non-loans. But the very essence of the banking business is to take deposits and make loans. Why loans? Because loans (if they are good) pay back the amount invested, plus interest. They are not supposed to fluctuate in value.

Banks also operate with a very high degree of financial leverage. This means that a bank may borrow up to 90 percent or more of its total capital. For example, at the beginning of 2010, Bank of America had well over 90 percent financial leverage. In other words, if you took the value of Bank of America's liabilities—mostly money owed to depositors—and subtracted that from the stated value of its assets (less "goodwill"), only about 6 percent of everything would be left over.

That kind of leverage means that even a relatively small drop in the value of the bank's assets can render it insolvent. As was demonstrated by the 2008 collapse, such small drops in the value of fixed income assets are possible. With equities, it happens routinely.

---

[10]http://emac.blogs.foxbusiness.com/2009/02/19/where-is-robert-allen-stanford.
[11]www.bizjournals.com/baltimore/stories/2009/02/16/daily19.html.

Let's return to SIB. If they were paying 15 percent on CDs, then they would have to earn significantly more than 15 percent on their assets in order to be able to pay that interest. It is all but impossible for a bank to earn that much on assets. For comparison, in a very good quarter, the first quarter of 2010, Bank of America earned *gross*, before expenses, about 6.5 percent on assets.

Anyone looking at SIB CDs promising 15 percent should have been able to detect that something may have been amiss.

In addition to the CD charges, SIB was also charged with fabricating historical returns on a proprietary mutual fund wrap program called "Stanford Allocation Strategy" (SAS) in order to help market the product to new investors.

According to the SEC, for the seven years ending in 2007 SIB claimed that its SAS Growth fund returned 11.03 percent, against S&P 500 returns of just 3.7 percent for the same period. Such performance is good, but not impossible. For example, during same period, the First Eagle Global Fund (now SoGen First Eagle) returned an average of 17 percent per year, compounded, according to Morningstar data.

For the investor, however, First Eagle Global would have been easier to understand. It was run until 2004 by Jean Marie Eveillard, one of the top international fund managers in the world. Morningstar's Russ Kinnel calls Eveillard "a legendary value investor who put together an impressive track record over the years of preserving his shareholders' money in down markets and doing very well in up markets as well."[12]

How could an investor distinguish between a legitimate fund offering, such as First Eagle Global, and fraudulent one, such as SAS? In this case, you would not be able to tell simply by looking at the track record. Remember that Madoff's so-called track record was essentially impossible given the stated strategy of the fund. That is not necessarily the case with SAS Growth. Its claimed returns were plausible for an equity fund over the period.

Still, according to the SEC, the returns reported by the SAS fund were simply lies. For example, "in 2000, actual SAS client returns ranged from negative 7.5 percent to positive 1.1 percent. In 2001, actual SAS client returns ranged from negative 10.7 percent to negative 2.1 percent. And, in 2002, actual SAS client returns ranged from negative 26.6 percent to negative 8.7 percent."[13] Compare these actual results to the results claimed by SAS. For example, SAS reported 16.04 percent for 2000, when the best actual client return was 1.1 percent. Using the presentation of these fabricated returns,

---

[12]www.marketwatch.com/story/fund-manager-eveillard-returns-to-first-eagle-de-vaulx-out.
[13]SEC filing Case 3:09-cv-00298-N Document 48, filed 02/27/2009, page 15.

within a short period of time, assets under SAS grew from under $10 million to $1.2 billion and generated fees in excess of $25 million.

Enron

Extremely high, seemingly unexplained returns can be a warning sign, even if you can't figure out what is wrong. For example, in the late 1990s and early 2000s, a Texas company in the utility and energy business was reporting consistently high and growing earnings. This was a large, public company that was SEC regulated, New York Stock Exchange (NYSE) traded, and audited by one of the Big Five accounting firms. Their consistent and growing earnings catapulted the stock from the mid-teens per share up to about $90 a share, which valued the company at a cool $68 billion. You may have heard of the company. It was called Enron.

We were curious at the time about Enron since we owned a few shares from the prebubble era when the company was known as Portland General, a rather staid electrical utility in Oregon. Enron merged with Portland General in 1997, although it amounted to a takeover by Enron.

At the time, we spoke with some very successful investors in the same industry who simply couldn't figure out what Enron was doing. These investors are some of the smartest and most successful people in the energy industry. They had long and deep experience in most of Enron's growth markets. They were losing employees and business to Enron. They just couldn't see how Enron was doing it.

We were far less sophisticated. But we looked at Enron and couldn't understand why a company in that industry could be trading for such a high multiple of earnings. We had no inkling of the fraud that turned out to be there, but we sold simply because it seemed out of whack. It turned out that the smart investors were right. Enron wasn't creating that much value in old and well understood markets. They were faking it.

From the time the Enron fraud was revealed, the whole house of cards collapsed relatively quickly, and the company's market value dropped from $68 billion to zero in a little over a year.

The Enron and SGC frauds have some similarities and some differences. They were both fraudulent, but these two cases showcase how no single fraud detection approach can work. Consider what each did. Each faked critical reporting numbers: SGC by simply conjuring them and reporting fictional or inflated investment results; Enron through elaborate, byzantine financial structures that fooled most of the outsiders (including a number of very successful fund managers, directors, and outside examiners).

Enron's reported results were not compatible with known industry standards. Very few, if any, large companies that have stock charts that looked like Enron's—parabolic growth with no clearly visible explanation—stay at those higher levels permanently. But Enron had all the outside credentials an investor could desire. It was in compliance with the SEC (except for the fraud); it had a clean bill of health from its auditors; it was in good standing with the NYSE; it was big; it had sophisticated investors; and it had a highly accomplished board of directors.

For an outsider, there was simply no way to tell that Enron was a fraud. The only warning available would have been the inability to explain the results.

The facts are almost the opposite for SGC. SGC did not have a big-name accounting firm, did not file SEC reports, and did not trade on the NYSE. Of course, many legitimate investment firms also don't have big-name auditors, don't file with the SEC (because they aren't required to), and don't trade on the NYSE. So the absence of those characteristics by themselves means nothing. Furthermore, SGC's reported investment results were well within the realm of the plausible.

So how could an outsider have spotted and avoided SGC?

One way would have been to be aware of and question the too-good-to-be-true returns on SIB's CDs. That scheme, as discussed above, with its claimed returns that were four times better than the market on what's normally a riskless investment, should certainly raise eyebrows. And if a company appears to have questionable practices or results in one of its investment operations, then that could be a red flag for investors in other programs run by the same company.

But what if you were looking at SGC, and missed the CD operation of its affiliate. Were there any other clues?

Yes, if you knew where to look. The SEC's investment adviser public disclosure forms[14] would have been a good place to start as they list and explain previous regulatory infractions and penalties (item 11, Form ADV, the Uniform Application for Investment Adviser Registration). For example, SGC had committed and settled without argument four separate regulatory infractions in 2007 and 2008. In November of 2007, FINRA charged SGC with distributing sales literature for their certificate deposits that "did not comply

---

[14]www.adviserinfo.sec.gov/(S(0yb03f45eyzkmq45tcajce45))/IAPD/Content/Search/iapd_Search.aspx (Investment Adviser Search).

with NASD advertising rules in that it failed to disclose . . . conflict of interest, [and] failed to present fair and balanced treatment of the risks . . . of a CD investment";[15] for this they were censured and fined $10,000. In July of 2008, FINRA charged SGC with failing to "report customer transactions in municipal securities within 15 minutes after execution," for which they were censured and fined $10,000. In November of 2008, two months before Stanford's operation came crashing down, FINRA again charged SGC with another infringement, alleging that they failed to disclose several items that are normally required in research reports, such as price charts, compensation, valuation methods, conflicts of interest, risks, and managers' financial interests in SGC's many affiliate companies. For this, they were censured and fined $30,000.

Baptist Foundation of Arizona Case

Charitable donors want to improve the world. Sometimes their donations make a difference, and, unfortunately, sometimes they don't. But no donor ever anticipates that the charity they are supporting will simply steal the money. Yet that is exactly what happened with the Baptist Foundation of Arizona.

When the Baptist Foundation of Arizona (BFA) finally blew up in 1999 and filed a Chapter 11 bankruptcy petition, it reported owing $590 million to 13,000 small investors, as well as another $50 million to other creditors. Against that liability it claimed assets of $240 million.

These small investors had been drawn to make investments with the Baptist organization by the lure of above-market returns, low risk, and the promise that at the same time they would be "doing good." For example, one of the BFA brochures read, in part,

> We are a ministry dedicated to serving the Lord and furthering Southern Baptist and other Christian causes. We re-invest your money and the profit we earn goes to further such ministries as Christian education, care for children and senior adults, missions and new church starts. Your investment actually touches the lives of countless numbers while you earn a very attractive interest rate.

Another proclaimed:

> You don't have to be a Southern Baptist and you don't have to live in Arizona to take advantage of our outstanding interest rates and unique

---

[15] www.adviserinfo.sec.gov/(S(0yb03f45eyzkmq45tcajce45))/IAPD/Content/ViewForm/ADV/Sections/iapd_AdvDrpSection.aspx#Regulatory.

"Stewardship Investing" opportunities. Nearly one fourth of our clients are not Southern Baptists.

The offer was relatively straightforward. BFA positioned itself as offering an alternative to a bank deposit. They said that they were investing the funds in real estate, which was true. However, they did not properly disclose the nature of the risks they were taking, nor did they disclose that more than $100 million of real-estate loans they made were actually made to insiders.

The law did not require that BFA comply with either banking rules or securities registration that typically is required for investment offerings of this type. However, BFA reassured its investors by having a major accounting firm audit its books. Year after year, this firm issued clean reports. You may have heard of the firm: Arthur Andersen. Andersen, of course, went down a few years later as a result of its involvement in Enron.

For a number of years in the 1980s and 1990s, BFA was able to operate without trouble as the Arizona real-estate market was steady or rose. However, in the late 1990s, trouble did begin to develop.

And unlike the Madoff, Stanford, and Enron frauds, you could have had warning about BFA before it went bust, just by reading the newspaper. In April of 1998, the *Phoenix New Times* published two articles that explicitly accused BFA of fraud, even revealing the modus operandi of their scheme.[16] That same month, with full knowledge of the article and its contents, Arthur Andersen signed off on their financial statements; apparently they had only asked BFA's managers if the allegations were true. In May of 2002, Arthur Andersen agreed to a settlement of $217 million to BFA victims.

The Bre-X Fraud

The cases of Stanford and Enron exemplify how fraud can occur through misstatements of income. The Baptist Foundation of Arizona case demonstrated how the same sort of results can come about by misstating assets. But falsely reporting the market value of an existing, tangible house is one thing; it's another thing entirely to create precious, liquid assets out of the air. The Canadian mining company Bre-X did just that: They conjured the discovery of what would have been the largest gold mine in the world and perpetuated the largest commodity fraud of all time.

---

[16]Terry Greene Sterling, "The Money Changers, A New Times Investigation," *Phoenix New Times*, April 16, 1998.

Canada has a long history of wildcat mining exploration companies. Searching for mineral deposits has always been, and continues to be, a difficult, risky, and frustrating process. When David Walsh started Bre-X in late 1988, he focused on finding minerals in Canada's Northwest Territories. A year later, the company, alongside a host of other no-name penny stocks, was listed on the Alberta Stock Exchange. Bre-X's price between 1989 and 1992 averaged a modest C$0.27.[17] Having had no luck in Canada, Walsh decided to follow the advice of his new partner, geologist John Felderhof.

Felderhof, who had experience in Indonesia, hired another geologist— Michael de Guzman. In November of that year, Bre-X announced that it had drilled some promising test holes at its Indonesian property known as Busang on the giant island of Borneo, one of the most remote and forbidding places on earth. The stock began to rise, and was near a dollar a share by year end.

The following two years brought a flurry of cores, assay results, test holes, and news releases. Bre-X, it appeared, had a very large gold discovery on its hands. The stock soared to over $14 by July 1995. The company continued to report finding more gold, and the stock continued to rocket.

By October, the company was claiming 10 to 30 million ounces, and the stock was at $50. In April of 1996, the stock was listed on the much larger Toronto Stock Exchange, where it traded hands at $180 a share. In June, they reported 39 million ounces. By July, the claim was sized at 47 million ounces.

During the summer and fall months of 1996, David Walsh, his wife, and John Felderhof sold 1.25 million shares of Bre-X for C$60 million. But the company attracted the attention of Wall Street, and in December Lehman Brothers rated Bre-X as a strong buy, "the gold discovery of the century" adding that this "growth story [is expected to] continue in a major way for the rest of this decade."[18] Like Enron a few years later, Bre-X attracted very smart institutional investors, including Fidelity, Invesco, and a number of large pension funds.

In February of 1997, the company announced an agreement with the Indonesian government, which demanded a hunk of the company, and the giant mining company Freeport-McMoRan, which would supply capital and know-how. The gold resources were now said to be 71 million ounces. A few days later Walsh unofficially estimated that there were 200 million ounces of gold present. The stock reached a high of $280 a share, which valued the company at about $6 billion.

---

[17] www.terry.uga.edu/~pirvine/files/Bre-X_fullcase.pdf.
[18] www.businessweek.com/1997/15/b352267.htm.

For comparison purposes, the proven and probable reserves of Anglo-Gold, the great old mining house whose history goes back a hundred years, are about 230 million ounces. Today, with gold many times the price it was in 1996, the market cap of AngloGold is about $17 billion.

Less than a month after Walsh's claim of 200 million ounces, the wheels came off the cart. On March 12, Freeport-McMoRan said its tests showed only trace amounts of gold.

On March 19, Guzman fell, jumped, or was precipitated, from a helicopter 800 feet above the Indonesian jungle. A suspicious fire also destroyed Bre-X's Busang office, destroying all of Guzman's geological records and almost all of the drilling results.

Two days later, the first public report, in an Indonesian newspaper, revealed that Bre-X might not have the gold. On March 26, trading in Bre-X was halted after Freeport-McMoRan announced that Busang contains "insignificant amounts of gold." When trading resumed, the price plunged to an equivalent of about $25.

The final straw came on May 5, when an independent analyst reported "only trace amounts of gold have been found in the sample assayed, and there were no samples that gave gold values of economic interest . . . the magnitude of the tampering . . . and resulting falsification of assay values at Busang, is of a scale and over a period of time and with a precision that, to our knowledge, is without precedent in the history of the world anywhere."[19] The day after the report was released, Bre-X opened at just pennies a share. It was soon delisted.

Walsh died the next year of a brain aneurysm. The Ontario Securities Commission filed charges of fraud against Felderhof. The case and others dragged through the court system until 2007, when Felderhof was acquitted of all charges.

Did Guzman carry out the fraud on his own? Was there an Indonesian connection? Was the Suharto government, or some of its officials, involved? We don't know.

What we do know is that many investors, including sophisticated, experienced investors, were deceived, and lost tens of millions of dollars as a result.

Were there any clues? Could a careful investor have smelled a rat, and avoided the Bre-X fraud?

A very careful investigator might have been able to discover that Walsh declared personal bankruptcy in 1993 because he had run up $60,000 in credit card debt. While not a clue to fraud (and we don't know whether Walsh was involved), you might want to think twice before betting on a company

---

[19] www.terry.uga.edu/~pirvine/files/Bre-X_fullcase.pdf.

run by a man who has such poor personal financial skills that he runs up such a huge credit card debt.

A careful investor might also have discovered that other companies had looked in Borneo and found economically infeasible amounts of gold. That, of course, doesn't mean it's not there, but it might provide some cause for pause. Some of Bre-X's operating procedures were also a bit unusual. For example, Felderhof did not invite any outside assayers, or any other large mining companies to visit the site with their experts. It is usual for a prospector to encourage such outside confirmations. Another irregularity concerned Bre-X's treatment of the same cores. It is usual to take a core sample, and divide it in half. One half is kept for future review and reference, and the other half is crushed and assayed. That appears not to have occurred in this case. Then, further adding to the suspicion, in August 1996, Walsh sold 1.25 million shares, netting about $60 million. If investors had known that at least some of the proceeds were used to buy property in the Bahamas, that might have been worrisome.

Allied Capital

There is a saying that "you can't fake dividends." The saying implies that a company that consistently pays dividends is probably not cooking its books because paying dividends requires cash. Of course, it is true that dividends require cash, and to pay them a company must have cash. For many businesses, the saying probably is persuasive. However, in the case of a lender, which almost by definition has cash available, or in the case of a company that is continually raising new capital, dividends may be very misleading. The case of Allied Capital shows that even years and years of high, stable, and growing dividends are no guarantee that the company is not a fraud.

The story of Allied is long and very complex. This brief account is based on the book-length treatment written by Greenlight Capital's David Einhorn. To make a long story very short, Allied Capital was a Small Business Development company (SBD). As such, it was in the business of making "mezzanine" loans to small businesses. These loans were usually insured by the Small Business Administration (SBA), meaning the U.S. taxpayer.

Allied, which failed in 2010, had been in business for more than four decades, and had enjoyed years and years of growth in assets, and in payouts.

In theory, such a business, like any lending business, can be profitable if it is well run. And Allied may have been run reasonably well for a number of years. It is hard to say when the fraud began, but it appears to have been ongoing for at least 10 years at the time of Allied's failure in 2010.

Allied appears to have been a complex Ponzi scheme. During the decade of the 2000s, Allied brought in over a billion dollars by selling stock to investors. As explained in great detail by David Einhorn in *Fooling Some of the People All of the Time* (John Wiley & Sons, 2010), Allied and its components made hundreds of millions of dollars of fraudulent loans and hid the fact through fraudulent accounting. Through a cynical combination of practices, including improper or fraudulent valuation of assets, maximizing taxable income, harvesting gains, refusing to write off losses, and repeatedly raising capital, Allied was able to generate enough new cash to keep up its payout and thereby maintain the stock price. Maintaining a high stock price, in turn, was essential to raising the additional capital necessary to keep the scheme going.

Allied was not an easy fraud for an investor to spot on his own. However, Einhorn, who is primarily a hedge fund manager, publicly stated as far back as 2002 his belief that Allied may have been a fraud. This was a relatively unusual instance in which you didn't have to ferret out the fraud yourself; all you had to do was read up on what was already publicly available.

The story is told in great detail by Einhorn in his book, which we highly recommend. The book discusses a fair amount of technical accounting, but also provides an important warning against relying on government oversight to protect investors. Einhorn documents the persistent failures of the Small Business Administration and the SEC, as well as the New York Attorney General's office, to vigorously defend the taxpayers' and investors' interests.

Fraudulent or Not? You Decide

Now that we've reviewed these five different frauds, all of which cost investors dearly, we'll present another situation that is ongoing. You decide whether or not it will turn out to be a fraud, leaving another generation of investors high and dry.

Here's the scenario. Suppose a broker you trust offers you the following investment opportunity. For now, we'll call it XYZ. You can begin investing now, and you can add to the investment for as long as you want. The sponsor and their spokespeople continually repeat that the investment is "guaranteed."

Your broker tells you that the rate of return is not guaranteed, but that in the past many investors have received a large multiple of their investments, and still get payments. He tells you, truthfully, that he has many clients who are now taking out every year more than the total that they ever invested. For example, he tells you about Fred, who put in just $6,958, and has so far taken out over a quarter of a million!

Your broker invites you to meet Fred, which you do at his yacht club. Fred looks pretty ordinary, not like a superstar investor. You buy Fred a drink, and chat. With the broker's approval, you ask Fred about his amazing investment in XYZ. Is it really true? To your surprise, Fred confirms that he put just $6,958 into XYZ, and that he now gets almost twice that *every year.*

After you leave, you ask your broker if you invest now, when will you be able to start collecting the loot. He tells you that once you invest, later, at a time partly of your choosing and partly of the sponsor's, you will receive cash payments every month, for as long as you live. If you die early, your family will receive cash payments, and if you get disabled, you will get cash payments starting soon after you get disabled.

Moreover, your broker explains that the sponsor of the investment has been in business for over 70 years, and they have paid off over a million investors.

How does it sound so far?

Now let me tell you a few additional facts you might want to consider.

What Backs Your Investment

The funds given to the sponsor are invested by being lent out at extremely low rates of interest to a related-party borrower who has no realistic way of earning the money to pay the loans back. This related party has lost money almost every year for decades. He stays in business by continuing to borrow more money. The sponsor claims that these funds are being invested, but the related party to whom they are being lent is actually spending them on current consumption.

Now forget about how the sponsor invests your money, and turn your attention to the sponsor's other main business. In addition to your investment, the sponsor runs an insurance scheme. This insurance scheme has future liabilities. The size of these future liabilities is indeterminate, but the best actuarial estimates show this liability to be far beyond the ability of the sponsor to pay under any reasonable scenario.

No Contract

Is your interest in investing cooled yet? If not, and you're still interested, you might want to know that this sponsor will not offer you a contract. You will have no contractual rights. The sponsor unilaterally decides when, whether, and how much to pay out. They can change their rules. If you don't like their changes, tough.

No Oversight

Neither the New York Stock Exchange, nor any other private exchange reviews or oversees the sponsor. The sponsor is exempt from SEC regulation. No foreign regulator or other body oversees or regulates the sponsor. Neither FINRA (Financial Industry Regulatory Authority) nor the NASD (National Association of Securities Dealers and predecessor to FINRA) regulates the sponsor. The sponsor's insurance activities are beyond the purview of the Insurance Commission of any of the 50 states. No foreign government or insurance regulator oversees the sponsor. The sponsor is not a member of FDIC, nor does the sponsor participate in any kind of private insurance. There is no private oversight group, committee, organization, or rating agency that reviews the sponsor's offerings. No Big Four accounting firm audits the sponsor. In fact, the only audit, which does not conform to Generally Accepted Accounting Principles (GAAP), is done by an affiliate; that is, by a related party. That's a bit like Madoff telling you, "Don't worry, my wife is doing the audit."

Source of Payouts

You will recall that Madoff was able to pay investors who wanted money only by using the money from other investors. Since Madoff was not truly investing the money he collected, there were no earnings to distribute.

The present opportunity, XYZ, is in some ways similar. XYZ does appear to have investments—those low interest rate loans to the related party. However, the related party is severely in debt, and the loans of XYZ could not be repaid by the related party, except by borrowing from someone else. So while it is true that people are being paid by XYZ, it is only because new investors continue to put in money. It is actually this new money that is going to pay the old investors.

What Is XYZ?

As you may have surmised, XYZ is a fairly accurate description of the U.S. Social Security system.

Social Security has an amazing number of features in common with a standard pyramid or Ponzi scheme. These include:

1. Great returns for early investors.
2. Lack of easy transparency.
3. Misapplication of investor funds (instead of being invested, the funds are turned over to a related party, who spends them on its own expenses).

4. Funds invested with a related party.
5. The related party is unlikely to ever pay the funds back in real terms (see below).
6. No outside audit.
7. Pay existing investors using funds from new investors.

How Will Social Security End?

Social Security, although fundamentally unsound, has several vitally important features that set it apart from privately run pyramid schemes. These include:

1. The sponsor, the U.S. government, can and does compel people to invest.
2. The sponsor has the ability to simply print the money to pay benefits.
3. There is no way that an outside investor can bring suit to put the whole system into receivership.
4. The sponsor, the U.S. government, can and does change the rules in the middle of the game.

Nevertheless, the combined liabilities of the Social Security system and the Medicare system are so staggeringly large that it is a virtual mathematical impossibility that the promised benefits, in real terms, will be paid.

Let us unpack that last sentence. To do that, we need to look at a few somewhat technical items. These technical items are what we mean by *promised benefits, real terms,* and *virtual mathematical impossibility.*

Promised Benefits

Unfortunately, most politicians either don't understand Social Security or deliberately mislead the public. In essence, Social Security is simple. The government forces you to "contribute" 12.3 percent of your wages to Social Security. This is officially not called a tax, because the government promises that you will receive benefits in the future.

Private insurance companies make similar promises all the time. You pay insurance premiums, or annuity premiums, in exchange for a promise to pay in the future (e.g., when you die in the case of life insurance, or when you retire with some annuities). Private insurance companies are required by good business practices and by law to invest the premiums they get from you so that they can be sure they have enough to make all the payments they've promised.

At any point in time, an insurance company is required to have sufficient assets to cover its future expected payouts. Those expected future payouts have a value today. Their value today can be estimated. That value today is called their "present value."

For example, a promise to pay $100,000 a year for 30 years is not worth $3,000,000 (i.e., 30 times $100,000) today. Rather, it is worth less. Depending on various assumptions, it may be worth $1,200,000 today.

If that insurance company has contracts that will require it to pay $100,000 a year for 30 years, it had darn well better have at least $1,200,000 in good assets today. If the insurance company had less than $1,200,000, it would have an *unfunded liability.*

When someone, some company, or some government has an unfunded liability, it means that it likely will not be able to pay the whole amount it owes or will owe.

The present value of the unfunded liabilities of the Social Security system, as of 2010, was approximately $8 trillion. That's $8,000,000,000,000. That number comes from the Social Security administration itself. That means that the government, if it were run the way it requires private insurance companies to be run, should have $8 trillion set aside *today*, just to fund Social Security. Instead, the government is over $9 trillion in debt.

But the true numbers are vastly worse. Social Security is not a stand-alone entity. It is part of the U.S. Government. And the U.S. Government, taken as a whole, has an unfunded liability of $60 trillion. That's $60,000,000,000,000. That number, which comes from the government itself—the GAO—may well be low. Other estimates put the true unfunded liability of the government at $100 trillion; that's $100,000,000,000,000!

Take a minute to reflect on the GAO number. The population of the United States is about 300 million. That works out to $200,000 of unfunded liability for every man, woman, and child in the United States.

The government should have $60 trillion today to meet the promises it has made. How much is $60 trillion?

It turns out that it is about $7 trillion more than the total wealth of all U.S. households combined.

Think about that for a minute. It means that even if the government owned all the private wealth in the United States, it still would not have enough to pass its own rules that apply to insurance companies!

Real Terms

What is inflation?

If you answered, "Rising prices," you are partially right. Although the word *inflation* has come to mean in popular usage rising consumer prices, rising prices are actually the *symptom* of inflation. They are not inflation itself.

What, then, is inflation?

Inflation is an increase in the supply of money.

Governments, and economists, often like to present economic issues as being more complex than they really are. Inflation is one of those economic issues that is often wrapped in mystery. In reality, inflation is really quite simple to understand.

At any given moment in time, there is a fixed amount of money, and a fixed amount of goods. If at that moment in time, you were able to record the price of every single good, you could then compute an average price level.

Now suppose that, magically, the quantity of money possessed by every single person doubled, and everyone knew it. Also assume that, magically, everybody immediately responds to the doubling of the money supply. Now when you compute the average price level, it will be twice as high as before.

The inflation was the increase in the money supply. The rise in prices, which we commonly call inflation, was the result.

If real-world inflation worked like this example, governments and central banks would not be interested in causing it.

But real-world inflation doesn't work this way. In the real world, some privileged people get the new money first. You and we are not allowed to create money out of thin air. That is called counterfeiting, and it is, quite appropriately, illegal. But the government, via the central bank, is allowed to create new money out of thin air.

When other people get new money first, they benefit at everyone else's expense.

Consider our example from a few paragraphs back. We're going to simplify it even further. Let us suppose that this economy is very simple. It contains 100 people, and 1,000 loaves of bread. Each person has $10, and each is willing to spend $10 to get 10 loaves of bread. This works out, and everyone has enough to buy his bread at $1 a loaf.

Now suppose that at a given moment in time, the supply of money doubles instantaneously. But this time, instead of everyone getting exactly double, 10 people in group A get all the additional money. They each get 100 dollars extra. Everyone else gets nothing. Also, this time there is no announcement that the people in group A got new money.

The people in group A will feel much richer. They will want to consume more bread, and they will have enough money to purchase more than the 10 loaves they could before.

But all the other people will still want their 10 loaves, and will still believe they can buy them. Some people get all the increase, and others get none.

The supply of bread is the same as before. But now there is more demand. What will happen?

The price of bread will rise.

Who benefits? The people in group A. They will end up with more bread than before.

Who is hurt? Everyone else, because they have the same amount of money as before, but the price of bread is now higher. So they will be able to buy less bread.

Now consider inflation in an economy in which people have borrowed money.

Consider a baker who generates his income by selling bread at $1 a loaf. He is able to make 10 loaves per period. Suppose he earns a profit of $.10 per loaf. Suppose also that he has borrowed money. He owes $100 on his mortgage. Not counting interest, he would have to sell 1,000 loaves of bread to pay back his mortgage.

How is Mr. Baker affected by inflation? Let's put him in group B, the group that does not get extra new money. The price of everything involved in his bread will go up. His costs will go up, and the price he gets for a loaf of bread will go up. For the sake of illustration, suppose the price of everything in the economy exactly doubles. Mr. Baker is in exactly the same position he was before, right?

Not so quick.

This table summarizes how things look to Mr. Baker before and after inflation.

	Before Inflation	After Inflation
Loaves sold	10	10
Cost per loaf	$.90	$1.80
Revenues per loaf	$1	$2
Profit per loaf	$.10	$.20
Inflation-adjusted profit per loaf	$.10	$.10

So it would appear that he is exactly where he was before. But we haven't considered his mortgage. The amount he has to pay back on his mortgage hasn't changed at all. Now instead of having to sell 1,000 loaves of bread to pay it, he has to sell only 500 loaves.

Mr. Baker, as a debtor, has benefited enormously from inflation.

Who is the biggest debtor in the world?

The United States government. The government has the means (the Federal Reserve), the motive (the giant, unfunded liability), and the opportunity (neither Congress nor almost anyone else is telling them not to) to inflate the money supply.

For these reasons, we believe we are almost certain to see continued monetary inflation, which will sooner or later show up in rising prices for most goods and assets. If you are a debtor, that might be good news.

But most charities are prohibited from being debtors. And that makes preserving a charity's assets in a time of high inflation even more challenging. Perhaps inflation indexing is a solution?

Inflation: A Brief History

When you studied history in school, the chances are that you spent a good deal of time going over material that is utterly irrelevant. Perhaps you were forced to memorize a list of ancient Egyptian rulers, or kings of England. You probably had to study lists of state capitals, or learn in what order states entered the Union.

It is also a good bet, unless you studied economic history, that you never learned any monetary history. You may never even have heard the term. So in the event that your recollection of the facts of inflation is a bit sketchy, we'll review some of the history of inflation very quickly.

Before the 1930s, with the exception of the sixteenth century and possibly the late Roman Empire, the world had never known persistent, ongoing, one-way inflation. Remember that the price inflation we see in goods, the kind that gets reported as the Consumer Price Index (CPI), is a symptom of an underlying cause. That underlying cause is an increase in the supply of money—monetary inflation.

Throughout most of recorded Western history, money has meant either gold, or silver, or both. The supply of each of these metals is relatively fixed over any short period of time. It is difficult or impossible to greatly increase it for a sustained period of time. Thus, for most of history, sustained inflation was simply not known, except when countries either printed paper money, or debased the coinage by adding base metals to the silver or gold, as the Romans did under many emperors.

The great exception is the inflation that accompanied the Spanish conquest of the New World. Giant new supplies of silver flooded into Europe, causing prices to rise about 300 percent in the course of a century. After Columbus discovered the New World in 1492, Spain rapidly followed up with voyages of conquest under the commands of Francisco Pizarro and Hernando Cortez. In lightning military actions, aided by internal strife among the Incas and Aztecs, respectively, as well as smallpox and other deadly Eurasian diseases, Pizarro and Cortez conquered what is now Central and South America within an astonishingly short period of time.

Columbus' driving hunger had been for gold in the New World. Columbus did not find gold. But his Spanish masters did find silver in the fabled silver mines of Peru. The center of this mining district, the city of Potosi (now in Bolivia, then part of what the Spanish called "Peru"), was founded in 1546. It soon became one of the largest cities in the world, and exported stupendous quantities of silver to Spain. Silver was also discovered at Guanajuato in Mexico.

Spanish treasure galleons brought silver (and some gold) literally by the boatload from the New World. But that gold and silver, having minimal uses other than as money, served mainly to increase the supply of money in Europe. Inflation is an increase in the money supply. And in the sixteenth century the increase was so great that it overwhelmed everything else that was going on and produced huge price inflation.

But even the terrible inflation of the sixteenth century was like a drop in the bucket compared to what has happened since the world abandoned the gold standard in the 1930s.

The huge influx of silver from the Spanish Main caused prices in western Europe to about quadruple (i.e., 300 percent increase) over about a century. That is compound annual growth of about 1.3 percent. Since the world abandoned the gold standard, annual price inflation has rarely been less than 1.3 percent!

In the United States, according to the official statistics, since Franklin Roosevelt abandoned the gold standard in 1933, prices have multiplied by about 16.5 times. That works out to an annual rate of about 3.7 percent per year.

In other words, in the periods prior to 1933 when money was usually gold or silver, the worst widespread, sustained inflation in recorded history averaged about 1.3 percent a year. Since 1933, when money is mostly unbacked paper, the average rate of price inflation has been nearly triple that previous record.

The above 3.7 percent likely understates the actual rate. Why? Because of inflation indexing.

Inflation Indexing

During World War I, Britain temporarily went off the gold standard. They printed large amounts of money, and inflation soared. High inflation is terribly damaging to a society. (It was hyperinflation in the 1920s in Germany that helped bring Hitler to power.) John Maynard Keynes observed that inflation engages "All the hidden forces of economic law on the side of destruction, and does it in a manner which not one man in a million is able to diagnose."[20]

While the average person may not be able to diagnose how inflation wreaks its havoc, hard-won experience has taught him the danger inflation poses to wealth.

During the period of high inflation of the 1970s, many people who had fixed income assets became painfully aware of the devastating effect of inflation on the value of those assets. The fate of the creditor is the mirror of the fate of the debtor.

---

[20] *The Economic Consequences of the Peace* (1919). Now in public domain and available online. The quotation appears in a paragraph worth reading. The full text of the paragraph and the one preceding it is:

> Lenin is said to have declared that the best way to destroy the Capitalist System was to debauch the currency. By a continuing process of inflation, governments can confiscate, secretly and unobserved, an important part of the wealth of their citizens. By this method they not only confiscate, but they confiscate – arbitrarily; and, while the process impoverishes many, it actually enriches some. The sight of this arbitrary rearrangement of riches strikes not only at security, but at confidence in the equity of the existing distribution of wealth. Those to whom the system brings windfalls, beyond their deserts and even beyond their expectations or desires, become "profiteers," who are the object of the hatred of the bourgeoisie, whom the inflationism has impoverished, not less than of the proletariat. As the inflation proceeds and the real value of the currency fluctuates wildly from month to month, all permanent relations between debtors and creditors, which form the ultimate foundation of capitalism, become so utterly disordered as to be almost meaningless; and the process of wealth-getting degenerates into a gamble and a lottery.
>
> Lenin was certainly right. There is no subtler, no surer means of overturning the existing basis of society than to debauch the currency. The process engages all the hidden forces of economic law on the side of destruction, and does it in a manner which not one man in a million is able to diagnose.

In 1975, under intense political pressure, Congress changed the law so that Social Security payments would be indexed to inflation. That is, each year's Social Security benefit would increase over the prior year's according to a measure of inflation. Similar indexing is applied to government pensions, and to some government borrowing. Furthermore, one of the government's biggest liabilities—Medicare—is essentially an open-ended promise to pay no matter how high prices go.

Indexing liabilities to inflation takes away the government's ability to inflate away its debts. It is as if Mr. Baker in our example had to increase his mortgage payment to match inflation. Poor Mr. Baker can only take the economic environment as he finds it. If there is inflation and he has a fixed mortgage, he can benefit. If the only mortgages available are linked to inflation (oddly, this is almost never done), then he'd have to take that if he wanted a mortgage.

But the government has much more flexibility. On the one hand, Congress wants to mollify (or perhaps we should say buy off) voters who receive Social Security payments. This they do by giving the so-called Cost of Living Adjustment (COLA) every year. But Congress also wants to be able to borrow, and spend, and then inflate its way out of the resulting deficit. But they don't want the voting public angry about rising prices.

When Congress (or staffers) look at indexation, they see a monkey wrench thrown into the works. As a result, almost as soon as the government agreed to index Social Security to inflation, it started fiddling with the calculations.

The government has strong reasons to want to inflate. Namely, monetary inflation provides a way for the government to pay its debts. At the same time, the government has a strong reason for the public not to perceive price inflation. But monetary inflation leads to price inflation.

So the government has done something clever, if dishonest: they have "improved" the way that inflation is measured.

Measuring inflation appears to be easy. If you were trying to measure inflation, one reasonable approach would be to select a basket of expenses—say bread, milk, gasoline, rent, taxes, insurance, and so forth. You would measure the cost of the basket at Time 1, measure *the same basket* again at Time 2, and the difference would be the amount of price inflation.

And, indeed, that is the commonsense way of doing it. In fact, it is arguably the only honest way of doing it. This commonsense method is pretty much the way the Consumer Price Index (CPI) was calculated since its creation in 1921 (World War I had put inflation on everyone's list of concerns), until the early 1990s.

As economist Walter John, per his web site Williams (publisher of the newsletter and web site Shadow Government Statistics) explains, Michael

Boskin (a Stanford economist, a former teacher of ours, and in the early 1990s the Chairman of President George H. W. Bush's Council of Economic Advisors) became the chairman of the Congressional Advisory Commission on the CPI. This was a group that Congress convened to look into ways to reduce the reported CPI, without actually changing what was happening to prices. A cynic would say the purpose of the commission was to figure out how to cook the CPI books.

The public did not take kindly to the idea of Congress fudging the inflation numbers, and Congress let the issue drop publicly. However, the idea did not go away. In 1997, for example, Alan Greenspan (who had with Boskin and others argued for a revision in the method of calculating CPI), addressed Congress on the issue. He argued, in his inimitable way, that the CPI needed to be revised because, he said, it was biased. That is, Greenspan claimed that the CPI overestimated the cost of living.

There is not necessarily a link between being clear and being right, but we want to give you a flavor for the clarity of Greenspan's argument. Then you can compare it with John Walter Williams' argument.

We're quoting Greenspan at some length because we don't want inadvertently to cut out a key point. He went on and on, so here's part of what Greenspan said to Congress:

> Although the concept of price is clear enough in theory, it is often extremely difficult to implement in practice. In order to construct a fully satisfactory measure of the price of a given item, one would first have to specify all the characteristics of that item that deliver value to consumers. Then one would have to reprice the identical bundle of characteristics month in and month out. In practice, both of these steps are difficult because we are often not precisely certain about what consumers value, and because the items that are available to consumers are constantly changing, often in subtle ways. As a result, virtually all of the components that make up the CPI are approximations, in some cases very rough approximations. But the essential fact remains that even combinations of very rough approximations can give us a far better judgment of the overall cost of living than would holding to a false precision of accuracy and thereby delimiting the range of goods and services evaluated. We would be far better served following the wise admonition of John Maynard Keynes that "it is better to be roughly right than precisely wrong."
>
> Estimates of the magnitude of the bias in our price measures are available from a number of sources. Most have been developed from detailed examinations of the microstatistical evidence. However, recent work by staff economists at the Federal Reserve Board has added strong corroborating

evidence of price mismeasurement using a macroeconomic approach that is essentially independent of the exercises performed by other researchers, including those on the Boskin Commission. In particular, employing the statistical system from which the Commerce Department estimates the national income and product accounts, this research finds that the measured growth of real output and productivity in the service sector are implausibly weak, given that the return to owners of businesses in that sector apparently has been well-maintained. Taken at face value, the published data indicate that the level of output per hour in a number of service-producing industries has been falling for more than two decades. In other words, the data imply that firms in these industries have been becoming less and less efficient for more than twenty years.

These circumstances simply are not credible. On the reasonable assumption that nominal output and hours worked and paid of the various industries are accurately measured, faulty price statistics are by far the most likely cause of the implausible productivity trends. The source of a very large segment of these prices is the CPI.[21]

Got that? Oh, you don't? Don't feel bad. Neither do we. But, here's John Williams (is it coincidence that Williams has to sell his services on the market, while Greenspan got paid by the government?) explaining both what the Greenspan argument is, and why it's wrong:

The Boskin/Greenspan argument was that when steak got too expensive, the consumer would substitute hamburger for the steak, and that the inflation measure should reflect the costs tied to buying hamburger versus steak, instead of steak versus steak. Of course, replacing hamburger for steak in the calculations would reduce the inflation rate, but it represented the rate of inflation in terms of maintaining a declining standard of living. Cost of living was being replaced by the cost of survival. The old system told you how much you had to increase your income in order to keep buying steak. The new system promised you hamburger, and then dog food, perhaps, after that.[22]

---

[21] www.federalreserve.gov/boarddocs/testimony/1997/19970304.htm. In addition to being opaque, Greenspan's claim that it is impossible to find the price of the same item month-in, month-out, is, to put it mildly, a load of horse manure. This might be true for some items, but it is also transparently false for many others. The problem is not a new one, and it is one that has been dealt with successfully by commodity exchanges around the world for well over 150 years.
[22] www.shadowstats.com/article/consumer_price_index.

Honest inflation indexing makes it harder for the government to profit from inflation. So the government, which gets to make the rules, has an incentive to fiddle with how the index is calculated. And fiddle they have. Williams calculates price inflation using the method that the government used pre-Boskin Commission.

In recent years, the official CPI numbers have been very low, in the 1 to 2 percent range. But you may have noticed that the things you buy seem to go up much more than that. Now you know why. The official CPI numbers are, as one wag put it, "Inflation after we take out everything that went up." Williams estimates that the reported official CPI would be about 6 to 7 percent per year higher if it were still calculated the old way.

The U.S. Government, as the world's largest debtor, has the world's largest motive to inflate. Is it really surprising that they're not going to let the arcane matter of an honest inflation index get in the way?

Foundations and Endowments Are Highly Exposed to Inflation

Inflation hurts creditors and helps debtors. So, everything else equal, if you expect inflation, you want to be a debtor. But this puts foundations and endowments in an awkward position, because foundations and endowments are generally prohibited from taking on debt. If you as a foundation manager fear inflation's effects on your foundation, you must emphasize this point in developing your investment policy (see Chapter 9).

Avoiding Fraud

At this point, you might be thinking that some fairly sophisticated techniques or knowledge would be necessary to avoid fraud. And you might be right. To understand why Madoff's returns were unlikely, you'd have to know something about split-strike strategies, which is very esoteric. Furthermore, you would have had to know something about normal and historical returns earned by other investors pursuing the split-strike strategy. And you would have needed the mathematical sophistication to understand how Madoff's returns did (or in the case did not) correlate with the returns from other managers' split-strike investment programs.

We're not going to tell you that avoiding fraud is as easy as flipping on the television money report. If it really were easy to avoid being taken for a ride, Madoff would not have numbered among his victims some of the biggest and most sophisticated players *in the world*, including:

- Royal Dutch/Shell Pension Fund. The second-largest company in the world, according to the 2010 Fortune Global 500 list.
- Swiss Reinsurance Co.
- Senator Frank Lautenberg.
- Henry Kaufman (formerly the chief economist of Salomon Brothers). Kaufman is a close friend of former Fed Chairman Paul Volcker. When Volcker was Fed Chairman, Kaufman was known on Wall Street as "Dr. Doom" and was so influential that his comments could and did move the markets for U.S. Treasury bonds.
- HSBC—Britain's largest bank and the third-largest bank in the world.
- BNP Paribas—the largest bank in the Eurozone (most of Europe, minus the UK).
- AXA—the largest insurance company in France and the ninth-largest company in the world, according to the 2010 Fortune Global 500 list.

Similarly, Enron counted among its shareholders some of the most sophisticated investors in the world, including many of the top mutual fund companies such as Fidelity and Janus, and sophisticated institutional investors such as the University of California.

Detecting the Stanford fraud in advance would have been similarly challenging. Bre-X raised eyebrows, but for too many investors greed overcame fear. Of the five we've looked at, only BFA had a public warning before the end.

So, should you hunker down and keep all your money, or all your foundation's money, under the mattress?

No.

Remember, these frauds are like airplane crashes: They are devastating when they happen, but they are, thankfully, quite rare. Of the tens of thousands of publicly traded stocks, only a handful are fraudulent. Of the tens of thousands of investment advisors, only a few are crooks. So while it's terrible if it happens to you, it might not be the biggest risk. Nevertheless, avoiding fraud is serious business. If you need to know more, you might turn to an expert for advice, or read further on the topic. One good source is Ken Fisher's *How to Smell a Rat*.[23]

Remember, having your money stolen is not the only, or even the biggest, risk for most investors. Even in the field of mutual funds, which, thanks to their careful separation of manager from custodian, clear disclosure, and limited mandates, are largely free of fraud, you can still lose your shirt. For example, the Vanguard Group is one of the biggest and most highly regarded mutual fund companies in the world.[24] Yet you can lose a lot of money with them, without anyone breaking any laws.

If you had invested your money in the Vanguard U.S. Growth Fund 10 years ago, you would have been investing in a large, proven fund that invested in large, proven American companies. The fund has been around since 1959, making it one of the oldest mutual funds in the world. It invests primarily in large-cap U.S. stocks, widely considered to be one of the safest, most conservative types of equity investment. But if you had made that investment 10 years ago, by now you would still have lost about two-thirds of your money. Ouch.

---

[23] Ken Fisher, *How to Smell a Rat* (John Wiley & Sons, 2010).
[24] Disclosure: As of this writing, both authors have funds invested with Vanguard.

CHAPTER 13

Other Planned Giving Vehicles

"Planned giving" is most often a fund-raiser's euphemism for gifts made after death. There are four major planned giving vehicles in addition to the ones we discussed in Chapters 1 and 4. These are charitable gift annuities, bargain sales, a life estate remainder, and charitable pooled income funds. All are designed to give the donor some benefit, or the appearance of some benefit, making it easier for charities to raise money. But it is incumbent on donors and their advisers to understand what these vehicles really offer in a given situation.

When the amount of money or property to be donated is relatively small and does not require the donor's or adviser's serious attention, one of these approaches may make sense. With larger amounts (and depending on the donor's goals and other factors) the donor's goals can be better achieved using one of the vehicles discussed in Chapter 1.

Charitable Gift Annuity

A charitable gift annuity is really two transactions. It is a gift of money or property to a charity and a promise by the charity to pay the donor (or donor's spouse) a certain fixed amount of money each year for the life or lives of the donors. The amount of the annuity payment will depend on the donation amount, the age of the donors, and the current market environment. The income tax deduction will depend on the donation amount, the donor's age, and the relevant IRS tables. Essentially, the tax deduction is for the expected present value of the remainder interest that will go to the charity. That is, the tax deduction is for the amount the charity expects to net after making all the required annuity payments and investing the cash available.

The Pitch

The basic pitch is that an annuity lets the donor have income, get tax deductions, and help the charity. The Salvation Army, one of the biggest sellers of charitable gift annuities, offers a fairly typical pitch. "Would you like to make a substantial gift to the Salvation Army but feel you cannot afford to do so … ? A [Salvation Army] Gift Annuity may be just the solution." The Salvation Army does provide considerable detail, although perhaps not enough to allow a donor to make a full analysis of the alternatives available elsewhere.

The Catch

The "catch" is a big one: In order for the charity to get a meaningful amount of money to invest, it must offer an annuity rate that's considerably lower than what you would get from a commercial annuity. Most charities offer annuity rates based on the recommendations of the Indianapolis-based nonprofit American Council on Gift Annuities, which meets periodically to set suggested rates. The Council sets the rates so that charities will, on average, net 50 percent of the amount of annuities they issue. This is considerably higher than the profit margin that a commercial company would earn on a comparable annuity. On the other hand, the donor does get an income tax deduction.

If the Council's recommendations seem to you like price fixing, you're too late. In 1995, a donor filed a suit alleging antitrust violations. But the courts didn't get the last word. Congress deemed the Council's approach to be not only acceptable, but also in the public's interest. The legislators were concerned that unrestrained competition between charities to offer the highest rates would weaken the charities' ability to carry out their public interest work.

Gift Annuities versus Regular Annuities

Since a charitable gift annuity in effect combines a gift and an annuity, it makes sense to evaluate the annuity against the alternative of making a gift and, separately, purchasing an annuity. Perhaps the major advantage of a charitable gift annuity is that it provides an immediate tax deduction for the donor, yet the donor doesn't suffer the cash-flow cost of the gift until he dies.

As of this writing, for example, a 75-year-old man could purchase a regular annuity from a commercial company and receive a guaranteed lifetime annual payment equal to 10.2 percent of the amount he put in. In contrast, the Council's recommended rate is 7.4 percent.

One interesting feature of the Council rates is that they don't change very often, compared with daily changes in commercial interest rates and frequent changes in commercially available annuity rates. This means, for example, that as interest rates fall, the Council rates become relatively more attractive. Conversely, when interest rates rise, the Council rates become less attractive.

Credit Risk

An important difference between a charitable gift annuity and a commercial annuity is the credit risk of the issuer. A donor buying a charitable gift annuity is, of course, buying an annuity issued by the charity. The promise to make the annuity payments is a general obligation of the charity. Depending on the charity's credit risk, the donor is taking on a small, or a big, risk. Considering that a 65-year-old has a life expectancy of about 20 years, and a 75-year-old about eleven years, this credit risk may be a vitally important consideration.

Commercial companies, of course, carry risks, too, but there is a critical difference: They are in the business of assessing these types of actuarial risks, and they are regulated by state insurance commissioners. Insurers issuing commercial annuities are also likely to be rated by one or more credit-rating agencies such as Standard & Poor's or A.M. Best. These ratings allow a purchaser to make an informed decision as to how much risk he is taking. It is very hard to get a comparable assessment for a charity.

Rarely, charities issuing charitable gift annuities go bankrupt. This occurred in 2009, when the National Heritage Foundation filed for bankruptcy. Eighteen of its 20 largest creditors were charitable gift annuity donors.

Partial Exclusion of Annuity Payments from Income Tax

One of the advantages of an annuity is that part of the annual cash flow is considered a nontaxable return of capital. In other words, a certain percentage of each annuity payment will be tax free to the purchaser. This is true for both commercial and charitable gift annuities.

The percentage of each payment that is tax free is called the exclusion ratio. It depends on two factors: the present value of the annuity, and the expected return to the purchaser. The expected return is the sum of the payments that the purchaser is expected to receive on an actuarial basis. For example, suppose a buyer purchased an annuity with a present value of $100,000 and was expected to receive $15,000 a year for 10 years, for a total of $150,000. The exclusion ratio would be 66.67 percent; that is, two-thirds of each annuity payment received would be excluded from taxable income. Note that once the purchaser has gotten back all that he put into the annuity, the payments become 100 percent taxable.

Treatment of Appreciated Property

As we discussed, a charitable gift annuity consists of a single transaction that is part charitable contribution and part purchase of an annuity. Another way to look at this, when appreciated property is used for the donation, is that the purchaser is selling property to the charity for less than its fair market value. In tax-speak, it is a "bargain sale," which we discuss further below. As we'll see, such a transaction will create some element of taxable income to the donor. How much depends on a number of factors.

Bargain Sale

The concept of a bargain sale to charity starts out simply enough. A donor who owns a piece of property sells it to charity at a price that is less than fair market value. However, this is where the simple part ends. The tax consequences of a bargain sale (as we've seen in one example above) can be byzantine, unexpected, and unwelcome. This is particularly true when debt-financed property such as mortgaged real estate is involved.

One answer to this complexity is to avoid bargain sales entirely. This is not necessarily a bad solution. However, bargain sale rules can show up in unexpected places, so donors and their advisers should know enough about this particular minefield that they'll have a fair chance of spotting such transactions.

The rules can be so pernicious that we feel it is worth going into some depth here.

"Allocation of Basis" Rules

To understand this rule, it helps to begin with an example of how bargain sale rules worked in the old days, before the 1969 tax reforms. Suppose a donor had property worth $100,000, in which he had a basis of $50,000. The donor, desiring to get his money back and also make a charitable contribution, sold the property for $50,000. It was the best of both worlds: He got only his money back, so he had no taxable gain, but he gave away $50,000 worth of value to charity, so he also got another $50,000 of tax deduction.

The current rules are complicated. We'll try to describe them as simply as we can, without distortion. Some readers may prefer to skip the English in the next paragraph and look at the mathematical formula instead, which says the same thing but in the concise, unambiguous language of symbols.

Under current law, the donor must now allocate his basis to himself and the charity in the same proportion as the fair market value of the property is split between donor and charity. The rule for apportioning the basis is spelled out in the tax law. Unfortunately, it is quite obtuse. This is the technical language from IRC Section 1011(b): When a bargain sale occurs, "the adjusted basis for determining the gain from such sale shall be that portion of the adjusted basis which bears the same ratio to the adjusted basis as the amount realized bears to the fair market value of the property."

We must resort to a little algebra to put this into a useful form. We'll assign symbols as follows:

B = the total amount of *basis*
D = the amount of basis that the *d*onor gets to use (this is what we're trying to determine)
R = the amount the donor is deemed to have *r*eceived
F = the *fair* market value of the property

Using these symbols, we can translate the code section as follows:

$$D/B = R/F$$

Solving this little equation for D gives us:

$$D = \frac{B}{F} \times R$$

In words, the amount of basis the donor may use is equal to the same fraction of the proceeds received (or deemed received) as the total basis is of the fair market value. Now let's do an example.

Suppose the donor gave to charity 50 percent of the fair market value of his $100,000 property, and kept 50 percent himself. The total basis, B, is $50,000. The fair market value, F, is $100,000, and the proceeds, P, are $50,000. We'd like to solve for D, the amount of basis the donor is allowed to use. D = \$50,000 × (\$50,000/\$100,000), or \$25,000. So, the donor would allocate \$25,000 of basis to himself. Now, when he sells the property for \$50,000, he realizes a taxable gain of \$25,000 (i.e., his proceeds of \$50,000, less his allowable basis of \$25,000). He still gets a deduction of \$50,000, but now he also has income of \$25,000. Overall, this is not as good a result for the donor as he would have had without the bargain sale rules.

As complicated as this is, it gets more complicated. As we'll see, the application of the rules for debt-financed property may be enough to make you tear your hair out. It certainly should make you think twice before making a contribution of debt-financed property to charity.

Caution: Contributions of Debt-Encumbered Property

Prospective donors run into the bargain sale rules most often when they contemplate a gift of debt-financed property (usually real estate) to a public charity. While these gifts are permitted (similar gifts to a private foundation would not be), they can create big tax problems.

The rules force the donor to calculate his contribution as though he had received the amount of the debt in cash. These rules apply whether the debt is recourse or nonrecourse to the donor (that is, whether or not the donor is personally liable for the debt) and regardless of whether the recipient assumes the debt.

Here's an example—based on an IRS Revenue Ruling—of how bargain sale rules can ensnare an unwary donor. Suppose a donor owns property with a fair market value of \$100,000, with a \$40,000 mortgage. Also assume that the donor had held the property for at least a year, and therefore it qualified as long-term capital gain property.

Absent the bargain sale rules (or if a donor were ignorant of them), the donor would expect to get a charitable deduction for \$60,000, or his total equity. However, even though the donor hasn't sold the property, the existence of debt means that the bargain sale rules apply, with the equity apportioned between the donor and the charity.

Thus, instead of a straight gift of \$60,000, we have the following:

- The donor is deemed to have received \$40,000 (the amount of the debt), giving us R for our formula.
- The total basis in the property, B, is \$60,000.
- The fair market value of the property, F, is \$100,000.

We need to calculate D, the amount of basis the donor may use, so that we can calculate his taxable gain on this gift. According to the formula,

D equals the fraction B/F, which is 60 percent, times the amount deemed received, $40,000. Sixty percent of $40,000 is $24,000. The donor is deemed to have received $40,000 in proceeds. He is permitted to apply $24,000 against the proceeds, leaving him with a deemed net gain of $16,000 on his gift of property.

In this example, the donor may still wish to make a gift, because his deduction, while less than it would be without the bargain sale rules, is larger than the deemed gain. However, it is not always that way.

The Same Problem, Only Worse: A Disastrous Example

If a donor decides to donate leveraged investment real estate that he has held for a while, the consequences may be even worse. Let us suppose that a donor owns real estate with a fair market value of $1 million, and a mortgage of $800,000. The donor has depreciated the property for a number of years, and has basis of only $50,000. What happens if the donor gives this property to charity? Many problems.

The donor will get a charitable deduction equal to his equity, or $200,000. However, he will also be deemed to have received proceeds equal to the mortgage, or $800,000. Against this gain, he will be able to apply only a fraction of his basis. Applying the formula, we find that the donor will be able to apply $40,000 of basis, leaving him with a net taxable gain of $760,000, and a charitable deduction of $200,000. The donor is almost certainly better off not giving the property to charity.

This section has just touched on the complexity of the bargain sale rules. There are many more aspects of this rule. (Please see the Real Estate section of Chapter 17.) Suffice it to say that donors, even donors who are not contemplating an actual sale, must consider the bargain sale rules and their tax impact.

Charitable Gift Annuity versus CRT

A charitable gift annuity has many similarities to a charitable remainder trust (discussed in Chapter 4), but there are important differences. Both allow a donor to make a gift, get a tax deduction, and receive an income stream. However, a charitable gift annuity makes the donor a general creditor of the charity. With a CRT, the donor becomes a creditor of a funded trust (that is, the charitable trust that is funded by the donation). Which is riskier will depend on specific circumstances. For example, the $10,000 a year annuity stream from a CRT that is initially funded with $1 million and conservatively invested will probably be more secure than the same annuity from a financially weak small charity.

Funding a charitable gift annuity with appreciated stock creates a bargain sale (with accompanying adverse tax consequences). In contrast, appreciated stock contributed to a CRT is not subject to such rules. However, annuity payments from a CRT do not enjoy the exclusion privilege that charitable gift annuity payments do. The combination of benefits that is better for the donor depends on the specific situation.

Any time a charitable gift annuity is being considered, the actual economics of the transaction should be compared with the alternative purchase of a commercial annuity combined with a gift to a charity, which could include a private foundation. And do the math, too, comparing a charitable gift annuity with a CRT.

Remainder Gifts with Retained Life Estate

As a rule, charitable contribution deductions are not available for gifts of partial interests (i.e., for gifts of less than complete ownership of an asset). However, there are exceptions, including some we've already examined, such as split-interest trusts (CLTs and CRTs) and charitable gift annuities. Another exception is remainder interests in a personal residence or a farm.

This kind of gift occurs when a donor makes an irrevocable gift to a charity of the title to a residence or farm, but keeps the right to use the property for a specified term. Generally, the term will be the life of the donor, or the joint life of the donor and spouse. The term can also be a certain number of years. At the end of the term, the charity gains full rights to the property. (Such gifts are sometimes called life estate agreements, since they typically use the life of the donor as the specified term.)

Life estate agreements may be appropriate for donors who want to obtain a current income tax deduction and continue to live in their house (or on their farm), but are willing to give the entire property to charity at their death.

Tax Deduction Is Based on the Present Value of the Remainder Interest

As with other gifts of remainder interests, the deduction for this kind of gift is based on the calculated present value of the remainder interest in the property. The calculation can be a bit complicated because of issues such as depreciation. But this is the basic equation: the fair market value of the property, discounted by the term of the life estate—using the Applicable Federal Rate as specified in the Internal Revenue Code, Section 7520. If there is debt on the property, the calculation is based on equity. (Note that, if there is debt, the bargain sale rules will apply.)

For contributions of such remainder interests to a private foundation, the deduction would be based on the lower of the donor's cost basis in the property or fair market value.

Potential Effect on Property Tax

A transfer of a remainder interest in real property may trigger a revaluation for property tax purposes, and/or may incur a transfer tax. If it does, this increase in property taxes should be factored in as a cost of making the transaction. As property taxes are local issues and rules vary by jurisdiction, donors considering a life estate gift should check with local experts or the local taxing authority.

Caveats

Life estate agreement gifts are complicated transactions with potentially complicated consequences. Donors and their advisers should think these through carefully. We emphasize two caveats in particular.

The first has to do with irrevocable gifts of an interest in a home. If a residence or farm constitutes a significant percentage of a donor's wealth, he should be very careful about entering into a life estate agreement. Such agreements are irrevocable, even if the donor's circumstances change. A life-threatening illness, for example, would not affect the agreement. When a donor enters into the agreement, he seriously limits his ability to use the property for his own financial purposes. Although such agreements can sometimes be terminated early (e.g., by buying back from the charity the remainder interest), the donor cannot get back the value that has been gifted away.

The second caveat concerns potential bargain sale problems. Donors contemplating remainder gifts of debt-financed property must be very careful. As we have commented, the bargain sale rules apply, and they may give rise to deal-killing problems. In one case, for example, a donor asked the IRS for guidance in a private letter ruling. While such rulings cannot be relied on as precedent, they do offer insight into the IRS's thinking. In this case, the donor planned to transfer the remainder interest in a farm to charity and retain a life estate. The property had a fair market value of $110,000 and an $80,000 mortgage. As expected, the IRS ruled that the present value of the remainder interest would be calculated based on the taxpayer's equity of $30,000.

However, the IRS also ruled that the donor would realize the whole $80,000 value of the mortgage for purposes of determining realized gain under the bargain sale rules. Even though the donor would remain liable for the $80,000, the IRS was treating it as though they were relieved of the debt. Obviously, this is a terrible outcome for the donor, because the donor's tax liability from the bargain sale could exceed the value of the deduction. And the donor would still be on the hook for the mortgage.

We now turn to two planned giving techniques. Although they cannot be used with private foundations, we discuss them briefly because advisers and donors may come across them and wish to consider their use as part of an overall plan.

Pooled Income Funds

As charities have worked to raise money through planned gifts, they have developed another tool that appeals to some donors wanting an income stream for life and an up-front tax deduction who are willing to leave the remainder to charity. This is the pooled income fund.

A pooled income fund is similar to a charitable remainder trust in that a donor contributes assets, the assets are invested, the donor gets an income stream for life, and the remainder goes to charity. Unlike a charitable remainder trust, however, in a pooled income fund the donor's assets are pooled with the assets of other donors. The charity keeps track of a donor's account. When the donor dies, the charity gets the amount remaining in the account. Essentially, a pooled income fund may be thought of as a charitable remainder mutual fund, run by a charity. In fact, the largest mutual fund company in the world, Fidelity Investments, has introduced a pooled income fund of its own.

A pooled income fund has units and unit values like a mutual fund, and distributes income to its income beneficiaries in much the same way a mutual fund does. When the investments do well, the value of the units rises, and when the investments do poorly, the unit value falls. Similarly, income can rise or fall depending on investment performance. The definition of income—in particular whether or not it includes realized capital gains—depends on the terms of the trust that establishes the pooled income fund.

Tax Benefits

Contributions to pooled income funds qualify as charitable income, gift, and estate tax deductions. The deductions are calculated as the present value of the remainder interest. Contributions of appreciated property qualify as deductible at fair market value, and the donor is not required to recognize any capital gain on appreciated property given to a pooled income fund.

Private Foundation Restrictions

Even though pooled income funds are not private foundations, and private foundations may not create pooled income funds, pooled income funds are subject to many of the same restrictions that apply to private foundations. These restrictions include the prohibitions on self-dealing, excess business holdings, jeopardizing investments, and prohibition on taxable expenditures.

Self-dealing applies to disqualified persons. Anyone who contributes $5,000 or more to a pooled income fund is a disqualified person with respect to that fund. Note that the prohibition on self-dealing must be carefully evaluated with many gifts of property other than cash or marketable securities.

Investment Options Limited

Because the donor's money is invested in exactly the same way as every other donor's money in the pool, the donor has little flexibility. At most, the donor may be able to choose from among a small number of different pools. This lack of investment flexibility is probably the biggest drawback of a pooled income fund as compared with a charitable remainder trust.

When to Use a Pooled Income Fund

Pooled income funds might make sense for donors with relatively small amounts to donate and who are prepared to live with the constraints. But few fully informed donors opt for a pooled income fund if the amount involved is sufficient to justify creation of a charitable remainder trust.

CHAPTER 14

Donor-Advised Funds

Until 2006, donor-advised funds were a de facto type of charitable entity, with considerable uncertainty surrounding the laws that should, or would, apply to them.

The situation was clarified, to some extent, by Public Law No. 109–208, which for the first time defined the term *donor-advised fund*. Congress, in its inimitable way, has helpfully defined the term for us, thus:[1]

> Under new section 4966(d)(2), a donor advised fund is defined as a fund or account owned and controlled by a sponsoring organization, which is separately identified by reference to contributions of a donor or donors, and with respect to which the donor, or any person appointed or designated by such donor ("donor advisor"), has, or reasonably expects to have, advisory privileges with respect to the distribution or investment of the funds.
>
> A sponsoring organization is defined under new section 4966(d)(1) as a section 170(c) organization that is not a governmental organization (referenced in section 170(c)(1) and (2)(A)) or a private foundation and maintains one or more donor advised funds.
>
> Pursuant to new section 4966(d)(2)(B), the term donor advised fund does not include a fund or account: (1) that makes distributions only to a single identified organization or governmental entity or (2) with respect to which a donor advises a sponsoring organization regarding grants for travel, study or similar purposes if:
>
> (a) the donor's, or the donor advisor's, advisory privileges are performed in his capacity as a member of a committee whose members are appointed by the sponsoring organization,

---

[1] www.irs.gov/irb/2006–51_IRB/ar11.html#d0e847.

(b) no combination of donors or donor advisors (or related persons) directly or indirectly control the committee, and

(c) all grants are awarded on an objective and nondiscriminatory basis pursuant to a procedure approved in advance by the sponsoring organization's board of directors.

Thus, a sponsoring organization that owns and controls a fund that meets these criteria may award a scholarship from the fund to a natural person without subjecting the sponsoring organization or its managers to excise taxes under new section 4966.

History

Donor-advised funds have been around, in one form or another, almost since the beginning of the permanent income tax was permitted. The permanent income tax was first given impetus by the Socialist Labor Party in 1887, and gathered critical momentum when the Democrats made the income tax a key platform plank in 1908. It was adopted in 1913.

The first vehicles that resembled donor-advised funds probably arose in the 1930s. Many community foundations and similar organizations have operated donor-advised funds since then. In the 1990s, commercial money management firms, led by Fidelity, and quickly joined by a host of other large names, established donor-advised funds to which they could provide for-profit management.

According to the *Wall Street Journal*, by 2009, the three largest donor-advised funds were Fidelity Charitable Gift Fund at $3.6 billion, Vanguard Charitable Endowment Program at $1.6 billion, and the Schwab Charitable Fund at $1.7 billion.[2]

In response to a number of questions and areas of uncertainty, Congress codified donor-advised funds in 2006, and the IRS issued guidelines in 2008.

Guidelines—Highlights

Under the new law and guidelines, donor-advised funds continue to be a sort of hybrid between public charities and private foundations.

Contributions and Deductions

In general, contributions to donor-advised funds are treated the same as would be contributions to any public charity. Thus, the 50 percent and

---

[2]http://online.wsj.com/article/SB124036165997141685.html.

30 percent deduction limitations apply. That is, a donor to a donor-advised fund may deduct contributions up to 50 percent of his adjusted gross income for contributions made in cash, and up to 30 percent for contributions of appreciated property. The corresponding limits for private foundations are 30 percent and 20 percent. It is possible to combine the two, so that, for example, a donor could contribute 20 percent of his adjusted gross income (AGI) to his private foundation in appreciated stock, another 10 percent of his AGI to his foundation in cash, and another 20 percent of his AGI in cash to a donor-advised fund, and it would all be deductible.

Self-Dealing, Annual Payout

Under the 2006 law, certain of the private foundation rules do not apply to donor-advised funds. These include the self-dealing rules under IRC Section 4941, and the 5 percent annual payout requirement under IRC Section 4942.

Excess Business Holdings

However, certain private foundation limitations do apply, which do not apply to ordinary public charities. Prominent among these are the limitations on excess business holdings outlined in IRC Section 4943.

Disqualified Persons

Although prohibited transactions rules do not apply per se to donor-advised funds, the concept of disqualified persons does. The IRS summary of who is a disqualified person reads:

1. "Disqualified persons" include the following with respect to a donor-advised fund:
   - A donor or any person appointed or designated by a donor (donor advisor) who has, or reasonably expects to have, advisory privileges with respect to the distribution or investment of amounts held in a donor-advised fund by reason of the donor's status as a donor. IRC §4958(f)(7)(A) (cross-referencing IRC §4966(d)(2)(A)(iii));
   - A member of the family of an individual described above. IRC §4958(f)(7)(B);
   - A 35 percent controlled entity. IRC §4958(f)(7)(C) (cross-referencing IRC §4958(f)(3)).

2. "Disqualified persons" include the following with respect to a sponsoring organization:
   - An "investment advisor," which is any person (other than an employee of the sponsoring organization) compensated by the sponsoring organization for managing the investment of, or providing investment advice with respect to, assets maintained in donor-advised funds. IRC §4958(f)(8)(B);
   - A member of the family of an individual described above. IRC §4958(f)(8)(A)(ii);
   - A 35 percent controlled entity. IRC §§4958(f) and 4958(f)(8)(A)(iii).

Payments to Disqualified Persons

Provided certain criteria are met, private foundations may pay certain reasonable amounts to disqualified persons. There is no such ability with donor-advised funds. A donor-advised fund is prohibited from making any kind of payment to or on behalf of a disqualified person that will result in a "more than incidental benefit" to the disqualified person. Such payments can result in an excise tax equal to 125 percent of any incidental benefit received, which tax is imposed on the donor, donor adviser, or related person under section 4967. There is also an excise tax equal to 10 percent of the incidental benefit imposed on the fund manager who agreed to the distribution, which is capped at $10,000. Section 4958 also imposes an excise tax for any "excess benefit transactions" engaged in by a donor-advised fund, which may include any grant, loan, or compensation that is paid to any donor, donor adviser, or related person. This excise tax is equal to 25 percent of the excess benefit, with an additional excise tax equal to 200 percent of the excess benefit if the transaction is not corrected on a timely basis. There is also an excise tax equal to 10 percent of the excess benefit that is imposed on any fund manager who knowingly participates in the transaction.

This is unlike a private foundation, which may directly pay, in cash, a donor, board member, or other disqualified person reasonable amounts for services actually performed.

This rule makes it infeasible for a donor to receive payments of any kind from a donor-advised fund.

Limitations on Grants

The permissible grants from a donor-advised fund account are more limited than those permitted to a regular public charity. Grants to individuals are prohibited, as are payments for any noncharitable purpose. In addition, several of the rules that pertain to private foundation grants apply also to grants from donor-advised funds. Foremost among these limitations is the requirement to exercise expenditure responsibility on grants to private operating foundations, Type II supporting organizations, Type I and Type III supporting organizations if the donor or a disqualified person controls the organization, and grants to non-501(c)(3) organizations. Note that any grant to a private foundation, even with expenditure responsibility, must be made only to private foundations of which the donor-advised fund advisor and his related disqualified persons are not also a disqualified person.

If a donor-advised fund makes a distribution to a charity that is not recognized under section 170 of the Internal Revenue Code or if the fund does not exercise expenditure responsibility over distributions, an excise tax equal to 20 percent of any taxable distribution is imposed on the sponsoring organization, and an additional excise tax equal to 5 percent of any taxable distribution is imposed on the fund manager who knowingly makes a taxable distribution. There is a $10,000 cap on the total tax that may be imposed on the fund manager.

Fees and Costs

Commercial Donor-Advised Funds

Most donor-advised funds charge the donor's account at least one level of fees or costs. For example, Fidelity charges 0.6 percent of assets on the first $500,000 of assets held in a donor-advised account.

Most commercial donor-advised funds charge further fees that may be hidden in the investment funds they provide for the donor to select among. For example, Fidelity makes available an All-Cap Equity investment fund, which incurred expenses (according to Fidelity's published information) as of September 2009 at the rate of 1.09 percent a year. So, a donor account at Fidelity with $500,000 invested in this equity account would incur expenses of 1.69 percent per year.

Nonprofit Donor-Advised Funds

Although there is quite a bit of talk of a distinction between commercial donor-advised funds and nonprofit donor-advised funds, we believe the distinction is arbitrary and misleading.

You might ordinarily think that you would get a better deal with a not-for-profit donor-advised fund. However, this may well not be the case. First of all, some commercial firms that run donor-advised funds, particularly Vanguard, are actually not commercial firms in the normal sense of the word. Vanguard is not a publicly traded company, and is not privately owned either. Vanguard is actually a mutual company, technically owned by the mutual funds themselves. Mutual companies are rarer than they used to be, but some of the big financial services companies still use the word in their names. Examples are Northwestern Mutual Life, and Mutual of Omaha.

Fees for Vanguard's Charitable Endowment Program drop sharply for accounts over $1 million, and Vanguard's funds, which are available for investment, are usually much cheaper (in terms of fees) than competing company funds.

Community Foundation donor-advised fund fees are often *much* higher than fees for commercial donor-advised funds. For example, the California Community Foundation, one of the nation's largest, offers a donor-advised fund, on which the fee for the first $1 million is 1.25 percent, and for the next $4 million is .75 percent.

Compare this to Vanguard, which charges .6 percent and .14 percent for the same levels. The second tranche of California Community Foundation's fees is *more than five times as high* as Vanguard's!

Another concern that some donors voice about nonprofit donor-advised funds, such as those run by community foundations, is the increased probability that the community foundation will exercise its legal right to do what *they* want, rather than what the donor adviser wants, with the funds. As a donor, you know that the Fidelities and the Vanguards of the world are in business to manage money, and the donor-advised fund is just another way for them to do it. You also know that community foundations are in business to fund whatever charitable causes their boards may decide from time to time.

Probably those twin concerns of cost and security are the driving factors behind the commercial donor-advised funds far outdistancing their nonprofit rivals in asset gathering.

CHAPTER 15

Building Assets with Charitable Planning

In the pantheon of professional advisers, financial planners and other investment professionals have a special understanding of and focus on the preservation and accumulation of capital. Precisely because private foundations are a powerful asset-growth tool, investment professionals need to be familiar with the uses and benefits of private foundations. This chapter focuses on how advisers can use foundations to help their clients build charitable wealth.

From our experiences with a variety of investment professionals, we have identified seven ways in which private foundations can help you enhance a client's assets. While some of the points we make here have been discussed in earlier chapters, we think it is valuable for investment advisers to see them presented in one place.

1. An immediate increase in total client assets (i.e., personal and foundation).
2. Significantly increased total client assets in the long run.
3. Excellent opportunities to diversify highly appreciated stock positions, without incurring capital gains taxes.
4. An opportunity to increase total portfolio after-tax returns by holding taxable-income-producing assets in a tax-exempt foundation.
5. An opportunity to cement lifetime relationships with client and heirs.
6. The opportunity to keep retirement plan assets intact for charity upon death of the client (without planning, these may be taxed at 80 percent).
7. The opportunity to create goodwill in the community.

Immediate Increase in Total Client (Personal and Foundation) Assets

When a client contributes to a private foundation, he receives an immediate income tax deduction. This income tax deduction, by cutting the amount the client must pay in taxes, immediately increases the value of assets under his control (see the following chart).

A client may deduct up to 30 percent of adjusted gross income each year. For a client who takes advantage of the maximum allowed deduction, the savings are significant. The following example shows the effect of the immediate income tax benefits on total assets. It assumes a client with income of $1 million who gives $300,000 to his foundation. The client immediately saves $135,000 in taxes (at a 45 percent rate).

Immediate Income Tax Savings

	Without Foundation	With Foundation
Gross income	$1,000,000	$1,000,000
Contribution to foundation	$0	$300,000
Taxable income	$1,000,000	$700,000
Income taxes	$450,000	$315,000
Net available to manage	$550,000	$300,000 (foundation) + $385,000 (personal) = $685,000 (a 25% increase)

Increased Total Client Assets in the Long Run

Over the long run, the increase in total assets is even more dramatic. For example, assume that a client has beginning assets of $12.5 million, which earn 10 percent a year. The client plans in any event to leave a bequest to charity, and with your assistance decides to create a foundation and begin funding it annually with 30 percent of his annual income. The client is giving to charity exactly what he would give anyway, but now he's taking advantage of the tax breaks available. The results are dramatic. Total assets available increase by over $26 million over 27 years. The table below summarizes the benefits.

Additional Assets Over 27 Years

	Without Foundation	With Foundation	Additional Assets
Total assets	$44.5 million	$71.1 million	$26.6 million

Diversifying Highly Appreciated Stock without Capital Gains Taxes

It is common for taxable accounts to accrue large capital gains, which present a significant tax burden when the positions are sold. Managers of taxable assets are faced with a difficult decision: Either hold positions they'd rather sell in order to avoid the taxes, or sell positions and create large capital gains taxes for the client.

If the client has a foundation, the manager can ease or eliminate this problem by encouraging the client to use appreciated stock, especially stock that the manager is planning to sell, to fund his foundation.

Using appreciated stock saves the client taxes *twice*. First, the client gets an income tax deduction. Second, he avoids capital gains taxes when the foundation sells the stock. The combined savings can be as much as 75 percent of the total value of the assets for clients in a 50 percent tax bracket who have zero basis stock.

Because a private foundation is a tax-exempt entity, it creates other opportunities as well.

Holding Taxable-Income-Producing Assets in Tax-Exempt Foundation

Managers of taxable accounts of high-net-worth individual investors usually like to minimize the taxable income the accounts produce because the expense of taxes creates such a drag on returns. This affects the money manager and the client in several ways, all negative. Avoiding taxes means that, other things equal, a dividend-paying stock is less attractive; it means that tax-free municipal bonds are usually preferable to taxable bonds even though munis yield less; and it means that sales of winners, as noted above, are costly and that investment decisions must be made with taxes, not just investment considerations, in mind.

When a client has a foundation, the foundation account can be run without worrying about these issues. Taxes constitute no barrier to investing in higher-yielding stocks. Bonds held, of course, can be fully taxable with the accompanying pickup in yield over municipal bonds. And buy and sell decisions can be made 100 percent by investment considerations.

Taken together, these additional degrees of freedom in a foundation could help produce at least 2 percent (200 basis points) in additional annual after-tax return on a long-term basis. Assets grow faster, resulting again in a happier client and more money to use for good purposes.

Cement Client Relationships

Few sophisticated investors today believe that any one adviser, or even any one firm, is an expert in all the areas they need. On the other hand, most of those same investors appreciate advisers who are widely informed and who have relationships with the variety of experts needed.

The ability to talk intelligently with clients about philanthropy and private foundations is still relatively rare among advisers and, as a consequence, is highly valued by philanthropic clients. The adviser who can be helpful to a client in the area of a foundation, and also handle the client's other investment-related needs, does the client a major favor by making his life simpler.

Perhaps equally important for the long-term continuity of the family investment enterprise, the private foundation may help the adviser develop a meaningful relationship with the client's heirs. Depending on the client's age, this might have significant long-run value for both client and adviser.

Keep Retirement Plan Assets Intact for Charity upon Death of the Client

Qualified plan assets (e.g., IRAs, Keogh Plans, 401(k)s, etc.) are subject to punishing levels of taxation when they pass through a taxable estate. It is not unusual for taxes (income taxes and estate taxes) to take 75 percent to 80 percent of the plan's assets. This is a particularly troublesome situation for estates with large qualified plans. For example, a $5 million qualified plan, left to a client's heirs through the client's estate, may result in only $1.25 million getting to the kids. This situation is bad for the children (incidentally, also bad for the asset manager) and is a hindrance to good estate and succession planning.

For a client who is interested in supporting charity, the solution is to leave the qualified plan to charity. If the client is interested, he may be able to effectively replace the money from the retirement plan with life insurance purchased outside the estate (see below). In fact, a private foundation created during life and funded annually may free up the cash with which to pay for the life insurance.

The following example illustrates how the approach, using life insurance, might be used. Assume the client has a $5 million qualified plan, annual income not counting extra qualified plan distributions of $250,000, and that the client gives $50,000 a year to charity. To implement the plan, the client creates a life insurance trust and funds it with an appropriate amount of life insurance. The client then withdraws an additional $100,000 from the qualified plan each year, bringing his income up to $350,000 annually. The client also contributes $100,000 to his private foundation, thus making the withdrawal from the qualified plan effectively tax free. The client now makes his charitable contributions from his foundation and allows the remainder to grow, income-tax-free, inside the foundation. The plan frees up $50,000 of cash at no tax cost, which can go to pay for life insurance. At death, the qualified plan goes to the private foundation, completely tax free, and the children get the life insurance death benefit, also completely tax free.

Opportunity to Create Goodwill in the Community

Charitable giving is universally admired and respected. By helping clients create and fund private foundations, investment professionals become facilitators of a great deal of charitable giving, and through the provisions of their expertise become indirect benefactors of causes that matter. This association with clients' charitable giving helps create goodwill in the community, which reflects well upon the investment professional who is conversant enough with private foundations and other philanthropic vehicles to make charitable dollars go further than they otherwise could.

Professionally Managed, Turnkey Private Foundations

It is highly desirable from a business perspective to provide the benefits of a private foundation in a way that creates a positive, hassle-free experience for the client. To ensure this, professional management is a must. The role of a full-service, turnkey foundation manager is to provide the client with a smoothly functioning, highly effective, and fully compliant foundation that requires very little administrative effort or attention from the client. Turnkey management provides the client with all the benefits and joys of a private foundation, without the hassles and worries of running it.

From the client's point of view, with the appropriate manager in place, the process of creating and running the foundation appears as follows.

Creating the Foundation

Clients need to make only three decisions to create their foundation:

1. Who they want the directors to be.
2. How much they want to contribute initially.
3. What they want the name of the foundation to be.

For the first decision, the board of directors will usually include the founder, often the founder's spouse, one or more of the founder's children, and occasionally others. There is no legal upper limit on the number of directors allowed, but there may be practical reasons for limiting the number of directors. For example, Don H. Twietmeyer, a Partner in the Rochester, New York, office of the law firm Hiscock & Barclay, points out that it may be difficult to obtain a quorum of directors for the transaction of any business coming before the foundation. "Generally, the quorum requirement is set forth in the by-laws, and for one foundation that I was on that had a large board of over 40 directors, we reduced the quorum requirement in the by-laws from one-half to one-third since we were having difficulty getting a quorum at meetings, especially during the winter months when a number of directors were vacationing in Southern climates."

The second decision is how much to contribute to the foundation initially. A good manager will be able to help clients and advisers navigate the complex tax issues involved in determining how much to contribute to the foundation, what type of assets to use, and when to make the contributions.

Third, the majority of founders name the foundation after themselves, their family, or particular members of their family. Since the foundation is a legal entity, the desired name must be available; that is, not already in use.

Operating the Foundation Each Year

With an investment professional managing the assets and with a full-service manager managing the foundation, the client is empowered to pursue the original objective: effective philanthropy. With professionals covering all the operational ground, the foundation is extremely simple for the client, who nevertheless maintains plenty of control and flexibility.

If the client wants counsel in determining the most effective opportunities for charitable giving, a good manager can provide expert help to discover, evaluate, and/or create attractive giving alternatives that meet the objectives of the clients or directors for giving money away.

The only other task for the client (assuming the client is an executive officer of the foundation) is the signing of compliance documents (such as tax returns). Such documents should be prepared by the manager.

Foundation Manager's Role

Behind the scenes, without the involvement of the client, the manager should handle all compliance and administrative issues that occur regularly, and others as they may arise. The following list gives a partial idea of what may be involved:

• Create the foundation and apply for exempt status.
• Determine the most tax-advantaged strategy for funding the foundation.

- Work with the client's financial advisers to make sure that the cash available in the foundation is always sufficient to meet the needs of the foundation.
- Communicate with the client's financial advisers to ensure that everyone understands any special or unusual requirements of the client.
- Prepare annual meetings, draft annual reports, and fulfill all corporate requirements.
- Maintain all required foundation records, including grant documentation.
- Provide the founders with proper donation acknowledgements from their foundation.
- Ascertain and document proper charitable status of foundation recipients.
- Provide all required bookkeeping and accounting.
- Calculate each year's minimum qualifying distribution.
- Ensure preparation and filing of annual federal and state tax returns.
- Ensure compliance with restrictions against self-dealing and excess business holdings.
- Confirm observance of fiduciary duty against jeopardizing investments.
- Monitor changes to IRS provisions regulating private foundations.
- Prepare required letters to grant recipients with required language as specified by Internal Revenue Code.
- Ensure foundation maintains compliance with IRS requirements.

In addition, a manager should provide the effectiveness tools discussed in Chapter 7.

Full-Service Management Makes a Private Foundation Feasible for Many Donors

Although the benefits of a private foundation are compelling, and the activity of a private foundation is conceptually simple, the compliance and accounting aspects can be formidable. Furthermore, the penalties for failing to comply with all the relevant requirements can be severe. Potential donors daunted by these obligations may postpone or forgo creating a private foundation. By offering comprehensive private foundation management to clients, professional advisers make it easy for wealthy individuals and families to gain all the benefits of their own foundation and to delegate, rather than be deterred by, the burdens and efforts of managing it.

Conclusion

Thanks to the tremendous creation of wealth in our economy, the market for experienced help in setting up and running private foundations has grown rapidly and will continue to expand as affluent families become more sophisticated about tax planning and wealth management. Private foundation management is an underutilized service—even by financial planners accustomed to bringing in other specialists such as accountants, tax attorneys, and family business experts—and its providers are fragmented. This makes it difficult at times for clients to find the right advisers. These are favorable circumstances for investment professionals and other advisers to add a valuable service for existing clients and to attract additional business.

As an alternative to becoming well versed in all the principles and practicalities of foundation management—a highly technical practice in itself—investment professionals can forge relationships with professional, turnkey managers and provide their clients with complete private foundation management along with everything else they are delivering. By giving this kind of comprehensive service to the foundations of new and existing clients, investment professionals can take better care of their client base, increase their clients' total assets under management, and contribute to the community, all without having to develop the necessary expertise and without requiring clients to manage their foundations themselves.

CHAPTER 16

How to Select a Foundation Manager

Donors who have decided to create their own private foundation have many decisions to make, but the first is very simple: Do you want to do it yourself? If not, how much help do you want?

You can do it yourself through a combination of personal effort and the use of required professionals such as attorneys and accountants. Or you can retain a full-service foundation management firm, which will provide turnkey foundation services but not invest assets. Or you can use a bank trust company, which will provide administration and investment services.

Until recently, some version of do-it-yourself was the most popular choice. Full-service management was hard to find, and for most people a bank trust company was not desirable because they didn't want the trust company managing the foundation's assets. But do-it-yourself places a heavy burden on the founder and directors. Unless you are willing to spend significant amounts of time educating yourself and your directors and then working on the foundation's business, the setup and running of such a complex venture is likely to be inefficient at best (see Chapters 7 through 10). At worst, you will end up violating the rules (see Chapter 11). Foundation founders who have the time and are fluent with all the topics covered in this book are well positioned to do it themselves. Others are better off with one of the alternatives.

Choosing a Full-Service Manager

Full-service foundation management, which until recently was available only to the ultrarich (with foundations of at least $100 million in assets), offers a focus different from that of bank trust company management. Full-service companies tend to specialize only in the administration and philanthropic effectiveness areas and do almost nothing directly on the investment front except, perhaps, to advise on investment policy. Bank trust companies, on the other hand, almost always approach the issue from the point of view of investment management. If a bank trust company offers any administrative or philanthropic assistance, it is typically an add-on. Rarely does a bank trust company have philanthropic effectiveness as a primary focus. Donors who want a full-service foundation solution but don't want to tie their investment management to a bank trust department need to go with a full-service foundation manager. That leaves them free to either hire a money manager or run the investment portfolio themselves.

Note that there are a large number of firms, many of which are really sole practitioners, offering partial services to foundations, such as accounting, administration, or grant assistance. These may be of use to the do-it-yourselfer, but will likely disappoint donors who want full service. In selecting a professional manager, there are a number of factors to consider, discussed in the remainder of this chapter.

- Time required to create a foundation.
- Range of services.
- Administrative systems.
- Experience.
- Philanthropic expertise.
- Reputation.
- Educational resources and attitudes.

Time Required to Create a New Foundation

Many donors wait until late in the year of inception to set up their foundation. Since foundation contributions must be paid by December 31 to be deductible in that tax year, speed in creating a foundation can be important. Inexperienced professionals can take up to three months to complete the process. Experienced specialist firms can sometimes accomplish it in as little as a day or two.

Range of Services

The first thing to look at in evaluating a manager is the range of services offered. Does the company create the foundation, or is the client left to fend for himself in getting the foundation created? Naturally, if "full service" includes creating the foundation, that means a smoother experience for the founder, avoiding a potentially troublesome transition at the beginning of the foundation's life.

So-called full-service management might be limited to just administrative functions. True full-service administration is comprehensive, encompassing all filing, paperwork, accounting, bookkeeping, legal work, tax return preparation, grant due diligence, and compliance activities. Leaving any of these services out of the mix means the founder or board will have to handle that work themselves.

Philanthropic effectiveness is the area of services most frequently given short shrift. Just as over the lifetime of a mortgage the cumulative interest payments exceed the principal, over the course of the foundation's lifetime, it will spend far more than the total capital value at any given time. How these monies are spent is therefore of great importance. When evaluating a potential manager's approach to managing philanthropic activities, it might be helpful to use the discussion in Chapters 6 through 10 as a guide.

Administrative Systems

The purpose of systems is to make sure that things don't fall through the cracks. Because there are a number of administrative and compliance details that must be accomplished, some of which have strict deadlines, it is very important that a foundation manager have effective systems. This goes far beyond mere accounting systems. As a review of Chapter 11 will quickly reveal, such systems must also cover areas such as due diligence on grants, proposed transactions and contemplated transactions between the foundation and disqualified persons, and the monitoring of investments.

Experience

Experience is, of course, a highly desirable prerequisite for a foundation manager. But it can be instructive to examine what kind of experience a foundation manager has. In particular, be aware that experience mostly or exclusively in the nonprofit world is not necessarily a good thing. In philanthropy, as in other industries, there is a buy side and a sell side. The charities are the sellers, trying to raise money. The donors—including private foundations—are the buy side. Donors are trying to make sure they accomplish as much good as possible. As with many businesses, there's much of value to be learned from both perspectives. The ideal private foundation manager will bring experience and understanding from both sides. A manager who knows the complexities of both giving and getting will help a donor more than one whose experience is limited to one or the other.

Philanthropic Expertise

As we discussed in Chapter 7, there is a wide range of philanthropic expertise. The more familiar a management firm is with these areas, the more effective the foundation will be. As you evaluate potential managers' expertise, keep in mind that you are not necessarily looking for deep experience in any particular area. It is unlikely that any manager will be the leading expert in the area in which you are interested. Rather, you are looking for a manager who has an approach that can work in a variety of areas so you ultimately get the high-level domain-specific expertise you require.

Reputation

Reputation is as important here as in any field. However, it's important to make sure that the reputation is earned for relevant work. An investment manager or bank with a terrific name, even if the organization also manages foundations, probably didn't earn that reputation for its foundation work. Find a manager whose reputation is based on the kind of work your foundation wants to do.

Attitude toward Education

Effective philanthropy requires an approach that is always open to new ideas, new information, and new ways of doing things. Look for a private foundation manager whose mission includes educating donors who want to learn. It is our view that an informed philanthropist is a more effective philanthropist.

Conclusion

A successful connection with a foundation manager will become a long-term relationship, in which directors, managers, and members of the founding family understand their goals and share their values. The right management can mean the difference between a mediocre foundation experience and a truly satisfying and meaningful philanthropic journey. It is worth the time to find a manager who will focus on the things you think are important, and who has the capability to help your foundation be as effective as it can be.

CHAPTER 17

What Can You Donate to Charity?

At some point, many high-end donors will think about contributing something other than cash to charity. This chapter examines some of the noncash assets donors may consider. We've tried to highlight the main issues, including tax implications, special private foundation considerations, and operational questions.

We will look at six categories of noncash assets: publicly traded securities, nonpublicly traded business interests, tangible personal property, intangible personal property, qualified retirement plans, and real estate.

Publicly Traded Securities

As a rule, publicly traded securities that have been held for at least one year can be contributed to a private foundation or public charity, giving the donor a deduction for the fair market value. If the property has appreciated, the donor does not realize the gain. Generally, appreciated publicly traded securities are an excellent asset to contribute to a private foundation or a public charity.

Conversely, if the property has lost value, the donor does not realize a loss. Therefore, it makes sense to give appreciated property, but not depreciated property. In virtually every case involving depreciated property, the donor would achieve better results by first selling the property and using the cash proceeds to make the gift.

The deduction the donor may take in a given year is limited to 20 percent of the donor's contribution base (in most cases, his adjusted gross income) for gifts to private foundations and 30 percent of his contribution base for gifts to public charities.

If the donor has not held the stock for at least a year, the deduction will be limited to the lower of two figures: the fair market value of the stock or the donor's basis. In this case, the property is treated like cash for the purposes of determining which deduction limitations apply. So a donor contributing short-term-gain property will be limited to a deduction of 30 percent of contribution base for gifts to a private foundation and 50 percent of contribution base for gifts to a public charity. The donor does not recognize a gain or loss on the disposition.

Types of Securities

Common and preferred stock that are traded on an exchange, open-end mutual funds, closed-end investment funds that are traded on an exchange, U.S. government bonds, and some exchange-traded corporate bonds are considered publicly traded securities for purposes of the charitable contribution rules. Given the right economics, all these are appropriate securities for charitable gifts.

Other publicly traded securities may not be appropriate for donations. This list includes certain zero-coupon bonds as well as Section 1256 contracts such as commodity futures and options to which the mark-to-market rules apply. The mark-to-market rules state that, for securities to which they apply, the owner must treat the securities, for income tax purposes, as though they were sold at the end of each tax year. The contribution of such property to charity will be deemed to be a sale, so a donor cannot avoid recognition of appreciation in such property. Therefore, such property is rarely, if ever, appropriate for a charitable contribution. (Note that this doesn't mean these aren't good investments for a foundation.)

Valuation

A donor of publicly traded stock is generally not required to obtain an independent appraisal of value. Instead, the donor may use the average of the high and low prices quoted on the exchange on the day of the gift. For mutual funds, the price is the closing net asset value on the date of the gift. If no such quote exists, it may be an indication to look more closely into the question of whether the property qualifies as a publicly traded security.

Date of the Gift

For a donor to receive a tax deduction in a given year, a gift must be completed in that year. For publicly traded securities, that means the security must be delivered into the recipient's account by year end.

Donors should not wait until the last minute. For operational reasons, many brokerage firms and other custodians take what may seem like an inordinate amount of time to transfer securities, even within the same firm. When a delivery to another firm is involved, even more time can be required. For year-end security donations, we generally recommend allowing a minimum of two weeks, and preferably a month, for the custodian to actually get the securities delivered.

Nonpublicly Traded Business Interests

Nonpublicly traded business interests generally include limited partnerships, closely held C corporations and S corporations, and limited liability companies. There are a number of considerations involved, and a donor should seek specialized counsel. That said, here are some of the general considerations.

Deduction Rules

For the most part, if an interest in a privately held business is donated to a public charity, it can be deducted at its fair market value, provided the interest has been held for at least one year. If the contribution is to a private foundation, it will be deductible only at the lesser of basis or fair market value. Keep in mind that privately held businesses, depending on their capital structure and the specific nature of the donor's interest, may be considered debt-financed property and subject to bargain-sale rules. (See Chapter 13.)

Valuation

Any deduction for nonpublicly traded business interests valued at more than $5,000 must be substantiated by a qualified appraiser. Such valuation issues are a study unto themselves, and a detailed discussion of the issues would easily fill a book. Suffice it to say that anyone considering a gift of nonpublicly traded business interests to charity should consider the valuation question early on. The valuation itself can be a time-consuming and expensive process.

Private Foundation Considerations

Contributions of nonpublicly traded business interests to a private foundation will not be deductible at fair market value. Furthermore, any gift of such an interest must be reviewed carefully in light of rules against prohibited transactions, self-dealing, and excess business holdings. These rules do not mean that such gifts are never allowed. Sometimes they are. And it is not uncommon to have such nonpublicly traded business interests held by the private foundation of a disqualified person.

Gifts of nonpublicly traded business interests are perhaps the most complex and hardest to analyze of any charitable gifts. They should be considered only when the size of the gift justifies a considerable expenditure on professional analysis of tax and other issues. In those cases, if the analysis shows it to be feasible, such gifts can be highly beneficial for recipient and donor alike.

Tangible Personal Property

Donors can also make gifts of items such as cars, jewelry, art, collectibles, gemstones, books, maps, and rugs. This category excludes real estate but includes items that may not immediately seem "personal": livestock, agricultural products, lumber (but not uncut marketable timber, called stumpage), harvested crops, and certain items of business inventory. In general, such property may be donated to charity with a tax deduction. However, there are a number of special cases (dealt with later in this section).

The general rule is that a donor may contribute tangible personal property and take a deduction for the fair market value at the time of the gift or for the donor's basis in the property, whichever is lower. For example, if a donor paid $100,000 for a ring, and it is now worth $150,000, if he gives it to charity he can deduct only $100,000. If it has fallen in value to $50,000, he could deduct only $50,000.

Related Use

The tax rules are different if the property is of a type normally used by the charity in its tax-exempt function. Then, if the donor has held the property for investment purposes for at least one year, the donation may qualify for a fair market value deduction. One example: an art investor who donates a painting to an art museum with the reasonable expectation that the museum will display the painting in the normal course of its business.

Deduction Limitations

For gifts of nonrelated-use property to public charities, the donor's deduction is limited to 50 percent of his contribution base. For such gifts to a private foundation, the limit is 30 percent. For gifts of related-use property that qualify for consideration as appreciated capital-gain property, the limits are 30 percent for gifts to a public charity and 20 percent for gifts to a private foundation.

Issues for Specific Assets

• **Art.** We often receive inquiries about artwork and how it should be treated as a gift. For art to be deductible at its appreciated fair market value, it must meet two tests. It must be held by a donor for investment purposes for at least one year. And it must be donated to a charity that expects to use it in a manner related to its charitable purpose. So, for example, a gift of art that the charity is expected to sell immediately will not qualify. Furthermore, an artist himself cannot get a fair market value deduction because he is deemed to be a dealer, and dealers are by definition not investors. An artist who donates his own art may deduct it only to the extent of his basis in the art. His time in creating it is not included in this basis. Finally, an artist who donates an original physical work but retains the copyright receives no deduction because this is a gift of a partial interest (that is, a gift of less than the donor's full rights in the property), and as a general rule, gifts of partial interests do not qualify for any deduction.

• **Timber.** Similarly, the treatment of timber depends on a number of factors. If the donor owns land with standing trees for investment, has held that property for at least one year, and contributes it to charity, the donation is not considered tangible personal property, and the gift is deductible at fair market value. If the same owner cuts the trees, the resulting cut timber will be deemed tangible personal property. Whether the gift is deductible at basis or at fair market value depends now on whether the recipient is expected to put the timber to a related use. If so, the donor may still deduct it at fair market value. However, if the recipient is expected to sell the timber (or put it to some other nonrelated use), the donation deduction is limited to the donor's basis.

• **Agricultural crops.** As with timber, the tax treatment of crops depends on several factors: whether the crops are sold with the land or are first harvested; whether the donor holds the cropland for investment purposes; how long the donor holds the land (but not the crops, which typically have a growing season of less than one year); and sometimes, whether the recipient puts the donated crops to a related use. To get a fair market value deduction, a donor must contribute land held for more than a year (with or without crops growing on it). If these conditions prevail and there are crops growing, the value of the land and crops is deductible at fair market value. If the crops are cut, they become tangible personal property and are then deductible at fair market value only if given to a charity that uses them for a related purpose. That might be the case, for example, if the crops were donated to supply meals for homeless people.

• **Livestock.** Certain types of livestock can qualify for long-term gain treatment, if they are held for breeding, dairy, or sporting purposes. Such livestock can be donated to charity for a fair market value deduction, even if the charity does not have a related use for the property. This area is quite complex, down to rules on which kind of animals are considered livestock; mink may be, turkeys and chickens are not. So donors and advisers should tread carefully in making any decision.

Valuation

Tangible personal property may be difficult to value. All gifts of such property worth more than $5,000 must be substantiated with a qualified appraisal. For some kinds of property—art is one example—it is advisable to use an appraiser who specializes in that kind of property.

Gifts to Private Foundations

In general, gifts of tangible personal property to a private foundation are permitted and are deductible at the lower of basis or fair market value, subject to the 30 percent limit. However, make sure that no such property will produce unrelated business income in the hands of the foundation. The better course for such assets may be first to sell them, then to contribute the proceeds. On the other hand, it may make sense to contribute appreciated tangible personal property to a foundation, because the unrealized gain may be realized in the tax-exempt foundation, avoiding income tax on the gain.

Intangible Personal Property

Intangible personal property is just what it says—and a bit more. The list includes copyrights, trademarks, patents, and other forms of intellectual property; as well as business assets such as databases, customer lists, formulas, royalties, or brand names; and contracts such as life insurance contracts, annuity contracts, and personal service contracts. Obviously, intangibles can be extremely valuable. It is difficult to generalize about the deductibility of intangibles, so we will review some of the more common types.

Copyrights

Donation to a public charity of a copyright that has been held for at least one year will qualify as long-term capital gain property, deductible at fair market value by the donor. As with art, this rule does not apply if the donor is the creator of the copyright. It also does not apply if the donor's normal business includes the buying and selling of copyrights. A copyright donated to a private foundation will be deductible at basis.

Patents

Generally, donations of a patent to a public charity will qualify for a deduction at fair market value regardless of the holding period. This exception regarding the holding period arises because IRS code section 1235 allows for this exception regarding the holding period. For patents that have been depreciated, the donor may face recapture of depreciation; that is, he will have to take as income some depreciation. This will reduce the donor's deduction by the amount of the recapture.

Unlike the case with copyrights, the creator of a patent is entitled to a fair market value deduction for a contribution to a public charity.

Royalties

Royalties for such things as copyrights, patents, and brand names are considered ordinary income assets, and as such are not deductible as capital-gain assets at fair market value, but instead at the donor's basis.

A gift of royalties without a gift of the property (such as a copyright) that produces them will be considered an assignment of income. When income is assigned, it is still taxable to the donor, even if it is received by a charity. For example, if a writer assigns the royalties from a book, but does not assign the copyright, the tax treatment for the donor is the same as if he was collecting the royalties and then giving them to charity. The donor should receive an income tax deduction for the amount donated. However, this deduction would be subject to the limitations applicable (30 percent of gross income for a private foundation, 50 percent for a public charity). Note that the donor in most cases will gain no tax benefit and may be worse off after making such a gift.

Oil royalties have different rules, relating to "working interests" and to "operating interests." A working interest is an interest in oil and gas in place (i.e., not exploration) that bears the cost of development and operation of the property. Operating interests are generally considered to be real property interests, and as such can be long-term capital gain property if held for one year. Royalties from such interests will also generally be considered long-term gain property, unless the donor uses the property in a trade or business. Donations of long-term gain property to a public charity are deductible at fair market value. Note that there are a number of variations in mineral interests, and any possible donation should be carefully examined.

Personal Service Contracts

Generally, a gift of a personal service contract will be considered an anticipatory assignment of income. The result is that the donor will be deemed to have received the income paid on the contract *as it is paid,* even though the donor does not get the cash. The donor should get a charitable deduction for the amounts as they are paid but, as previously noted, these deductions will be subject to the normal limits. For example, assume a donor has $1 million of income a year from a contract and assigns that contract to a public charity. The donor will be treated as if he has received income of $1 million and then made a gift of $1 million. The 50 percent deduction limit will apply, and the donor will only be able to deduct $500,000 that year, with the other $500,000 carried forward.

Installment Notes

When someone sells property on an installment basis, an installment note is created. Contributing such a note to charity is considered a taxable sale, and the donor will be deemed to have received all the remaining unrealized gain in the note. The donor will receive a tax deduction for the fair market value of the note.

Life Insurance and Annuity Contracts

A donor may contribute a cash-value life insurance contract to charity. The donor is entitled to a deduction equal to the lesser of his basis in the contract and the contract's fair market value, which will usually approximate its cash value. The calculation of fair market value depends on several factors, and for large donations a qualified appraisal may be required.

Note that if a contract has any outstanding loan against it, it may be considered debt-financed property, and donation of debt-financed property will subject the transaction to the bargain-sale rules.

The gift of an annuity contract issued after April 22, 1987, will be considered a sale and will result in the owner being deemed to receive ordinary income equal to the fair market value of the annuity, less his basis in it. The gift would be deductible at fair market value. Thus, it will rarely be beneficial for a donor to make a gift of an annuity contract. For contracts issued before April 22, 1987, the donor may be limited to a deduction only for his basis, which is an even worse outcome.

Employee Stock Options

Frequently, donors who hold large positions of employee stock options wish to donate these to charity. Unfortunately, this is not possible in most instances because of contractual prohibitions. Even when it is possible, it will generally have no tax advantage because the donor will be deemed to receive income for the value of the option.

Qualified Retirement Plans

Qualified retirement plans, such as IRAs, 401(k)s, and Keogh plans are powerful wealth accumulation tools due to their tax-deferred status. So it is not uncommon for donors to have large qualified plans and to seek to give all or part of such plans to charity. Under the current law, it rarely makes sense for a donor to give a plan to charity during his life. Conversely, upon death such assets are often excellent choices. Let's look at these in more depth.

Congress has been changing the rules regarding contributions from IRAs to charity on a very frequent basis. As of this moment, it is generally possible for donors over age $70\frac{1}{2}$ to contribute up to $100,000 from their IRA without adverse tax consequences. If this might appeal to you, ask your tax adviser about your specific situation.

Lifetime Contributions

During a donor's lifetime, to contribute plan assets to charity a donor generally must first receive the money from the plan as income. For example, if a donor wants to give $50,000 from his IRA, he must first take the $50,000 out of the IRA, and it will be considered taxable income. The donation will be a charitable contribution and deductible subject to the limitations. Currently, contributions directly from an IRA to charity are only allowed under limited circumstances pursuant to section 408(d)(8) of the Internal Revenue Code. While that provision expired on December 31, 2009, section 725 of the 2010 Act passed in December 2010, extended the provision to December 31, 2011, so contributions directly from an IRA to a charity are allowed in the limited circumstances previously allowed. The taxpayer must have attained the age of $70\frac{1}{2}$ years, the amount is limited to $100,000 per taxpayer per year, the amount counts toward the required minimum distribution (which was usually the hook for making the contribution, especially if the distribution was not needed), and a charitable contribution deduction can't be claimed. There was also a special rule that the taxpayer could elect that distributions directly from an IRA to charity in January 2011 would be treated has having been made in 2010.

There are a few situations in which it might make sense to take distributions from a qualified plan to contribute them to charity. We'll consider distributions of employer stock (as from an ESOP), a lump-sum distribution that qualifies for 10-year forward averaging, and distributions taken as part of a "wealth replacement" plan involving life insurance.

Lump-sum distributions of employer stock from a company retirement plan may qualify for long-term capital gain treatment in the hands of the employee. Unlike most distributions from retirement plans, this distribution isn't automatically deemed income and taxed. The employee receiving the stock does not have to hold it for a year to qualify for long-term capital gains. So the stock, when received, can be contributed to charity for a fair-market value deduction.

A somewhat similar situation may arise when a retirement plan beneficiary receives a lump-sum distribution that qualifies for 10-year forward averaging. This is special tax treatment that results in plan distributions being taxed at between 15 percent and 22 percent. A donor could take these distributions, pay tax at the lower rates, and then donate the proceeds to charity. The charitable deduction would be usable by the donor against his highest marginal tax rate, which is around 45 percent for top-bracket donors in high-tax states.

The third situation involves life insurance planning designed to eliminate the estate tax on a large qualified plan. The donor purchases life insurance in a life insurance trust outside his estate. The death benefit on the life insurance is designed to equal the amount in the qualified plan. Because qualified plan assets can be left to charity upon death without income tax or estate tax (see the following section), the donor plans to leave the qualified plan to a private foundation. To help pay the life insurance premium, the donor withdraws an amount each year from the retirement plan, gives part of it to the foundation, and uses part to pay the premium. At death, the qualified plan goes to the private foundation, completely tax free, and the heirs get the life insurance death benefit, also completely tax free.

Testamentary Gifts of Qualified Plans

While lifetime gifts of qualified plans seldom make sense, testamentary gifts (gifts made upon death) often do. One of the major benefits of qualified plans is that they offer tax deferral. However, the death of an owner of such a plan often triggers income tax on the amount of income that has been deferred. If the amounts involved are large, this income tax will be at high marginal rates, and combined state and federal rates may approach 50 percent in some states.

In addition to income taxes, the plan value may be subject to estate tax, which is also on the order of 50 percent. Fortunately, these two taxes are not quite additive, or the plans would be completely wiped out. However, the combined effect of income taxes and estate taxes can still devastate the value of such plans. The combined tax bite can be upwards of 75 percent of the predeath value of the plan.

When a donor gives a qualified plan to charity, both the income tax and the estate tax are avoided. This allows 100 percent of the plan value to go to charity. If the donor contributes the plan to a private foundation, his heirs can continue to control 100 percent of the plan value. Often the best way to make sure that a charity, such as the foundation, receives the assets without tax is to name the charity as the beneficiary of the plan.

If less than the whole plan is to be contributed to charity, care must be taken to address issues of minimum distributions required from the plan, as well as to provide for the payment of the taxes that may result.

Real Estate

Gifts of real estate to charity are filled with opportunity and fraught with complexity. The complexity arises from the bewildering array of ownership structures, the variety of tax rules, and the bedeviling bargain-sale rules, which apply, perforce, to gifts of debt-financed real estate. Nevertheless, we summarize some of the key issues and highlight the key opportunities and pitfalls.

Basic Rules

Contributions of real estate to public charities are deductible up to 50 percent of contribution base for contributions valued at basis, and up to 30 percent if contributions are of appreciated long-term gain property held for at least one year. If the contribution is to a private foundation, the deduction will be limited to the donor's basis and will be deductible up to 30 percent of contribution basis. These are the basic rules. However, there are a number of potential complications.

Ordinary Income Traps

As noted, contributions of appreciated property to public charities normally qualify for deduction at fair market value. But there are several important exceptions. They include donor's dealer status, a donor's short-term holding period (i.e., less than one year), or a depreciation recapture situation. If one of these applies, the deduction will be for the lesser of basis or fair market value.

A donor will have dealer status if his business is buying and selling real estate. For example, if a home builder who donates a house to charity is in the business of buying lots, building homes, and selling them, it is likely that he will be considered a dealer. Dealer status can have important tax consequences for reasons other than deductions, so it is likely that a donor will be aware of this issue if it applies to him. A donor will have a short holding period if he has not held the property in question for at least one year. Depreciation recapture is a potentially hidden trap. Because the rules for depreciating real estate have always been complicated and have changed over the years, any given real estate holding may or may not be subject to depreciation recapture upon disposition. If it is, the deduction will be reduced by the amount of the recapture.

Debt-Financed Property

We have already discussed the potential pitfalls involved in contributing debt-financed property to charity. At best, it triggers the bargain-sale rules. Note that the debt-financed property rules will complicate or scuttle most contemplated contributions of partnership interests in real estate.

Partnerships

Often donors own real estate limited partnership interests that they consider contributing to charity. Proceed carefully. Partnerships often have debt financing on their property. Because partnerships are pass-through entities for tax purposes, the limited partner in such a case is considered to own a debt-financed interest in the property. This means that a contribution will trigger the bargain-sale rules. In addition, limited partners may have very complicated basis situations that include some amount of potential basis recapture.

Partial Interests

In general, the donation of partial interests to charity are not deductible. However, there are several exceptions, two of which apply to real estate: contributions for qualified conservation easements and so-called life estate gifts.

A qualified conservation easement consists of a perpetual easement on property for purposes of conservation. Such an easement must be granted on suitable property to an appropriate agency; for example, a governmental unit or a qualified land trust. A typical easement may prohibit a parcel of land from ever being developed, while still allowing a donor to continue living in an existing house and sell the property in the future. However, the easement will continue to go with the property, and a future purchaser must abide by its terms.

Life estate agreements are also permitted contributions, as discussed above. While such agreements may permit a deduction for a gift of a future interest, we would counsel great caution for donors who are considering making a gift of a future interest in their principal residence. Such gifts are irrevocable and may significantly limit the flexibility of the donor to deal with unforeseen developments. Life estate gifts are discussed more fully in Chapter 13.

Conclusion

In this chapter we have touched on the more common types of property that donors consider giving to charity. For the most part, only gifts of cash and publicly traded stock can be considered "simple." Donors considering any other type of gift, if the amount is significant, would be well advised to consult with an expert before committing to such a gift.

CHAPTER 18

When the Shoe No Longer Fits

What to Do If You Get Tired of Your Private Foundation, Donor-Advised Fund, Charitable Remainder Trust, or Charitable Gift Annuity

Typically, donors create new private foundations, donor-advised funds, and charitable remainder trusts in an atmosphere of excitement, or at the very least optimism. And usually that optimism is justified, if not forever, then for a good many years.

But as people are living longer, they sometimes experience changes in their circumstance, the circumstances of their family, or developments in the world at large that cause them to re-evaluate their ongoing charitable involvements.

In this chapter, we examine common circumstances that often cause donors to re-evaluate their giving strategy, and sometimes make dramatic adjustments.

Private Foundations

It occasionally happens that the creator of a private foundation decides that he just doesn't want to deal with the foundation anymore. Among the reasons for such a decision may be a change in health; determination that the children are not interested in becoming involved; unforeseen shrinkage in the foundation's assets; family distress; business distress; and divorce or remarriage.

In most of these circumstances, there are still significant assets in the foundation. This raises the question of what to do. There are two main alternatives. These are:

1. Arrange new management for the foundation.
2. Terminate the foundation.

Arrange New Management

If a donor wishes to keep his foundation going, but be far less involved, he can accomplish this by bringing in additional foundation directors who will take over the responsibility of a board. This should be done with care. For more information, see the discussion of Foundation Governance in Chapter 7.

Terminate the Foundation

Terminating the foundation is another option to consider. There is sometimes confusion around the meaning of *termination of a foundation.*

The Internal Revenue Code (IRC) recognizes a private foundation as distinct from a public charity, and from an ordinary taxable entity. It is possible for a private foundation to become a public charity, and it is also possible for a private foundation to become an ordinary taxable entity. In either event, the Internal Revenue Service (IRS) considers such a transition as a "termination of private foundation status."

The IRS recognizes four distinct ways in which an organization once classified as a private foundation can lose that status. These four ways are governed by Section 507 of the IRC. It is sometimes confusing, because two of these ways can give rise to tax liability, while the other two do not. In practice, as long as the foundation is run properly, it is easy to terminate without any tax being owed.

Method 1: Voluntary Termination

The IRS describes this method as follows:

1. Voluntary termination by notifying the IRS of intent to terminate and paying a termination tax: To voluntarily terminate under section 507(a)(1), the organization must send a statement to the Manager, Exempt

Organizations Determinations (Internal Revenue Service, Exempt Organizations Determinations, P.O. Box 2508, Cincinnati, OH 45201) of its intent to terminate its status under section 507(a)(1). The statement must provide, in detail, the computation and amount of private foundation termination tax. Unless the organization requests abatement, it must pay the tax at the time the statement is filed.

In practice, voluntary terminations of private foundation status are almost always planned so that the termination tax is zero.

The tax itself, if applicable, is designed to eliminate the possibility that a donor could benefit from creating and funding a private foundation, and then later voluntarily giving up private foundation status. The IRS describes the tax thus:

The tax imposed under section 507(c) on the termination of a private foundation is the lesser of:

The combined tax benefit resulting from the section 501(c)(3) status of the organization, or

The value of the net assets of the organization.

The combined tax benefit resulting from the section 501(c)(3) status of any private foundation is the sum of:

The combined increases in income, estate, and gift taxes that would have been imposed on all substantial contributors if deductions for all contributions made by those contributors to the foundation after February 28, 1913, had been disallowed, and

The combined increases in income tax that would have been imposed on the private foundation's income for tax years beginning after 1912 if—

a. The foundation had not been tax exempt, and
b. In the case of a trust, its charitable deduction had been limited to 20 percent of its taxable income, and

Amounts received from private foundations to which transferee liability applies, and

The interest on the tax increases in (1), (2), and (3) from the first date the increase would have been due or payable to the date the organization ceases to be a private foundation.

In figuring the combined increases in tax under (1), all deductions for a particular contribution for income, estate, or gift tax purposes must be included. For example, if a substantial contributor had taken income tax and gift tax deductions for a charitable contribution to the foundation, the amount of each deduction must be included. The combined tax benefit may be more than the fair market value of the property transferred.

The value of the net assets of the organization is generally the greater of:

The value on the first day action was taken to terminate private foundation status, or

The value on the date the organization ceased to be a private foundation.

If all the assets of the foundation are given away to charities prior to the termination, in general the termination tax will be zero. A filing is still required.

Method 2: Involuntary Termination

As discussed in Chapter 11, there are many, many rules with which private foundations must comply. Failure to comply can ultimately result in loss of private foundation status. Private foundation status can be involuntarily terminated by the IRS for repeated willful violations or flagrant and willful violations of certain of the sections of the IRC concerning private foundation excise taxes. You do not want to choose actions that will lead to this route.

Method 3: Transfer of Assets to Certain Public Charities

If a foundation wishes to close its doors and go out of business, the easiest way is to give away all its assets to one or more public charities, all of which have been in existence and classified as public charities (under Section 507(b)(1)(A)) for at least 60 continuous months prior to the gifts. A foundation that gives all its assets away in this manner will terminate automatically, does not need to notify the IRS of intent to terminate, and does not owe termination tax.

Method 4: Become a Butterfly

In general, there are two ways for a caterpillar to go out of existence. One is to die, and the other is to turn into a butterfly. The latter is the most glorious method, especially from the point of view of the caterpillar (or so we assume, not being privy to the thoughts of any actual caterpillars).

Similarly, a private foundation can terminate by becoming a butterfly, as it were. In this case, the butterfly is a public charity as described in Sections 509(a)(1), (2), or (3) of the IRC. If a foundation thinks that it might go this route, it needs to notify the IRS in advance of its intention, and then meet the criteria for qualifying as a public charity for 60 continuous months.

It is quite unlikely that a private foundation that is not achieving the goals of its founder will go this route. The process takes five years, and in most cases requires raising significant amounts of money from the public.

Donor satisfaction with private foundations tends to be quite high. Donors understand up front that the money they contribute to their foundation is gone from their personal ownership forever. In contrast, when a donor creates a Charitable Remainder Trust (CRT), the donor retains an ongoing personal financial interest in the assets.

Charitable Remainder Trusts

A donor to a CRT actually owns the right to receive cash from the CRT, usually for life, sometimes for a set term of years. As a result of this lively interest in the financial fortunes of the CRT, donor satisfaction with his CRT is far more likely to wane as compared to satisfaction with a private foundation.

In most cases when a donor funds a CRT, the donor is looking not only for charitable benefits, but also for tax benefits. One of these tax benefits occurs immediately, in the form of an up-front tax deduction for the portion of the CRT that is considered a charitable gift (see Chapter 4). The other tax benefit is the deferral of income taxes into the future, and the spreading of those taxes over many years.

As a result, changes in the donor's circumstances over time, as well as changes in federal tax rates, state tax rates, and the investment markets, can all cause a donor to re-evaluate the desirability of continuing with the CRT.

If a donor decides that it does not make sense to continue with the CRT, she generally has three options. These are:

1. Contribute it all to charity.
2. Terminate the CRT.
3. Sell her income interest in the CRT to a third party.

Contribute It All to Charity

All CRTs have to have at least one charitable beneficiary. If a donor wearies of the CRT, and does not wish to receive any value for her income interest, the donor can simply gift the income interest in the CRT to the charitable beneficiary. This will generally result in an additional tax deduction to the donor, and the termination of the CRT. Tax returns will need to be filed, but there would generally be no tax to the CRT or the grantor.

Termination

In general, it is possible to terminate a CRT by dividing the assets of the CRT on a strictly pro rata basis between the noncharitable and the charitable beneficiary. There are a number of Private Letter Rulings that have been issued on this topic. In general, the IRS has ruled that if the charitable beneficiary is a public charity, the division will not be a prohibited transaction.

Each case is unique, the terms of the trust must be taken into account, and the division must comply with procedures established by the IRS. The rules in this area are evolving. If you want to go down this road, you need to seek professional guidance at the time.

Sell the Income Interest

The newest and most exciting way for a donor to be finished with a CRT is to sell his income interest. As we write, there is a thriving private market for such transactions. From our vantage point, that market has been growing rapidly as donors and advisers discover the option that they never previously knew about.

Perhaps the best way to convey a flavor for the kinds of situations and transactions that occur is to examine a number of case studies.

Getting Out of a Sticky NIMCRUT

Brenda had always been fascinated by one of Los Angeles's unique attractions. So much so that she decided to name its associated museum as one of her CRT beneficiaries. Little did she suspect, when she funded her CRT, that she would one day come to feel like one of the museum's display creatures.

As you drive down Wilshire Boulevard, one of Los Angeles's main thoroughfares, from the beach to downtown, you pass by high-rise condos, commercial strip shopping centers, churches, synagogues, stores, a golf course, and even the odd oil well. You also pass, wedged between the LA County Museum of Art on the west and a commercial development on the east, one of the most unusual geological and paleontological sites on the planet.

Here, at the La Brea tar pits, during the last ice age over 10,000 years ago, an almost unimaginable bestiary of fantastical creatures came from miles around to drink at the area's watering holes. The kings of this menagerie were the gigantic woolly mammoths. The males stood 13 feet high, and sported eight-foot helical tusks weighing close to a ton each. These gentle giants were grass eaters. To eat all that grass, perhaps a thousand pounds a day, required enormous grinding teeth. The teeth on one side of a mammoth's upper jaw were easily bigger than an entire human head.

Beside mammoths, there lived mastodons, woolly rhinoceroses, powerful saber-tooted tigers that brandished razor-sharp fangs six inches long, giant

10-foot-tall ground sloths, the dread-inspiring carnivorous dire wolves, and dozens of other smaller and exotic creatures.

All of these incredible animals came to the tar pits seeking succor in the form of water. They got their water, but they also got more than they bargained for. Picture, if you can, a majestic mammoth bull, with his long woolly reddish coat of fur, slowly and ponderously approaching the watering hole, as he has done so many times before during his 40-odd years of life. Smaller mammals scatter out of his way. The flutter of birds' wings fills the air immediately around him as they part to make way. He comes to the water's edge, sucks up a trunkful of water, and greedily drinks it down. He takes another step into the shallow water. Then another. He feels his right foot sink into the mud, three, four, five, six inches. That is not unusual for an animal weighing over five tons.

But as he takes another step, he stumbles a bit. His right foot is stuck. He can't pull it out. Seeking better leverage to use his massive strength, he places his left foot nearer the right. As he pushes down on the left to free the right, the left foot sinks deep into the muck. But he cannot free the right foot. He decides to move the left foot, and finds that it too is stuck. He struggles and struggles; he bellows; he roars his rage. But there is no answer. The silent, deadly monster has him in its iron grasp and will not let him go.

Zed, as he will be named by scientists, is stuck in the tar. He will perish there, be covered by tar, and lie undisturbed for 40,000 years until his bones, complete with tusks, are discovered by a construction crew.

Zed walked unknowingly into a trap from which he was unable to extricate himself. Brenda also found herself in a trap, although this trap, fortunately, threatened only her wealth and not her life.

Brenda's trap, like Zed's, was attractive initially. Brenda received significant and valuable income tax deductions when she set up and funded her NIMCRUT.[1] And also like Zed's trap, Brenda's offered her real benefits for quite a while.

Zed got water for drinking and spraying, and did not suspect or realize that he was in a trap. It was only when he tried to get out that he realized that there was a big downside to his drinking hole. Only then, if we can attribute that much awareness to a mammoth, did Zed realize he was stuck in a tar pit.

---

[1] A Net Income with Makeup Charitable Remainder Trust (NIMCRUT) is a type of CRT that distributes the lesser of income or a stated payout rate (5 percent minimum), with any deficiencies (i.e., amounts by which the trust's income falls short of the stated payout rate) to be made up in later years when trust income exceeds the required set percentage amounts for such years.

Similarly, Brenda was very pleased with the performance of the NIM-CRUT, which paid out very little, but kept on building up its value.

When the Great Recession hit in 2008, Brenda learned that for her, the NIMCRUT was a tar pit. Outside the NIMCRUT, she held some investment real estate that was leveraged to about 75 percent of its value. Because of the market collapse, the lender both tightened its lending standards and decreased the level of loan-to-value it would finance. Brenda was lucky, because she was able to refinance the loan, but the bank's double-whammy meant that instead of the former 75 percent loan-to-value (LTV) ratio, she would now be able to get the equivalent of only about 50 percent. That meant she needed to come up with the missing 25 percent in equity.

The rainy day for which Brenda had been building the CRT was here. She confidently called her investment manager, and told him of her need. She needed him to change the way the CRT was being invested so that it could distribute.

That was when Brenda discovered that she was in the tar. She hadn't realized how long it would take to get her cash via income distributions. She turned to her tax adviser, Al, who had put her into the NIMCRUT in the first place. Again, Brenda was lucky, because Al knew just what to do. As soon as he heard her issue, Al told Brenda that she could probably get all the cash she needed by selling her CRT interest.

Al called us. The trust was fine, and in fact the investment manager had been investing quite well. Within a matter of weeks, we had located a buyer who was willing to pay a fair price that worked for Brenda. Brenda sold her interest, and her cash was wired directly into her account at the bank. She was then able to use that cash to increase her equity, the bank refinanced the loan, and Brenda held the property, which, thanks to the extra equity and low interest rates, is producing good cash flow for her.

Believe it or not, people still occasionally get stuck in the tar at La Brea. Fortunately, nowadays there is someone around to help, and modern tools and techniques to extricate people from the tar, which is unbelievably sticky.

Fortunately for Brenda, she got stuck in the modern era, when tools and techniques exist that can be used to extricate people from the tar pit that some NIMCRUTs can become.

"There's Gold in Them Thar CRTs!"

James Marshall built things. He was a contractor, and contractors start work early. So there was nothing unusual in the fact that Marshall rose at dawn on Monday morning, January 28, 1848, and proceeded directly to his current construction project. Marshall was building a sawmill. In those days, mills were still powered by flowing water, a technology then already almost 2,000 years old.

Not surprisingly, water mills require water. Mills are typically built near a source of moving water, such as a river. But until the advent of modern hydroelectric dams, it was not customary to block the entire river. Instead, some of the water flow would be diverted and run through the mill and then drained back into the river. The water reached the mill in a specially built watercourse called a mill race.

Marshall was inspecting his mill race that Monday morning, when he found something that made him totally forget about sawmills and water wheels. Beneath six inches of water, something reflected the morning sun brightly into Marshall's eyes. He bent down for a closer look. Intrigued, he reached in, and grasped the object. Pulling it out of the water, he recognized it immediately: gold.

The gold rush was on, and California, the United States, and even the world would never be quite the same. Marshall, and his better-known partner, John Sutter, immediately recognized that they could greatly increase the value of their property by changing strategy.

A bit more than a hundred years later, a woman was born in the great city most affected by the gold rush: San Francisco. She grew up in the Golden State, and acquired millions in one of a number of latter-day California gold rushes, this one involving technology stocks. Her name is Sue.

Unlike Sutter and the gold barons of the nineteenth century, whose main obstacle in being wealthy was to earn the money, Sue also has to face that nasty invention of the twentieth century: the income tax.

Sue has an excellent adviser, Tony, whose firm advises both established and nouveau riche. Tony has understood all along that Sue's primary goal is growing her pile, along with maintaining a lifestyle to which she has become accustomed.

Toward the end of the 1990s bull market, but before the bubble burst, Sue had accumulated some very large unrealized gains in her portfolio, including making many times her money in Cisco. She didn't need the money, but wanted to convert some of the new wealth into spendable form. Tony was wary of the market and thought it might be a good idea to diversify. He also took into account the fact that Sue didn't want to pay a huge capital gains tax. So Tony suggested that Sue consider a CRT.

Tony showed Sue that by contributing her Cisco to a regular charitable remainder unitrust (CRUT), she could generate an income tax deduction, diversify her Cisco holdings, and generate an annual cash flow. Tony ran the numbers, and they made sense. Sue set up the CRUT and funded it with her Cisco stock. According to their plan, the CRT then sold the Cisco and invested in a portfolio that was capable of generating the CRT's annual distribution, which was more than 5 percent.

In the late 1990s, Tony was drawn to Real Estate Investment Trusts (REITs) because of their high yields and apparently low valuations. The CRT invested heavily in REITs.

When the tech bubble burst within a year or so, while Cisco and everything tech-related were plunging, Tony's REITs helped Sue's CRT hold its own, and even rise. When we complimented Tony on his brilliant timing, he modestly replied, "Better lucky than smart." Indeed.

For almost the entire first decade of the current century, Sue's CRT hummed along. As REITs reached what Tony considered stratospheric heights in 2004, Tony cut back the position, only to see some of his former holdings double in value. "Can't win 'em all," he explains.

But Sue wasn't complaining. Tony noticed, however, that it was becoming harder and harder, without the REITs and with bond yields so low, for the CRT to earn the distribution amount. He was forced to sell assets to make the payments, which he didn't like but thought was preferable to making investments he felt were overvalued.

When Tony learned that it was possible to sell the income interest in a CRT, he reacted with almost as much alacrity as James Marshall did when the gold glittered in the mill race.

Tony did his own valuation of the CRT, and determined what he thought Sue's interest was worth, at current tax rates. He contacted us, and we also valued her interest. We told Tony that we thought we could sell Sue's interest for at least as much as its current value. Tony explained the idea to Sue, who grasped the benefits. Tony is a very matter-of-fact, fee-only adviser. He doesn't sell. He thinks for his clients about things they don't want to spend time on, or don't have the necessary knowledge that Tony does have.

Tony says that it was so obvious that selling made sense, that Sue suggested it before he had even finished his explanation. Sue made the decision right away. We quickly found a buyer, and the transaction closed within a few weeks of Tony's first considering it.

In fact, once he saw what a great strategy selling was, Tony contacted all his CRT clients to make them aware of the potential. He reviewed his cases one by one with his clients, and with us. In the end, about three-quarters of his clients wound up selling their CRT interests.

Like John Sutter, they realized a gold strike when it stared them in the face. They changed strategy accordingly, and came out far ahead. As Tony says with a gilded twinkle in his eye, "There's gold in them thar CRTs!"

Ordinary CLAT, Unusual Usage

Lee Wing's mother and father never imagined that they would live in a 5,000-square-foot house, on an acre of land, with a swimming pool and a tennis court, and a three-car garage.

When they grew up in post-war China, only in distant America, so it was rumored, did ordinary people sometimes become millionaires and live in big, new houses on lots of land.

Lee's parents were fortunate to survive the Japanese occupation and the Second World War, and still more fortunate to make it to the United States. Lee was born here. His parents were very demanding, and drilled Lee an hour a day in math from the time he was seven.

They felt their efforts were vindicated when Lee was accepted into Stanford in 1985. Lee, of course, went. After a stab at math, Lee was drawn to electrical engineering, and then to the relatively new field of computer science. Lee excelled. After graduating with a double major in computer science and electrical engineering, Lee faced excellent job prospects in the burgeoning computer industry of Silicon Valley.

After working for a couple of companies that didn't make it, Lee landed at one of Silicon Valley's success stories. (The company is one of those whose name has the same letter in positions two and three.) After Lee had been there a few years, he was surprised and delighted to find that his stock plus options were worth well over $50 million.

It was at this point that Lee purchased a mansion for his parents. He lives in a modest house and drives a Toyota.

Like almost all people, Lee doesn't like paying taxes. In the year he exercised a large chunk of his options, he was looking at a multimillion-dollar tax bill. He set up a private foundation and funded it with a modest amount of cash. He then sought the counsel of his advisers. He wanted to provide further for his parents, especially when they were old, and also reduce his taxes. Was there a strategy that could accomplish both these goals?

After several meetings and great deal of thought, his team of advisers concluded that a Charitable Lead Annuity Trust, or CLAT, could accomplish the dual objectives.

A CLAT is a split-interest trust in which a series of lead payments (sometimes called the income interest) goes to a charitable beneficiary, and the remainder (whatever is left over at the end) goes to a noncharitable beneficiary. A CLAT is usually used to transfer value from parents to children or grandchildren in a way that minimizes or eliminates the estate tax or generation-skipping tax, or both.

Most large gifts go from parents to children. But the way the tax laws are written, large gifts between other people could be taxable, too. For example, a large gift from a child to a parent could conceivably result in a tax. This is a rare occurrence, because in most situations a large, taxable gift from a child to a parent could reasonably be expected to cause a similar large taxable transfer (probably via the estate tax) from the parent back to the child.

This could, depending on the numbers and tax rates involved, result in a total tax of near or even greater than 100 percent. For example, suppose that a child made a taxable gift to his parents of $10 million. At 45 percent, this would generate a gift tax of $4,500,000. Assume that the child paid this tax out of other resources. The parents then invested the $10 million, and lived off the proceeds. This would often be quite feasible, as $10 million, invested in tax-exempt bonds earning 3 percent, would generate $300,000 of net spendable income for the parents.

Eventually, in the natural order of things, the parents will die roughly a generation before the child. That $10 million will still be in the parents' estate, at which time it will (assuming it is taxable at 45 percent under the law then in effect) be subject to estate tax of another $4,500,000. Under this scenario, the total gift and estate taxes caused by the gift of $10 million from child to parent equal 90 percent of the amount of the gift. In the days when the gift/estate tax rate was over 50 percent, such a scenario would have resulted in a tax of more than 100 percent of the amount of the gift. This perverse outcome is a big reason why large gifts from children to parents occur rarely.

Lee wanted to give a significant amount to his parents, but also didn't want to pay gift tax. So Lee decided to set up a CLAT and name his parents as the remainder beneficiaries. The annual income would go to Lee's private foundation for 15 years; and the remainder would go to Lee's parents.

CLATs can be set up as regular trusts, or as grantor trusts. The main difference is in how the income tax deductions for the gifts to charity are treated. In a regular CLAT, the trust can deduct up to the full amount of the distribution to charity each year against its taxable income. There is no income tax deduction for the person who sets up the CLAT.

In a grantor CLAT, the trust itself gets no income tax deductions each year. Instead, the full present value of all the future gifts of the CLAT to charity becomes an upfront tax deduction for the grantor. That full present value of the charitable interest is deducted from the value of the trust for gift tax purposes. By setting the terms of the trust appropriately, the gift tax can be brought as low as desired.

By setting up his CLAT as a grantor trust, Lee was able to generate a large up-front tax deduction. Each year, the trust funds his private foundation. And, if, as Lee expects, the trust's assets grow at 7 percent per year, his parents will receive a large sum at the end of 15 years.

CRT Case Study: Divorce (Hell Hath No Fury Like a Woman Scorned)

Consider this scenario: A mature British gentleman, a millionaire, falls passionately in love with a lively, hot-blooded Latin-American woman who is many years his junior. After a short romance, they marry. They enjoy a short period of married bliss, then his ardor cools, but hers remains unabated. He wants out. She is determined to stop him. When she realizes she can't keep him, she determines to make the cost to him as high as possible.

If this reminds you of a Victorian romance, you're right. So far, we've outlined part of the plot of Arthur Conan Doyle's Sherlock Holmes story "The Problem of Thor Bridge."

If you've read that story, you know what happens. If you haven't, I won't spoil it for you here.

I am reminded of "Thor Bridge" by a case we recently saw. To protect the people involved, I've changed some of the names and specifics in what follows. But the key facts and lessons are presented as they occurred.

It began when I received a call from Jeb, an adviser who had worked very hard in the mid-1990s to set up a CRT for his client, Chuck. Jeb told me Chuck was married to Marta, a Peruvian woman 15 years younger than Chuck. They had a couple of kids, a huge house by the beach in San Clemente, and a $15 million CRT. And now they were getting divorced. What could we suggest?

We asked a few more questions, and learned that Chuck was 68 and Marta 53. The kids would stay with Marta, who although not a U.S. citizen had a green card. Marta was living in the San Clemente mansion, which was worth about $17 million. There was another $17 million in assets beside the house and CRT.

A bit more inquiry revealed that the divorce had already proceeded quite far, and in fact they had divided most of the property except the CRT. They were quarreling over the CRT because Marta's divorce lawyers argued that she was entitled to more than half the CRT value because she was younger and her life expectancy was therefore longer.

Under the terms of the CRT, Chuck and Marta were each to receive half of the annual distributions, which amounted to nearly three quarters of a million dollars each, per year. The trust provided that if one of the spouses were to die, the entire amount would go to the remaining spouse. (Do you see a motive for mischief?)

But Chuck and his lawyers refused to see it that way. They assumed that since Chuck was so much older, he was going to die first. They further argued that if Chuck did die before Marta, and she got extra payments, then to make it fair, a larger percentage of the remainder should go to Chuck's charity than to Marta's.

Neither side wanted to be in the long-term relationship with the other that would result if they kept the CRT intact. Chuck's lawyers suggested splitting the CRT, so that Marta would have her own CRT, for her life, and Chuck would have one for his. Marta's lawyers didn't reject the idea, but insisted that Marta's half should get more than half the assets, because of her greater life expectancy.

They were deadlocked. That's when Jeb called us. He explained the situation, and suggested that both sides might be made better off if they could sell the CRT income interest, and then split the cash.

We analyzed the numbers, and reached several important conclusions. First, we concluded that in a sale, both Marta and Chuck could get about a million dollars more, each, than they could expect otherwise.

Second, we analyzed what would happen if the trust were split into two trusts as suggested by Chuck's attorneys. The result was eye-opening: Splitting the trusts would result in the loss of about $1.5 million in joint expected net present value (NPV) for Chuck and Martha together. While on the surface this looks like a mystery worthy of Sherlock Holmes, it has a simple explanation.

The income interests in two trusts, one for Marta's life and the other for Chuck's, each with one-half the assets, are worth less together because splitting the trusts in this way removes the joint life expectancies. This is true for the same reason that second-to-die life insurance is generally much less expensive than a comparable single-life. The joint life expectancy of two people is generally longer than the single-life expectancy of either one of them separately.

In our case, even Marta, much younger than Chuck, has a life expectancy on her own that is several years less than her joint life expectancy with Chuck. And for Chuck, the difference is even more pronounced.

Jeb understood this clearly, and explained it to Chuck's lawyers, who also understood it clearly. They explained that splitting the trust would destroy about $2 million, which could otherwise be divided between Marta and Chuck. Compared to a sale, which we believed was feasible, the destruction would be over $3 million.

Marta was unmoved $3 million be damned, she said. Her lawyers made a full-court press and the trust was split, and the value lost.

In "The Problem of Thor Bridge," the marriage issue is settled by a bullet to the head. In the problem of Marta and Chuck, the property issue was settled, not by a bullet, but by a vicious financial body-blow inflicted by Marta on the value of the estate. Despite the fact that she was hurt more than Chuck, Marta valued revenge more than money.

The ending of this case recalls the words of another famous English writer, William Congreve. It is Congreve to whom we owe the unfortunate epitaph to this story: "Hell hath no fury like a woman scorned."

Monaco Sunrise

Dr. Michael Rupert was feeling pretty good about life. A Virginia physician, Rupert was enjoying a life of leisure. Well, leisure by his standards anyhow. Several years back, Rupert had sold the medical devices business he and a partner had started and built to the number three player in the industry. He still lectured all over the world.

Rupert's share of the company had been well over $10 million. He now toured the world, sometimes lecturing to groups of doctors, sometimes simply enjoying the scenery. Today he was in Monte Carlo. Any other doctors there were present by coincidence; the only conferences going on, at least as far as Rupert knew, were going on around the craps tables and were far more likely to concern wine, women, and song, than medical devices.

But Rupert wasn't at the casino. He was sitting with his young wife at a café, overlooking Monte Carlo's famous, glittering yacht harbor. As he enjoyed his drink and chatted, his eye spotted a ship entering the anchorage. He watched, surprised at the unscheduled arrival of a cruise ship. Since being overwhelmed by thousands of cruise ship passengers in Georgetown during a visit to the West Indies a few years previously, Rupert had paid attention to cruise ship schedules and avoided them when he could.

His curiosity aroused, Rupert watched the ship slip slowly through the calm water. He did not recognize the liner, which he estimated at 400 feet long. He did not recognize its colors either. A casual inquiry yielded the amazing revelation that this cruise ship was actually a private yacht. And not just any yacht, but Larry Ellison's *Rising Sun*. Rupert decided on the spot that he wanted his own yacht. Of course, it would be considerably more modest than the $200 million *Rising Sun*, but still, he figured, a million bucks ought to buy quite a bit of yacht. Which indeed it does.

Rupert worked on the idea on the long plane ride back to Virginia. By the time he landed, he had it all worked out. He would have his CRT buy a yacht and lease it out. When the yacht wasn't leased, he figured, it would be available for his personal use. The day after his return, he excitedly called his financial adviser to tell him of the new strategy for the CRT.

Rupert's adviser demurred, and was happy to refer this idea to a lawyer. So Rupert called his longtime lawyer, Harold. Harold is an old-time business lawyer, now in his 70s. He's seen a lot, and he's known Rupert for many years. He had helped Rupert sell the business. When Rupert called Harold with his great idea, Harold burst out laughing. "I gotta give 'im credit." Harold laughed as he recounted the story, "If it worked, it would be great. But part of my job is to make sure he stays within the lines."

Harold gently explained to Rupert some of the reasons his idea of having the CRT own his yacht wouldn't work. Among these reasons are that such a program would almost certainly run afoul of prohibited transactions rules and unrelated business income tax (UBIT) rules. The program would also likely create issues of excess distributions, and the investment in a yacht might run afoul of restrictions on jeopardizing investments.

Rupert backed off. But his heart was still fixated on the yacht. He had his eye on a 50-footer. Admittedly, his boat would not quite be the 453-foot yacht that Rupert had momentarily mistaken for an ocean liner. But, Rupert figured, a million-dollar yacht would still turn heads at the yacht club.

Harold asked why Rupert wanted to have the CRT buy the boat. Why not just buy the boat himself?

"Harold," Rupert said, "I don't have much liquidity. We've got some very exciting investments in bio-tech and med-tech ventures. But they're not liquid. We also have quite a bit, too much, in the angel fund I put together. My wife says I should wait till my ships come in. She thinks it's funny. But I don't. I want it now. But today, and for the foreseeable future, I don't have the cash, or the liquid assets."

Harold suggested that Rupert borrow against the assets.

"Not so easy today," Rupert answered. "Especially when they know you intend to invest the proceeds in a yacht. You know what the bank said when I told him that? He said buying a million-dollar yacht was the opposite of an investment. He said I wouldn't believe the number of clients he's had over the years who admitted that the old saw was true."

"What old saw?" asked Harold.

"The one about a boat being a hole in the water into which you pour cash."

"There is that," agreed Harold.

Rupert's glum face fell even further. Then Harold brightened his day. "I have an idea. Let's see if we can sell your CRT interest."

Harold proceeded to explain that what Rupert owned was the right to receive income from his CRT. That right, usually referred to as the income interest, was considered a capital asset. As such, the income interest could be sold, if the language of the trust didn't prevent such a sale.

Harold contacted us and provided the full information. The trust was well drafted and presented no obstacles. We located a buyer and concluded a sale that enabled Dr. Rupert to purchase his yacht for cash. Rupert was delighted with the transaction and was also very happy with Harold. Harold, for his part, was thrilled to collect his fee promptly and without the usual chiseling he had come to expect from Rupert.

Rupert named his new acquisition *Monaco Sunrise*, in honor of that day in Monte Carlo.

Getting Rid of Other Charitable Vehicles

Occasionally donors may have some other type of charitable vehicle that they are tired of dealing with, such as a charitable gift annuity or a donor-advised fund account. In each of these cases, the donor doesn't really have to do anything.

In the case of the CGA, the donor could, if he really wanted to be rid of the annuity, give the remaining income interest to the charity. This should generate a tax deduction. In theory the interest could probably be sold, although in practice it seems to occur fairly rarely.

The donor-advised fund is even simpler. The donor actually owns nothing and has no responsibilities. Since the assets are actually and legally owned by the donor-advised fund itself, if the donor does nothing, eventually (see the specific language of your specific fund) the assets will simply become part of the general, undifferentiated assets of that charitable entity, and the trustees of the donor-advised fund will decide how they are to be given away. The donor need do nothing.

Conclusion

Philanthropy and its challenges are not new. Aristotle, who lived 2,400 years ago, was aware that "to give away money is an easy matter and in any man's power. But to decide to whom to give it, and how [much], and when, and for what purpose and how, is neither in every man's power nor an easy matter." Today the opportunities in the philanthropic sector are larger and more varied than ever.

As discussed in Chapter 7, one of the modern world's wisest observers, management guru Peter Drucker, sees in the philanthropic world much evidence that Aristotle's observation still holds. Drucker's insights are worth repeating here. In an interview in *Philanthropy Magazine*, he said, "Nonprofits today are probably pretty much where American business was in the late 1940s, with a few outstandingly effective, well-managed companies, and the great bulk of them at a very low level. In the business world, the average has risen dramatically. Yet today, the vast majority of nonprofits are not so much badly managed as they just are not managed at all."

Drucker, who has worked with the philanthropic sector more than five decades, is as biting as ever in his criticism. In the same interview, he goes on to say, "One of the reasons I spend so much time on nonprofits is that it is so incredibly easy to improve them, because you start from such a low base." This applies to both the public charity and private foundation sectors.

But as we've seen it is not easy. Only part of the difficulty is poor management. Many of the problems charities seek to address are deep, entrenched, hard problems.

In the private sector, if a task is too difficult to do profitably, it simply won't be done, even if the technical hurdles can be overcome. For example, as challenging as it is to build a commercial jetliner that can cruise at 1,000 miles an hour, the technical challenges were met. However, there is nowhere in the world today commercial supersonic travel, because the market won't support it, and the British and French taxpayers won't support it, either.

But intractability in the task does not necessarily deter philanthropists. And there is an argument that it should not. In this book, we've reviewed the key problems. In the foundation sector, the inefficiencies start at the funding level. Thousands of Americans are forfeiting millions of potential charitable dollars (collectively, billions) each year because they are not taking advantage of the numerous tax benefits for funding a foundation. These inefficiencies get compounded at the grant-making level. Few foundations take even half of the steps for effectiveness that were outlined in Chapter 7. And there's ample room for improvement at the grantee level, too. "The main shortcoming," says Drucker, "is that far too many nonprofits believe that good intentions are sufficient. They lack the discipline—the imposed discipline of the bottom line."

The good news is that despite these tremendous inefficiencies, wealthy individuals and families are willing to give of their resources, and private foundations are ideally positioned to address these problems in the arenas of both the foundation and public charity. Improvements in foundation efficiency, combined with the ongoing growth in the number of foundations and the willingness of foundations to impose a bottom line on recipients, will make possible dramatic improvements not only for those who are most needy in society, but for everyone.

It would be nice to conclude that the improvements in foundation efficiency and effectiveness that are possible are also inevitable. But they are not. In the for-profit sector, improvements by one company in an industry compel the rest of the industry to improve or perish. In the nonprofit sector, there is no such force.

In education, for example, both the government and thousands of private charities continually throw more money at the problem. All this funding masks the fact that for the most part, high tech bells and whistles notwithstanding, education still follows the same outmoded Prussian/factory model that it has for over a century.

For improvement in the way charitable activity is carried out, we must look to the particularized self-interests of philanthropists to see their good ideas spread.

There are lots of good ideas already out there. We discuss a number of them in this book. More are being developed and tested all the time. We hope that this book will help you to find and implement some of the good ideas that already exist, and inspire you to develop new ones. We look forward to hearing from you.

Selected Resources

"Charitable Giving Decision Flowchart," Sterling Foundation Management, 2002.
   Sterling has created a decision flowchart that donors and advisers can use as a guide to the decision-making process for charitable giving. Request a free copy of this flowchart by sending an e-mail to Flowchart@SterlingFoundations.com and mentioning this publication. Include your full contact information and phone number.

The Foundation Center
   This site provides an abundance of resources for grant makers, including a searchable database containing more than 20,000 full bibliographic citations for books, periodicals, and Internet resources on philanthropic topics.
   www.fdncenter.org

Guidestar
   A useful site that includes information on more than 600,000 charities. Often includes copies of public documents, including some financial information and informational tax returns.
   www.guidestar.org

IRS Publication 78
   A useful site for checking on the continuing tax exempt status of a charity. This is found by using the "Search for Charities" link at the following web site address: www.irs.gov/charities/topic/index.html

Philanthropy News Digest
   A philanthropy news source provided by The Foundation Center.
   www.fdncenter.org/pnd/index.jhtml

The Philanthropy Roundtable
   The Philanthropy Roundtable site contains several interesting publications on the establishment and management of private foundations.
   www.philanthropyroundtable.org

PNN Online
   A source for information on nonprofit organizations.
   www.pnnonline.org

Sterling Foundation Management
   Sterling Foundation Management provides comprehensive foundation management services, including grant-making procedures, cash management, expert knowledge, best practices management, leverage, tax planning, effectiveness measurement, and general

support. The web site contains a great deal of information about creating, administering, and managing private foundations.

www.sterlingfoundations.com

Council on Foundations

The Council on Foundations (CoF) is a comprehensive organization that assists family and corporate foundation staff, trustees, and board members with the legal, financial, and managerial challenges. Member services include access to an array of publications addressing problems frequently confronted by private foundations, grant-making information, annual conferences for board members and trustees of family and corporate foundations, and in-depth research on the staff and endowment management practices of other member foundations. The CoF also sponsors the Philanthropic Advisors Network, where legal and financial professionals can discuss issues that are pertinent to foundation management.

1828 L Street, NW

Washington, DC 20036

202-466-6512

The Philanthropy Roundtable

A national association of individual donors, corporate giving representatives, foundation staff and trustees, and trust and estate officers. Member benefits include consulting and referral services, complimentary copies of Roundtable studies, and a series of regional meetings.

1150 17th Street, NW, Suite 503

Washington, DC 20036

202-822-8333

BNA Income Tax Planner

High-end, expensive software from one of the leading tax information services. Designed for tax professionals, possibly the most comprehensive tax-planning software available. Call 800-372-1033 to order.

About the Authors

Roger D. Silk, PhD, CFA, is chief executive officer of Sterling Foundation Management, LLC. A leading expert in the field of private foundations, his articles have appeared in magazines such as *Estate Planning, Philanthropy, Investment Advisor, Journal of Financial Planning, Journal of Personal Financial Planning,* and *Trusts and Estates,* where he is a member of the Philanthropy Advisory Committee. As the founder of several nonprofit organizations and former CEO of a national public charity, Silk has spoken to audiences around the country on the benefits of private foundations. He earned a PhD and an MA in applied economics from Stanford University, as well as a BA in economics, and was awarded the esteemed CFA (Chartered Financial Analyst) designation by the Association of Investment Management and Research. Silk is a current or past director of several charitable organizations, including the George Mason University Foundation.

James W. Lintott, Esq., is chairman of Sterling Foundation Management, LLC. Previously he was head of one of the nation's largest private foundations. Lintott received his JD from Stanford Law School, as well as an MA in applied economics and BA degrees in economics and political science from Stanford University. Mr. Lintott serves on the boards of a number of nationally known charities, including Best Buddies International, and is chairman of the Children's National Medical Center in Washington, DC.

AN OFFER FROM STERLING FOUNDATION MANAGEMENT

Sterling Foundation Management is the country's leading, and oldest, national, full-service, foundation-management company.

Sterling provides its clients with comprehensive foundation management services so that they can enjoy all the pleasure, gratification, and satisfaction that come from an effective, well-run foundation. Sterling can quickly create a foundation and free the founder from the administrative burden of maintaining a foundation. We help our client foundations in all the areas discussed in this book—including grant-making procedures, cash management, expert knowledge, best practices management, leverage, tax planning, investment policy, effectiveness measurement, and general support—as well as other more specialized issues not covered in this book.

Sterling creates value in a wide variety of ways, some of which are measurable in saved money, some in saved time, and some in saved lives. Our clients find that our services more than pay for themselves in actual savings and added value.

Free Resources: Sterling offers free resources for donors and advisors. Donors wishing to learn more specifically about Sterling's services can request a copy of "Managing Your Foundation" from Sterling by e-mailing a request to us at BookOfferD@SterlingFoundations.com.

Advisers may request a free copy of "What Every Investment Professional Needs to Know about Private Foundations," which covers adviser-specific material not discussed in this book. Requests should be e-mailed to BookOfferA@SterlingFoundations.com.

All requesters should identify themselves as readers of this book.

Index

"Bogus" certificates of deposit, 157–159
Bonds:
  high-grade, 131
  high-yield and emerging-market, 132
  tax free vs. taxable, 203
  Treasury Inflation-Protected Securities
    (TIPS), 131
Borneo, 164, 166
Boskin, Michael, 178, 179
Bre-X fraud, 163–166
Buffett, Warren, 54, 81, 137
*Building the Corporate Community
  Development Team* (Alperson), 87
Bush, George H. W., 40–41, 178
Bush, George W., 41
Business holdings, excess, 151
Business income, unrelated, 151
Business of philanthropy:
  best practices, 83–84, 146
  dirty work, foundation doing, 98–99
  feedback, 91
  foreign deductions, 96–97
  generally, 71, 99
  getting started, 74–75
  governance, 77–81
  grant making approaches, 81–82
  knowing your charities, 75–77
  leverage, exercise of, 95–96
  measurement of effectiveness, 86–90
  measures, establishing, 90–91
  mission, 71–74
  negotiation, 82–83
  outside experts, 84
  public relations, 97–98
  strategic giving, 93–95
  support, types of, 84–86
  tax-exempt financing, 98
  wisdom, skills and, 91–93
Buy and sell side, 211–212

California Community Foundation,
  200
Capital gains tax:
  estate tax advantage, 24–25
  generally, 23
  highly appreciated stock and, 203
  income tax advantages over time, 24

  income tax benefit, appreciated stock
    gifted, 24
  income tax benefit in single year, 23
Carnegie, Andrew, 15, 53, 62, 74, 94
Carnegie Foundation, 124
Carry-forward rules, 26
Cash assets, 130–131
Cash flows in, anticipated, 114–115
Cash flows out, anticipated:
  cash management, 119
  fluctuating investment returns, 119–120
  grant planning, 120–121
CDs (Certificates of Deposit), 157–159
Chairs, endowed, 5
Charitable beneficiary, 43
Charitable gift annuity:
  vs. CRT, 189–190
  generally, 183–184
  pitch and catch, 184
Charitable Lead Annuity Trust (CLAT),
  237–239
Charitable Lead Trust (CLT):
  defined, 43
  flexibility and irrevocability, 52
  gift/estate taxes and, 43–44, 46–47
  as grantor/nongrantor trusts, 44–45
  private foundations and, 46
  scenario using, 44–45
  as split-interest trust, 190
  tax-saving power of, 45–46
  time-saving power of, 45
Charitable planning. *See also* Tax planning
  cementing client relationships, 203–204
  foundation manager's role, 206–207
  generally, 201, 207–208
  goodwill in community, 205
  highly appreciated stock and, 203
  increased total client assets, immediate,
    202
  increased total client assets, long term,
    202
  professionally managed private
    foundations, 205–206
  retirement plan assets, death of client
    and, 204–205
  taxable-income producing assets in
    tax-exempt foundation, 203